A **PENNY TASSONI** HA

SUPPORTING CHILDREN WITH
SPECIAL NEEDS

HODDER EDUCATION
AN HACHETTE UK COMPANY

Every effort has been made to trace the copyright holders of material reproduced here. The authors and publishers would like to thank the following for permission to reproduce copyright illustrations: photo on page 4 © TopFoto; photo on page 5 © Jonny White/Alamy; photo on page 19 © Ariel Skelley/Blend Images/Getty Images. All other photos were taken specially for this book by Jules Selmes Photography.

Orders: please contact Bookpoint Ltd, 130 Milton Park, Abingdon, Oxon OX14 4SB. Telephone: (44) 01235 827720. Fax: (44) 01235 400454. Email education@bookpoint.co.uk Lines are open from 9 a.m. to 5 p.m., Monday to Saturday, with a 24-hour message answering service. You can also order through our website: www.hoddereducation.co.uk.

ISBN 978 1 4718 5469 9

Copyright © Penny Tassoni 2015

First published in 2015 by

Hodder Education,

An Hachette UK Company

Carmelite House

50 Victoria Embankment

London EC4Y 0DZ

Impression number 10 9 8 7 6 5 4 3 2 1

Year   2018   2017   2016   2015

Hachette UK's policy is to use papers that are natural, renewable and recyclable products and made from wood grown in sustainable forests. The logging and manufacturing processes are expected to conform to the environmental regulations of the country of origin.

Cover photo © Ariel Skelley/Blend Images/Getty Images

Typeset in India.

Printed in Italy.

A catalogue record for this title is available from the British Library.

Contents

About the author

Penny Tassoni is a well-known education consultant, author and trainer who specialises in the whole spectrum of learning and play. Penny has written more than thirty books, many of which are bestsellers in the childcare sector. Penny is a sought-after speaker both in the UK and internationally, where she has worked in Istanbul, China and Japan. She is also President for PACEY, the Professional Association for Childcare and Early Years (formerly the NCMA).

❱ Acknowledgements

There are a number of people that I need to thank who have supported me in this project. Firstly, I would like to thank the team at Hodder Education including Stephen Halder, Jane Adams and also Peter Banks. I would also like to thank the Bilston Nursery School for being inspirational and a great base for our photoshoot. There were also many professionals and organisations who have contributed to this book, but I would particularly like to thank Anne-Marie Tassoni, SLT, Kent Community Health, and Karen Brotherton, Area Inclusion Co-ordinator, Hampshire, for their time and support. Finally, I would like to thank Wendy Bristow for sharing her journey as a parent with me.

Introduction

By their very nature, all children are special and unique. This is reflected in the way they smile, what makes their eyes light up and also how they respond to new situations. It is the differences between children that make working in this sector so interesting and also rewarding.

Working with children means recognising that these differences also play out in the level of support that children may need. Support may come in a variety of forms including changing the environment or using particular resources, but also the need for some children to work alongside adults who have specialist knowledge.

For many years, children who needed such additional support as a result of learning difficulties, medical conditions or disabilities were neglected and discriminated against by both society and the education system. Today, there have been some improvements in this situation as there is a legal requirement for all education settings to identify children who need additional support and to involve them and their families in making the necessary provision.

This book is designed as a practical handbook for those working in early years settings. It is an updated version of an earlier book *Supporting Special Needs: Understanding Inclusion in the Early Years*, published in 2003.

It is divided into three parts:

Part 1 Special Needs – Key Issues This section looks in detail at the current SEND Code of Practice 2014 and its implications for early years settings. It begins by considering the key issues surrounding inclusion.

Part 2 This section focuses on practical strategies for supporting children who may need additional support in one or more areas of development.

Part 3 This is a reference section designed to provide background knowledge about some common medical conditions and disabilities.

I hope that you will find this book useful, but do remember that it is a starting point for your work with children and their families. Children are wonderfully complex and to work in their best interest, we need to gain additional information from their parents, other professionals and of course from the child themselves.

PART 1

Special needs – key issues

The recent Special Educational Needs Code of Practice, as well as other recent disability legislation, is changing the way that children with special educational needs are educated. It is important that all adults working with children understand the implications of the new Code of Practice as well as other recent legislation aimed at combating discrimination against disabled people. This section is designed to help practitioners understand the concept of inclusion and its history. It also provides a step-by-step practical guide to the process of identifying and making plans for children who may have special educational needs.

Chapter 1

Key issues in special educational needs and disability

▶ Introduction

There are some key issues and perspectives that all adults working with children need to understand in order to work effectively with children and their parents. These issues and perspectives reflect the way in which our society is trying to become more inclusive and valuing of diversity. Isolating children because their learning or physical needs are different to those of the majority of children is now seen as being discriminatory and therefore morally wrong. The latest Code of Practice reinforces the concept that all children should be educated together apart from in exceptional cases and that early years settings, schools and other education providers have a duty to adapt their provision to allow for this.

This chapter is designed to give you an understanding of the background of inclusive education and it covers the following areas:

- Definitions of special educational needs and disability
- Being sensitive to language
- Attitudes and stereotypes
- Models of disability
- The concept of inclusive education.

▶ Definitions of special educational needs and disability

Definitions by their nature can create stereotypes and as such are often very controversial. Many professionals and parents dislike the labelling that definitions generate and also the tendency of definitions to focus on a deficit model, i.e. what children cannot do. Policy makers, on the other hand, would argue that without definitions, it would be impossible to create any enforceable laws and policies. Funding and legislation are often therefore tied to definitions and so it is very difficult for settings to avoid using them.

The following definitions are used in current legislation and are referred to in the current Equality Act 2010 and the Special Educational Needs and Disability Code of Practice 2014.

Disability

'A person (P) has a disability if:

(a) P has a physical or mental impairment, and
(b) the impairment has a substantial and long-term adverse effect on P's ability to carry out normal day-to-day activities.'

Special educational needs (SEN)

This term came into existence as a result of the 1978 Warnock Report. The committee was anxious to avoid labelling children or using words that had negative connotations. The term 'special educational needs' was used as an all-encompassing term to describe any child who needed some extra support. It is worth noting that many organisations campaigning for inclusiveness are unhappy with this term. The current definition of SEN used in the Children and Families Act 2014, from which the Code of Practice derives its legal status, is as follows.

'● A child or young person has special educational needs if he or she has a learning difficulty or disability which calls for special educational provision to be made for him or her.
● A child of compulsory school age or a young person has a learning difficulty or disability if he or she:
   (a) has a significantly greater difficulty in learning than the majority of others of the same age, or
   (b) has a disability which prevents or hinders him or her from making use of facilities of a kind generally provided for others of the same age in mainstream schools or mainstream post-16 institutions.'

There is also a definition which states that children under two years may be considered as having special educational needs if they are likely to have difficulty when they reach compulsory school age.

▶ Differing points of views in respect of defining children

There is some unease about whether the terms 'special needs' or 'SEN' should be used at all. It is worth understanding the concerns shared by some parents and organisations that promote children's rights. Organisations such as the Alliance for Inclusive Education (ALLFIE) suggest that all children have needs and, as such, they have an automatic right to be met. The argument is that if society were more inclusive in its structure and nature, there would be no need to have 'special needs' policies or even to label children as having 'special needs'. Interestingly, Scotland uses the term 'additional needs', which has been adopted by some early years settings and schools in England.

Being sensitive to language

As we have seen, definitions can be controversial and damaging. This is because language can be a very powerful tool. Understanding and reflecting on your language is therefore an important part of working effectively with children and their parents. This section is designed to help you feel more confident in your use of language. As attitudes and language evolve, it will be essential for you to continually check that your language is effective and accurate.

A good starting point is to understand that language reflects attitudes and values. Take the term 'invalid' as an example: it actually means something that is not valid! Barriers to communication can appear quickly if someone feels that they are being labelled or negatively viewed. There has been a shift in thinking about disability over the past 20 years and this has been reflected in the language we use; terms such as 'spastic' or 'physically handicapped' are no longer acceptable. Language use and preferences continue to evolve. A good example of this is the way that some organisations prefer to use the term 'disabled children' while others prefer 'children with disabilities'.

This collection box dates from a time when children with disability were seen only as victims

Defining disability

'Impairment' refers to the lack or abnormality of development or of growth. While this term is used widely, it is worth noting that it is not always favoured by all organisations. A good example of this is the Royal National Institute of Blind People, which uses the term 'sight loss' rather than 'visual impairment'.

'Disability' refers to the restrictions that an impairment causes – for example, a person with a hearing loss has a disability in hearing.

'Handicap' refers to the disadvantage that the person has in relation to others in certain situations. Note that the person is not themselves 'handicapped' – he or she is being handicapped by the situation. For example, a person with hearing loss is being handicapped when announcements are broadcast in an airport because he or she has a hearing disability. His or her disability does not prevent him or her from reading the signs and getting on to the aircraft, and so he or she is not handicapped all the time.

▶ Changes in the use of language

Some language which was frequently used a few years ago is no longer considered to be appropriate. The chart below shows the ways in which language has shifted.

Shifts in language use

Avoid	Preferred
'The disabled' to describe a group of people or children	Disabled people or disabled children
Able-bodied	Non-disabled
Wheelchair-bound	Wheelchair-user
Mental handicap	Learning difficulty or learning need
Suffering from	'Living with' or 'has' and name the medical condition or impairment
Spastic	A person or child with cerebral palsy
Congenital	Genetically impaired
'Fit' when a person has epilepsy	Seizure
An epileptic, diabetic, asthmatic, etc.	A person or child with epilepsy or diabetes, etc.
Disabled toilet	Accessible toilet

This child is a wheelchair user. It allows them to be more independent.

After a disastrous incident where a member of staff managed to offend a parent of a child, we have now put in place a rigorous induction process. One of the things that we focus on during induction is ensuring that adults new to our setting really understand the issues around children who have SEN and/or disabilities. This includes being sensitive to the language that is used as well as what it means to have an inclusive setting. We have learnt the hard way that not all staff will have had really good training about equality issues including SEN and disability awareness.

Julie, daycare nursery manager

What this means in practice

- Remember that the child is always far more important than any condition or syndrome. Make sure that your language reflects this.
- Avoid drawing attention to a child's disability, difference or condition needlessly! Ask the child or their parents about their preferences in terms of language.
- Contact support groups or voluntary organisations if you are unsure about the best language to use, especially when writing plans or policies. Some organisations have a section on their website which briefs journalists about terms to use and to avoid.

▶ Attitudes and stereotypes

The way we think about disability affects the care and education of disabled children. This is why it is important to examine the stereotypes and attitudes that are common in society. A good starting point is to understand that discrimination against people with disabilities is not new, but is centuries old. In the past, disabled children were left to die, physical differences were mocked, and later institutions were built to house the 'defective'. Disability was seen as a 'curse', bringing shame and stigma upon the child and his or her family. Attitudes towards disability were probably founded on ignorance, poverty and religious bigotry. Today, we are faced with the remnants of those attitudes but we no longer have the excuse of ignorance and poverty as we are a relatively well educated and prosperous society.

▶ Stereotypes

Stereotypes are the images that we hold of groups of people. They tend to reflect society's prejudices and lack of knowledge. They are unhelpful because they lead people to assume that they 'know' about a person who is part of a stereotyped group. These assumptions can prevent us from considering each person as an individual. The controversy surrounding definitions relates to the way that they can reinforce stereotypes. There are common stereotypes that are still prevalent, many of which apply to disabled children. It is important to be aware of them as vestiges of them may influence practice with children and their families.

Parents as heroes and angels

Many parents and carers resent the common stereotype that they are heroes or angels. This common stereotype creates unrealistic expectations for them to live up to and also misses the point that they do things because they love their children. This stereotype also allows society to conveniently forget that parents need support, as there is the idea that parents will bravely soldier on.

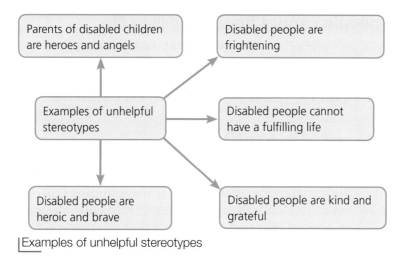

Examples of unhelpful stereotypes

Disabled people are helpless and dependent

This stereotype tends to mean that disabled people are to be pitied and are seen as needing others. Traditionally, this stereotype was used by charities in order to raise funds. The other reason behind the stereotype is that barriers were put up which prevented disabled people from being able to do things for themselves, e.g. coat hooks being positioned at the wrong height.

Disabled people are heroic and brave

This stereotype puts a lot of pressure on disabled people to be cheerful, accepting and ready to 'make the most of their condition'. It is propagated by media stories of disabled people who 'despite the odds' have achieved in some way. This stereotype does not allow for people to have complex emotions and sees disabled people as being different rather than ordinary.

Disabled people are kind and grateful

As with the stereotype of a disabled person being brave, this stereotype assumes that all disabled people have the same personality and temperament. The reality is that each and every one of us is different. The idea that disabled people are expected to be grateful is also interesting. It harks back to a time when charity was given to disabled people, rather than equal rights. Non-disabled people are not grateful that they can enter a shop; their assumption is that they should be able to do so.

Disabled people cannot have a fulfilling life

This stereotype promotes the assumption that disabled people cannot have 'quality of life'. It assumes that disabled people will not be able to have a family, get a job or take on responsibility. The focus remains continually on the barriers and the person's difficulty, rather than on the person themselves.

▶ Models of disability

There are two models or ways of thinking about disability: the medical model of disability and the social model of disability. Understanding both models is important as they reflect underlying attitudes towards disability. As a practitioner, it is important that you understand that the medical model of disability is considered by disabled people to be oppressive.

▶ Medical model of disability

The medical model of disability has its roots in seeing people with disabilities as being imperfect. It reflects society's faith in doctors and came about because of the historic fear of disability, combined with scientific advances. The medical model views disability as something that must, whenever possible, be cured. Where this is not possible a feeling of failure results, unless the person can be made to 'look' normal or 'act' normally. The medical model of disability therefore treats people with impairments as victims and patients; words such as 'handicapped', 'incurable', 'suffering' and 'wheelchair-bound' are associated with this attitude. The medical model of disability tends to put the emphasis more on the condition than on the person. This results in labelling people according to their impairments, for example, 'a person who's wheelchair-bound' rather than 'James, who uses a wheelchair'.

▶ Social model of disability

The social model of disability reflects a new attitude towards disabled people. It has been developed by disabled people themselves and aims to challenge the historical view of disabled people as being less worthy. It considers first and foremost that they are people with rights and feelings. The social model of disability looks to empower people as it emphasises their rights to make choices and be independent. It also challenges society to become more inclusive so that disabled people are not seen as being 'problems that need sorting out' or as 'victims who need pity'. The social model of disability has meant that terms such as 'mentally handicapped' and 'wheelchair-bound' are now considered unhelpful. The case study below shows clearly how attitudes have changed and how the social model of disability is increasingly now being accepted as the way forward.

Case study

Emma was born with one arm foreshortened above the elbow. Her mother was determined that this should not affect Emma's life and she refused to let anyone feel sorry for Emma or consider her a victim. Emma was given a prosthesis (false limb) which although uncomfortable and restricting, made her look like all other children. At home Emma never wore her prosthesis as her family completely accepted the way she looked without it.

Emma learned to ride a horse, manage everyday tasks and was a very happy and confident child. She left school and started to work in a restaurant. As she became older, she gradually started to question society's attitude towards disability and began to feel unhappy that she was in effect disguising her disability. One day she decided that she would no longer wear her false arm. Her employer was unhappy about this decision. He said that seeing a person with only one arm would make customers feel uneasy and it could affect his business. Emma turned the argument around and said that if she had spent her life learning to cope without an arm, perhaps his customers could spend five minutes learning to see her without one, especially as they had already learned to cope with seeing his bald head!

What this means in practice

- What images and representations do you have of disabled people?
- Do the images reinforce the traditional stereotypes?
- Do you carry out fundraising for organisations such as Scope or Epilepsy Action?
- If so, are you doing so in ways that reinforce the stereotype of 'poor disabled children'?
- Do you challenge stereotypes when you come across them?

▶ Understanding the concept of inclusive education

The medical model of disability has up until now affected the way in which children are educated. Children with any disability or learning difficulty were seen as a 'problem' and were segregated. This resulted in many children not fulfilling their potential as expectations of their abilities were often lowered. Segregation also meant that children in mainstream schools grew up without ever meeting a child who had needs that were different to their own. This has served to perpetuate many myths about disabilities.

The concept of inclusive education is the result of parents and disabled people putting pressure on successive governments to change the education system so as to allow all children to have fair and equal access to education. It is important to realise that the campaign for inclusive education is not limited to children who have special needs, but extends also to a wider range of children who have traditionally been discriminated against, such as those from travelling families or who are being 'looked after' by the local authority.

The concept of inclusive education signals a significant mind shift. Instead of expecting children to 'come up to standard' or otherwise be segregated, the emphasis is on schools and settings to adapt and be flexible enough to accommodate each and every child. Organisations seeking inclusive education also point out the importance of significant funding as poor resources, both physical and human, are often barriers to inclusive education.

❱ Principles of inclusion

One of the leading organisations that promotes inclusion in education is the Alliance for Inclusive Education. They have a very clear vision of what inclusion in education should look like. You may find it interesting to visit their website at www.allfie.org.uk where you will find their principles, which include the following:

- Inclusive education enables all students to participate fully in any mainstream early years provision, school, college or university.
- Inclusive education provision has training and resources aimed at fostering every student's equality and participation in all aspects of the learning community.
- Inclusive education aims to equip all people with the skills needed to build inclusive communities.

❱ Inclusion and legislation

Over a number of years, we have edged more closely towards inclusion in education. The Equality Act 2010 is clear that all education settings are required to make reasonable adjustments to ensure that their provision is accessible for disabled children. Interestingly, this is anticipatory, for example early years settings need to think ahead to what might be needed.

Inclusive education is based on nine principles:
1 A person's worth is independent of their abilities or achievements.
2 Every human being is able to feel and think.
3 Every human has the right to communicate and be heard.
4 All human beings need each other.
5 Real education can only happen in the context of real relationships.
6 All people need support and friendship from people of their own age.
7 Progress for all learners is achieved by building on things people can do rather than what they can't.
8 Diversity brings strength to all living systems.
9 Collaboration is more important than competition.

Alliance for Inclusive Education, reproduced with kind permission

Inclusive education means all children having the same opportunities to play and learn together

The Special Educational Needs and Disability Code of Practice states in its section on principles:

As part of its commitments under Articles 7 and 24 of the United Nations Convention of the Rights of Persons with Disabilities, the UK Government is committed to inclusive education of disabled children and young people and the progressive removal of barriers to learning and participation in mainstream education. The Children and Families Act 2014 secures the general presumption in law of mainstream education in relation to decisions about where children and young people with SEN should be educated and the Equality Act 2010 provides protection from discrimination for disabled people.

Special Educational Needs and Disability Code of Practice

Chapter 2
Key legislation

▶ Introduction

The laws of a country often reflect the underlying attitudes and beliefs of its society. Over the past few years, legislation relating to disability in the UK has changed enormously, mainly as a result of powerful campaigning by disabled people and parents of disabled children. The most recent legislation has built upon preceding Acts so it is helpful to understand the chronology of and legal background to its formation. This chapter provides a chronological overview of some of the key legislation that has shaped the journey towards the current Code of Practice 2014.

▶ The background to current legislation

While this book is designed to provide a practical approach to working with children, it is worth understanding the background to current legislation. Here are some of the key parts of legislation that have had a profound effect on the lives of disabled people and children, as well as people and children with learning difficulties.

▶ Mental Deficiency Act (1911)

This Act is significant as it is a powerful reminder of the attitudes that existed – and to some extent still exist today – towards people with learning difficulties. This piece of legislation was developed in response to an idea known as eugenics. Eugenics was seen to be the way in which society might be improved by selective breeding and also by preventing those who were seen as weak in some way from reproducing. The idea, which is now of course abhorrent, was widely promoted and was supported by politicians including Winston Churchill. The Act allowed for the permanent detainment (effectively imprisonment) of children and adults who from an early age appeared to fit into one of four categories: Idiots, Imbeciles, Feeble-minded or Moral Defectives. There was no appeal system in place. The Act was replaced in 1959 by the Mental Health Act after campaigning by organisations such as the National Council for Civil Liberties (now Liberty).

What this means in practice

While the Act is no longer in force, interestingly the words 'idiot' and 'imbecile' are still used, but they are offensive because of this.

◗ Chronically Sick and Disabled Persons Act (1970)

This Act required local authorities to keep a register of disabled people and to provide services for them. The Act is still current, although it has been strengthened by other pieces of legislation such as the 1986 Disabled Persons Act. Section 2 outlines the range of services that local authorities need to provide if a person is assessed as requiring them. These services include holidays and transport, as well as practical assistance in the home. This Act had a significant impact as it suggested that disabled people had the right to a reasonable standard of life.

◗ Education Act (Handicapped Children) (1970)

This piece of legislation made all disabled children the responsibility of the local education authority. Since 1944 they had been the responsibility of the health service, as children with a learning difficulty were considered to be impossible to educate. As a result of this Act, many special schools were built in the 1970s in order to give such children an education for the first time.

◗ The Warnock Report (1978)

Reports are not pieces of legislation and many findings in reports are often 'forgotten'. This was not the case with the Warnock Report and it is often considered to be a landmark in the education of disabled children. In 1978 a Report was published by a committee chaired by Mary Warnock. The committee had undertaken a comprehensive study of the whole area of disabled children, their education and their needs. The committee took evidence from parents, the voluntary sector, educationalists and the medical profession. The Report was to prove highly influential and subsequent legislation, including the SEN Code of Practice 2001, evolved from the findings of this Report. For years, people had talked about handicapped children or had labelled children according to their disability. The Report suggested a title of 'special education need' (SEN), which would include any child who needed some form of extra support. The Report suggested that there might be three types of support:

1 Special means of access to the curriculum.
2 Changes to the curriculum.
3 Changes to the environment, including emotional or social support.

Terminology

The term 'special educational need' was an all-encompassing term and included children who had slight difficulties with their reading and writing, as well as children who had major care needs. It also included children who had short-term needs that were causing them to have difficulties in fulfilling their potential, alongside children who had long-term needs. In this way it focused professionals on the idea of how to meet the needs that the children might have, rather than on the condition or cause of them. This was a major breakthrough and one that the Warnock Report is noted for.

It is worth remembering that prior to the Report and subsequent legislation, children were categorised and educated according to their disability rather than according to their potential. This meant that a partially sighted child would be educated in a school for the blind and would not have access to the same curriculum and qualifications as other children.

The Warnock Report introduced the following terms in an attempt to remove the previous labelling of children according to their medical condition:

- speech and language disorders
- visual disability and hearing disability
- emotional and behaviour disorders
- learning difficulties: specific, mild, moderate and severe.

Key proposals of the Warnock Report

Assessment

The Report suggested that early diagnosis and help were essential. It suggested that a team of multi-disciplinary professionals should assess the child's whole needs and these should be reviewed annually.

Supporting pre-school age children

The report emphasised that children and parents in the first five years would need support. It suggested that each family should have a 'named person', a social worker or a health visitor, who would support the family.

Integration

The Report proposed that the integration of children into mainstream education should happen wherever possible.

Parents

The Report pushed for parents to be more involved in decisions about their child.

❱ Education Act (1981)

This Act was heavily based on the recommendations of the Warnock Report and gave local education authorities (LEAs) legal duties to fulfil. The Act placed a clear responsibility on the LEAs to provide support for children who have special educational needs. It also introduced the process now known as 'statementing'. This is the process by which children are assessed by a team of professionals alongside their parents, and a statement of how the child's needs are to be supported is drawn up. The statement of special educational needs was a legally binding one and committed the LEA to providing for the child. The Act is also important because it gave parents power for the first time. Parents were to be involved in the process of producing a statement and deciding on the best course of education for their children, but more importantly, parents were given the legal power to challenge LEAs. The process of statementing continued until September 2014 when statements of need were replaced by the Education, Health and Care plan (see pages 00–00).

❱ Disabled Persons Act (1986)

This Act continued the trend towards placing duties on local authorities by requiring them to assess people for services that could be provided under the 1970 Act, if asked to do so by the disabled person or their representative or carer. This Act strengthened the Chronically Sick and Disabled Persons Act of 1970.

❱ Education Reform Act (1988)

This Act introduced the National Curriculum into all state schools, including special schools, in England and Wales. This measure was at the time met with some consternation amongst teachers, but the Act allowed schools to modify the curriculum or even not to use it if it was not deemed to be appropriate. It was a significant step as many disabled children were not fulfilling their academic potential.

❱ Children Act (1989)

The Children Act has generally been a well received piece of legislation. It is still current and many practices, such as the compilation of a register of 'children in need' by LEAs, are carried out to comply with this Act. It brought together many pieces of legislation that related to children and was based on the idea that children had rights. It sought to protect all children, but also looked at the needs and rights of vulnerable children. The Act is wide ranging and covers issues such as child protection, registration of childcare settings and parental responsibility.

Key proposals of the Children Act

- The welfare of the child must at all times be considered paramount.
- Wherever possible, children should be brought up and cared for within their own families.
- Parents with 'children in need' should be helped to bring up their children themselves (disabled children are considered to be 'in need').
- Children should be consulted and kept informed about decisions that affect their future.

Disabled children are seen as children 'in need' and as such the LEA has legal duties towards them and their families. This means that LEAs are obliged to maintain a register of children and to offer them support. Many disabled children therefore have a social worker who visits the family from time to time. The requirement of the Act for LEAs to support children and help them to remain with their families meant that respite care, play schemes and funded places in pre-schools began to be offered. The 1989 Children Act also set the trend for parents and children to be seen as important in the decision-making process.

❯ NHS and Community Care Act (1990)

Under Part 3 of this Act (which is still current), the government sought to help people who previously would have been in residential care to have their needs met at home and thus to remain in the community. Services such as domestic help, equipment and modifications to accommodation are examples of the help that can be provided.

❯ Education Act (1993)

The 1993 Education Act was based on the 1981 Education Act. Its key points are summarised below and are important because they form the basis of the Education Act of 2001.

Code of Practice

The Act required that the Secretary of State for Education publish a code of practice to give LEAs and others practical guidance in following the legislation. The Code of Practice came into effect between September 1994 and December 2001.

Parents

The 1993 Act made it clear that local education authorities needed to work alongside parents. It also established SEN tribunals to hear cases where parents and local authorities were unable to agree. Parents' rights of appeal were extended and information was published to help parents understand their rights.

Definition of special educational needs

The Act also defined what was meant by special educational needs. It stated that to be defined as having special educational needs, children had to have a learning difficulty that required special educational provision because the learning difficulty was greater than that for the majority of children of the same age, or because of a disability that prevented them from using the same provision as other children. It also made it clear that children who had a different home language to the one used in the setting were not to be classified as having SEN.

Co-operation between agencies

The Act stated that where health services identified that a child under five years old might have special educational needs, they had a duty to both the LEA and the parents to inform them. It also stated that they should pass on information about voluntary organisations that might be able to assist parents. This was significant because it encouraged voluntary, education and health services to work together in the interests of the child.

Assessment of children under two years

The Act gave parents the right to ask for their child to be assessed and, if appropriate, to be given a statement of special educational needs

As a result of the 1993 Education Act, a Code of Practice was produced. This legally binding document was available to everyone involved in the care and education of children with special needs, including parents. The availability of this information meant that parents were able to challenge schools and LEAs that were not fulfilling their obligations. The Code of Practice introduced a new role into settings, that of the Special Educational Needs Co-ordinator or SENCO (a named person responsible for co-ordinating support for children with SEN). The Code also required all maintained schools (schools receiving public funds) to have a policy on special needs. These two measures gave SEN a higher profile in schools that has since been built upon by the current Code of Practice.

▶ Disability Discrimination Act (1995) and Disability Rights Commission Act (1999)

The Disability Discrimination Act 1995 (DDA) came into force on 2 December 1996. It is considered to be a landmark in terms of addressing discrimination against disabled people. For the first time, it was against the law for shops, employers and landlords to discriminate against disabled people. The Act gave disabled people new rights in the following areas:

- employment
- goods and services, including transport
- education
- buying/renting of property.

The Act also created a Disability Rights Council, but this did not have statutory powers. After campaigning from many groups, a Disability Rights Commission was created in April 2000, following the Disability Rights Commission Act 1999. This Commission has statutory enforcement powers, which means that it can conduct investigations into discrimination and also support an individual in bringing court proceedings where unlawful discrimination is alleged to have taken place. The Commission also has a key role in educating employers, service providers and the general public in order to prevent discrimination occurring.

The DDA is divided into seven parts. It defines disability as a physical or mental impairment that has a substantial and long-term adverse effect on a person's ability to carry out day-to-day activities. To allow shops, restaurants and other service providers time to make 'reasonable' adjustments, different parts of the Act were phased in gradually.

The Act ensures recognition of the needs of disabled people who wish to study and the provision of better information for parents and students. The aim is that students will not be discriminated against because of their impairments. This Act was strengthened further by the SEN and Disability Act 2001.

Schools have to explain their arrangements for the admission of disabled students, how they will help these students gain access and what they will do to ensure they are treated fairly.

- Further and higher education institutions funded by the Further and Higher Education Funding Councils have to publish disability statements containing information about facilities for disabled people.
- LEAs have to provide information on their further education facilities for disabled people.

Making reasonable adjustments to premises is a requirement of current legislation

◗ Education Act (1996)

This Act incorporated all previous Education Acts since 1944. Part 4 of this Act included the main elements of the 1993 Education Act in relation to SEN. It gave parents more rights to appeal and also set a limit of 26 weeks to complete the legal process for identifying and assessing special needs. This Act is still current, but it has been amended by the Special Educational Needs and Disability Act 2001, which gives parents and children stronger rights to be included in mainstream education.

◗ Human Rights Act (1998)

This Act came into effect in October 2000 and incorporates provisions from the European Convention on Human Rights. It has wide-ranging implications for many areas of people's lives, as all government initiatives and decisions must be interpreted in line with the agreed Articles and Protocols of the Convention. These include the Right to Education (Article 2 of Protocol 1) and the Prohibition of Discrimination (Article 14).

◗ Carers and Disabled Children Act (2000)

This Act came into force on 1 April 2001. The aim is to recognise the role of carers and to provide for their needs, as well as the needs of children. Parents of disabled children are therefore asked about the family's needs, as well as the needs of the disabled child. The Act also allows councils to make direct payments to families so that they can purchase services. As well as direct payments to the family, short-break vouchers are also provided, which are intended for families to use to gain respite care.

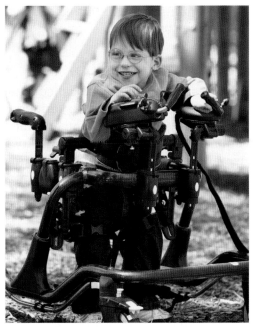

◗ Special Education Needs and Disability Act (SENDA) (2001)

This Act is divided into two sections. The SEN Code of Practice 2001 is the product of this Act as it gives practical guidance to LEAs, schools and parents about the implementation of the Act. Part 1 of the Act reforms the framework of SEN to strengthen the rights of parents and children to access mainstream

There is a presumption for children to attend mainstream education rather than special schools education. Part 2 extends the Disability Discrimination Act 1995 to education, extending the civil rights of disabled children and adults in schools, colleges and universities.

Key features of the Special Education Needs and Disability Act (SENDA) 2001

- The right of children with special educational needs to be educated in main-stream schools (where this is what parents want and where it is appropriate for the child).
- The requirement for LEAs to arrange to provide parents of children with special educational needs with advice and information, and a means of resolving disputes with schools and LEAs.
- The requirement for LEAs to comply with orders of the Special Educational Needs Tribunal.
- The requirement for education settings to tell parents where they are making special educational provision for their child and to request a statutory assessment of a pupil's special educational needs
- The introduction of disability discrimination rights in the provision of education in schools, further education, higher education, adult education and the youth service.
- The requirement not to treat disabled students less favourably than non-disabled students.

▶ Equality Act (2006)

The Equality Act 2006 established a new commission to replace the separate commissions that dealt with various aspects of discrimination, such as the Disability Rights Commission and the Equal Opportunities Commission. The new commission is known as the Equality and Human Rights Commission (EHRC). As well as the setting up of the commission, the Equality Act 2006 also made it illegal to discriminate on the grounds of religion and belief when providing services and goods.

What this means in practice

The Equality and Human Rights Commission is a useful source of information and it is worth visiting their website at www.equalityhumanrights.com. You will find out more about:

- your obligations as an early years setting
- your obligations as an employer
- your rights as an employee
- your rights as a consumer (in relation to discrimination).

❱ Equality Act (2010)

The Equality Act 2010 brought together under one single Act more than one hundred separate pieces of anti-discrimination legislation, including those covering disability, gender, race and age equality. In terms of practice in early years settings and schools, the Equality Act 2010 reinforces the duties that are already in existence as a result of SENDA 2001 and the Disability Discrimination Act 1995. As we have seen, education settings already had duties to make reasonable adjustments and to be proactive in ensuring that children were not discriminated against because of disability or learning needs.

❱ Children and Families Act (2014)

The Children and Families Act 2014 is a significant piece of legislation relating to several aspects of the care and education of children. Its aim is to reduce disadvantage among children and to support families. While Part 3 of the Act is the most important in relation to this book, other parts of the Act cover other topics such as adoption and employment rights in relation to parents. It also allowed for the setting up of child-minding agencies, the introduction of free school lunches for primary school children up until Year 2, and reformed the function of the Children's Commissioner.

Part 3 of the Children and Families Act 2014

Part 3 of the Act contains the legislation relating to children with special educational needs and disability. Part 3 contains some significant changes, including:

- The support of young people is extended to the age of 25.
- The duty of local authorities to develop a Local Offer of provision in response to the needs of children, young people and families.
- The replacement of statements (see the Warnock Report) with Education, Health and Care plans.
- The opportunity for parents to request a direct payment known as a 'Personal Budget' in place of the local authority making provision for the child or young person.
- A new Code of Practice.

What this means in practice

It is important that you check your policies and procedures in the light of the latest legislation to ensure they are accurate.

Chapter 3

Special educational needs and disability Code of Practice 2014

▶ Introduction

The Code of Practice took effect in September 2014 and is a key document in planning and providing for children who have special educational needs and/ or disabilities. It is important to look carefully at this document and to read it alongside the statutory requirements of the Early Years Foundation Stage if you are working in early years. The Department for Education has also published a guide for early years settings called 'Early years: guide to the 0 to 25 SEND code of practice' which is also useful to read.

In this chapter we look at:

- The principles and structure of the Code of Practice.
- How the Code of Practice affects early years settings.
- Developing and reviewing a SEND policy.
- The role of the SENCO in early years settings.

▶ Legal status of the Code of Practice

The Code of Practice translates into practice the legislation contained in the Children and Families Act 2014. When reading the Code of Practice, it is important to understand that it has a legal basis even though the word 'guidance' is in its title. Throughout the document, it is important that you pay attention to any sentence containing the word '**must**'. The word 'must' denotes that this is a legal requirement for all the organisations and bodies identified in the code. You should also keep an eye out for the word '**should**'. This denotes that there is an expectation that the relevant bodies and organisations will follow the Code and, in situations where they do not do so, they have to be able to give a valid explanation of why it was disregarded.

 Do all early years settings have to follow the Code of Practice?

 Yes, the Code of Practice requires all early years settings to have regard to the Code of Practice, which in effect acts as a requirement.

Can we use elements of the previous Code of Practice?

No! You must use this Code of Practice and disregard the previous Code of Practice.

 Do we have to follow the Code of Practice as it does say it is guidance?

 Yes, the term 'statutory' means that you must follow it as it has a legal status.

Principles of the Code of Practice

A good starting point when looking at the Code of Practice is to understand the principles behind it. These principles are based on those within the Children and Families Act 2014. These principles should underpin your practice and policies. Here is a summary of the principles.

- The views, wishes and feelings of children or young people and their parents are central.
- The importance of children or young people, and their parents, participating as fully as possible in decision making and being given the information and support to do so.
- The importance of identifying the needs of children and young people.
- The need to work collaboratively with other services, including health and social care, to provide support for children and young people.
- The importance of providing high quality provision that is inclusive and removes barriers to learning.
- The need to support the child or young person in ways that will allow them to achieve the best possible education or other outcomes, including preparation for adulthood.

The structure of the Code of Practice

The Code of Practice is divided into 11 chapters. There is a specific chapter for early years providers, but you should also be familiar with the other chapters in order that you can support both the parents and the child.

How the Code of Practice affects early years settings

All early years settings are required to have regard to the Code of Practice. While some parts of the Code of Practice do not relate directly to early years settings,

This nursery provides an inclusive environment through careful resourcing

there are plenty of aspects that do. Here are some of the key aspects that you should particularly note and be ready to demonstrate in your practice. While I have provided the relevant paragraphs from the Code of Practice, you should still refer to the Code.

◗ Working with parents (1.4, 1.7, 1.9, 2.4, 5.5, 5.37)

One of the features of the Code of Practice is the stress put upon working with parents so that they can be involved in decisions about their child. The Code also stresses the importance of respecting parents' knowledge. There is a clear requirement for early years providers to ensure that parents and, where appropriate, children are involved in assessments which may lead to an Education, Health and Care (EHC) plan and also to contribute to the development and review of an EHC plan. There are also requirements to value parents' contributions and knowledge about their child even when children do not have an EHC plan. Paragraph 2.4 requires local authorities to build on existing Parent Partnership Services so that parents can have access to advice and information. It will be important for you to know the contact details of your local Parent Partnership Service. Do note, though, that the names used for this service vary from area to area.

There are also requirements for local authorities and the joint commissioning group to engage with parents when planning services. To this end, paragraph

1.9 states that all local authorities have to create a parent–carer forum. You might like to encourage parents to become involved with this group.

What this means in practice

You will need to show that parents are at the heart of your systems and that their voice is reflected when planning interventions or referring children.

▶ Children's rights to participate in decision making (1.6)

As the Code of Practice is very person-centred, there is a focus on the importance of taking children's and young people's views into consideration. This paragraph reinforces that children, even at a young age, already have the right for their opinions to be taken into consideration under the United Nations Convention on the Rights of the Child. There is a caveat that considerations of their views do need to take into account their age, maturity and capability.

What this means in practice

You will need to make sure that your systems and paperwork clearly take into consideration children's thoughts, views and ideas. It will be important that you find age-/stage-appropriate ways of doing this.

▶ Identifying children's and young people's needs (1.15, 5.4, 5.12, 5.22, 5.23, 5.27, 5.28, 5.29, 5.30, 5.31, 5.36)

One of the principles of the Code of Practice is that children with SEN and/or disabilities will gain the support needed. To this end, there is a focus on the importance of identification. There is an expectation that early years providers as well as schools will have a role in identifying children with special needs and bringing them to the attention of the local authority.

In addition, paragraphs 5.4 and 5.12 reinforce the need for early identification in line with the requirements of the EYFS. Paragraphs 5.22 and 5.23 remind us that there are already assessments built into the EYFS: the two-year-old check and the EYFS profile.

Later, paragraphs 5.27 onwards provide further advice about identifying SEN and disability. It is worth noting paragraph 5.30, which looks at identifying and assessing SEN for young children whose first language is not English. The guidance states that you should establish whether the delay is linked to SEN or disability, as opposed to simply having difficulties learning English. Children whose difficulties are due to having EAL are not considered to have SEN.

What this means in practice

You will need to have systems in place to identify children who may have SEN and/or disabilities and bring them to the attention of the local authority. This may mean finding out more about your local authority's services and systems.

▶ Using a graduated response to support children (5.38, 5.39, 5.40, 5.41, 5.42, 5.43, 5.44, 5.45, 5.48, 5.49)

Once a child is identified as not making expected progress, guidance is given as to how early years settings should work with the child. In line with the principles of working with parents, several paragraphs emphasise the importance of involving parents. The graduated response consists of Assess, Plan, Do and Review. If it becomes clear that the interventions made are still not meeting a child's needs, then paragraph 5.48 states that practitioners should consider involving other specialists, but the decision to do so should be taken with the child's parents. In a situation where the child continues, despite interventions, not to make expected progress, the next step is for a setting to request an Education, Health and Care needs assessment. Paragraph 5.45 states that a SENCO should lead the graduated response process (see page 36, Role of the SENCO).

This team is reviewing the session and planning for individual children who need additional support

What this means in practice

You will need to develop a way of assessing, planning and reviewing interventions. There are many ways in which you might do this, which we will look at in Chapter 6.

 What has happened to Early Years Action and Early Years Action Plus?

 These are no longer being used and so your paperwork and systems will need to be revised to reflect the graduated response approach.

▶ Tailoring practice including assessment to support children and young people with special educational needs (1.25, 5.4, 5.31, 5.32, 5.33, 5.34, 5.35)

In addition to the need to adopt the graduated response of Assess, Plan, Do and Review, there are also paragraphs within the Code that emphasise the importance of tailoring practice to support children. Paragraph 1.25 contains several expectations for early years settings and schools to meet. It is worth reading and reflecting on each of these expectations. These include the requirement for precise assessment of children's learning and development, tracking children's progress and reviewing provision for them. There is also a requirement to work closely with parents and children and to check that approaches are having an impact on children's progress.

Paragraphs 5.32, 5.33, 5.34 and 5.35 look at the importance of matching provision to children's needs and also look at the importance of reviewing interventions.

What this means in practice

In order to achieve precise assessment, you may need to look for a range of sources of information. For language, for example, consider downloading a free copy of the poster 'Stages of Speech and Language Development' from www.ican.org.uk. Look out too for the *Early Years Development Journal* available from www.councilfordisabledchildren.org.uk. This links the EYFS more precisely to ages/stages and will help with precise development.

❱ Inclusive practice (1.26, 1.27, 1.31, 1.35, 2.38, 5.6, 5.10, 5.11)

Paragraphs 1.26 and 1.27 emphasise the presumption that children with special educational needs and/or a disability will be educated in mainstream provision, although parents of children with an EHC plan have the right to ask for a place at a special school.

Paragraph 1.31 also states that those working in early years settings and schools should have high expectations of children with SEN or disabilities and that they are to be included in opportunities that are available to other children. In addition, paragraphs 1.35 and 5.10 remind settings that they have a responsibility under the Equality Act to ensure that reasonable adjustments are made for children with disabilities.

Paragraph 2.38 reminds maintained nurseries, academies and schools of their duty to provide information about how they eliminate discrimination between disabled and non-disabled children.

There is also a reminder in paragraph 5.11 that all early years providers need to take steps to ensure that children with medical conditions get the support they need. This is already a requirement of the EYFS.

A sensory room at a nursery school

What this means in practice

You should check that everyone in the setting understands the term 'inclusive practice' and that admission processes, policies, resources and activities all reflect inclusive practice.

▶ Education, Health and Care plans (EHC plans) (5.46, 5.49, and all paragraphs within Chapter 9 of the SEND Code of Practice)

Where you have tailored provision and employ a graduated provision approach, but children are still needing substantial additional support, under this Code of Practice a plan called an Education, Health and Care plan (EHC plan) can be requested. We look at this process in detail on pages 57–61. The EHC plan has a legal basis and is drawn up in conjunction with parents by the local authority once an assessment process is completed. The EHC plans replace the statementing arrangements from the previous Code of Practice. The EHC plan is reviewed at least once a year by the local authority. Paragraph 5.46 states that the local authority can ask early years settings (or maintained nurseries) to carry out the review on their behalf.

 How is an EHC plan different to the statements that children used to have?

 The EHC plan has a different focus. It is more person centred and also focuses on outcomes for the child or young person

What this means in practice

You will need to understand the process by which a child can be put forward for an EHC plan and the evidence that you will need to provide to support the application. You will also need to have systems in place to review the needs of children who have an EHC plan.

▶ Partnership working (3.28)

One of the key features of the Children and Families Act that is reflected in the Code of Practice is the need to join up services and also that the provision for services should be commissioned according to local needs. A range of information is needed to commission services. This includes data from the statutory check for two year olds and the EYFS profile.

What this means in practice

As data from the two-year-old check is being used to commission services, it is important that assessments are accurate and reflect children's needs.

❱ Personal Budget (3.38)

One of the features of the Children and Families Act is the ability of parents to request a Personal Budget. The idea behind this is that parents and carers can then have the flexibility to choose which services will best meet the needs of their child.

What this means in practice

In theory parents may choose use their Personal Budget on additional hours of care to add to their existing free entitlement of 15 hours a week.

❱ Training for staff (3.40, 3.41, 3.63, 4.32)

These paragraphs mention the possibility of training being commissioned so that professionals working with children have the skills and knowledge to better identify and support children with SEN or disabilities.

What this means in practice

It will be important for you to let your local authority know of your setting's training needs in respect of children with SEN and/or disabilities. You should also keep an eye out for courses that will help you gain more knowledge and skills in respect of SEND.

❱ Social care (3.49)

There is a requirement for local authorities to provide early years providers with a contact for advice if a child has a social care need.

What this means in practice

Some children and their families may also need further support for social care, e.g. respite care or advice about housing or parenting issues. You should find out the contact details and also the process for referring children and their families for this support.

❱ Local Offer (1.19, 4.16, 4.31, 4.32, 4.38, 4.39, 4.42, 5.7)

One of the key changes is the 'Local Offer'. This is information that is provided so that parents and other interested parties know what provision is available in the local area. The Local Offer also includes information about how parents can request an EHC plan. In order to prepare and also review the Local Offer, your local authority will need to gather information about your setting's provision for SEN and disabled children. You have a duty to provide this information. It is worth looking at your area's Local Offer so that you can advise parents and also find out more about what is available locally. The Local Offer should also show the arrangements in place for training.

As part of the Local Offer, there is a duty for local authorities to secure sufficient childcare for working parents and to work with early years settings to manage local provision. Paragraphs 4.38, 4.39 and 4.42 also require local authorities to publish information in the Local Offer about childcare options and the range of expertise available, including specialist provision.

What this means in practice

You should have a good understanding of what you are already providing in terms of support for children with SEN and/or disabilities and also what, in theory, you could provide if requested.

❱ Reviewing support (5.7, 5.51)

Paragraph 5.7 asks that early years providers regularly review their provision in terms of its quality and breadth. This will also help in terms of providing information for the local authority and for the Early Years Census.

What this means in practice

You should review your practice, resources, knowledge and also training needs. This is good practice as part of aiming for continuous improvement.

❱ SENCO (5.52, 5.53, 5.54)

As in previous Codes of Practice, the role of the SENCO is a key part of SEN and disability provision. Paragraph 5.54 outlines the role of the SENCO. There is a requirement for maintained nurseries to appoint to this post a qualified teacher who also has an additional qualification. These requirements do not apply to other early years providers. For childminders in a network or agency, there is the suggestion that the SENCO role may be allocated to someone within the network or agency.

What this means in practice

You should have someone in post who can take on the role of SENCO. If you are a maintained nursery, the person may now also need to complete the new qualification.

 Is there any difference in the SENCO role from the previous Code of Practice?

 No, not really, although they would need to make sure that the systems are in place that reflect this Code of Practice.

◗ Area SENCOs (5.55, 5.56, 5.57, 5.58)

An Area SENCO is normally someone employed by the local authority who can give additional advice or support to settings. While there is no requirement for local authorities to employ someone in this role, these paragraphs look at this role.

What this means in practice

You should find out if your local authority has employed an Area SENCO and find out how, if needed, you would contact them.

◗ Funding (5.31, 5.59, 5.60)

Interestingly, though paragraph 5.31 puts the onus on early years settings to make provision for children with SEN and disability, there is no mention of funding. Paragraph 5.59 refers to the legal requirement for local authorities to ensure that adequate funding arrangements are in place to provide support for SEN and disabled children. Paragraph 5.60 states that early years providers should make best use of their resources.

What this means in practice

You may like to check if you are supporting a child with SEN and/or disabilities that you are receiving the funding that has been set aside by the local authority to support children. You should also be thoughtful in how you use any additional funding.

Developing and reviewing an SEN and disability policy

A good starting point when implementing the Code of Practice is to consider your setting's SEN and disability policy. While the EYFS statutory framework does not require any written policy unless you are a maintained nursery, the reality is that most early years settings do have a policy. This is because it is a requirement of the EYFS and also of the Code of Practice that you have arrangements in place to identify and support children who have special educational needs and/or a disability. The EYFS also requires you to share this information with parents, while the Code of Practice requires you to provide information about your provision to the local authority.

Developing an SEN and disability policy

Policies outline the attitudes as well as the actions that settings should take about various areas that are important to their everyday practice. While there has been a significant reduction in the number of policies that early years settings are required to have, most early years settings find having policies and procedures clearly written and understood to be a useful tool. In addition, there is a requirement for parents to be given information about a range of topics including safeguarding, food and drink, as well as about how your setting supports children with special educational needs and disabilities. Good policies are like road maps: they help everyone in the setting to understand the direction that the early years setting wishes to take and how it intends to get there.

Who should write the policy?

The policy is best written and thought about as a team effort, although in many settings the manager, owner or SENCO will co-ordinate the actual writing of the policy. If you are a childminder and belong to a professional organisation such as PACEY, you may find that you can work with others or use exemplar materials to help you. Settings that plan and write policies together tend to find that they work more effectively because everyone understands the purpose of the policy. It is worth reminding any reluctant members of staff that the Code of Practice expects a shared involvement in relation to SEND and that they will have a day-to-day responsibility to make sure that every child is given opportunities to make progress and access the provision.

Here is a step-by-step guide that might help you review or write an SEND policy.

Step 1 Begin by considering what information is needed

The key starting point is to jot down the type of information that will be helpful and what information will be required by others.

Your policy is likely to need sections on the following:

Useful information for an SEND policy

SEND policy topics to consider	Possible content
Roles and responsibilities for SEND	This will vary according to the provision that you work in but could include the role and responsibilities of the SENCO, the role and responsibilities of the key person and also, where appropriate, the role and responsibilities of others, e.g. committee members, senior team.
Training	Additional training may be required to support children with SEND. In an SEND policy, a statement about the importance of continued training and how this is to be accessed could be useful.
Implementing the graduated approach	The Code of Practice requires settings to take a graduated approach using four stages: Assess, Plan, Do and Review. Explaining how you will implement this approach should be included in your policy. You should pay particular attention to explaining how you will identify children who need additional support (Assess) and how you will draw up plans for these children (Plan).
Involving children	A key feature of the Code of Practice is the requirement to involve children when drawing up plans for them. You should consider writing about how this might take place in practice.
Involving parents	A key feature of the Code of Practice is the importance of fully involving parents. Your policy should focus on this as well as on practical ways in which this will happen.
Liaising with other professionals	Your policy could include the reasons why and the procedure by which you would liaise with other professionals and how you would do this.
Applying for an EHC assessment	As some children may need additional support and require an EHC plan, you could also include how you apply for an assessment and the procedures you would follow.

Step 2 Review what your setting is currently doing

For many settings, the SEN policy should simply put into words what they are doing in practice. Look at what is currently happening; consider what is working well, what needs to be changed in line with the Code of Practice and how this might happen. If changes are needed, you will need to consider these with the other staff and also seek advice from your Area SENCO or local early years team.

Here are some questions that are worth reflecting on which may help you write your policy.

- What is the setting's overall belief in terms of anti-discriminatory practice and meeting children's needs?
- What is your admissions policy regarding children with SEN and how does this reflect the Code of Practice?
- Who has the overall responsibility for the SEN policy?
- Who is acting as the SENCO?
- What is the responsibility of the SENCO in your setting?
- Who will be responsible for identifying children with SEN and how will this occur?
- How will parents be informed of any concerns that staff have about children?
- How can parents raise concerns that they may have about their child?
- How will parents be made aware of services in the local area, including their right to ask for an EHC assessment?
- How are targeted plans to support children drawn up and reviewed?
- How do targeted plans reflect the views of parents and children?
- How will records relating to children be stored and who will be responsible for updating them?
- How will the setting make sure that staff are given on-going training so that they can meet the needs of children?
- Who will monitor the effectiveness of the SEN policy and when will it be reviewed?

Step 3 Order your headings and produce the first draft

Use clear headings and stick to these. Check through your draft with the staff involved to ensure that the text is clear and that everyone is in agreement. This can be a good time to gain feedback from an early years adviser or an Area SENCO. It is also useful to ask sympathetic (but objective) parents to make some comments, as the policy will be needed when working with parents.

Step 4 Revisit the Code of Practice and EYFS. Produce the final policy

It is always worth revisiting the Code of Practice and EYFS requirement before finalising the policy to check that nothing has been overlooked. You should also have steps in place to review the policy and to help new adults in the setting understand the policy. This should be part of the induction process.

▶ The role of the SENCO

Every early years setting and school in receipt of government funding has to have a named person who is responsible for co-ordinating support for children with SEN and/or disabilities – this is the Special Educational Needs Co-ordinator (SENCO).

The position of the SENCO is regarded by the Code of Practice as an essential role. For many early years settings, the role of the SENCO is a promoted post as it requires an experienced practitioner, although not necessarily someone who has had any specific training in SEN. The exception to this is in maintained nurseries, where the SENCO is required to be a qualified teacher with a SENCO qualification. There are some key skills and qualities that are essential in a SENCO. These are shown in the figure below.

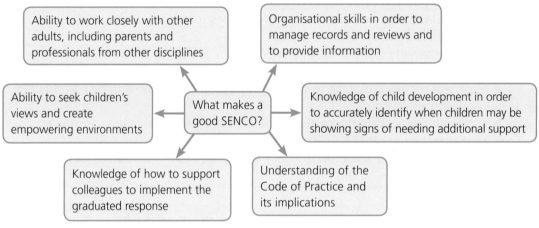

What makes a good SENCO?

▶ The Code of Practice and the role of the SENCO

There is significant focus on parents' views and ideas in the Code of Practice

Paragraph 5.54 of the Code of Practice says that the role involves the following:

- Ensuring all practitioners in the setting understand their responsibilities to children with SEN and the setting's approach to identifying and meeting SEN.
- Advising and supporting colleagues.
- Ensuring parents are closely involved throughout and that their insights inform action taken by the setting.
- Liaising with professionals or agencies beyond the setting.

Source: Special Educational Needs and Disability Code of Practice 2014

▶ What the SENCO role means in practice

There are several practical aspects that SENCOs will need to do which link to the Code of Practice's explanation of the role. In large settings, additional time will need to be allocated so that the SENCO can properly fulfil the role. Here are some of the practical aspects of the SENCO role.

The role of the SENCO includes liaising with parents, practitioners and other professionals

Implementing the Code of Practice

One of the most important roles of the SENCO is to ensure that the setting complies with the Code of Practice and also the EYFS in respect of children with SEN and disabilities. This in practice means being involved in the writing of the SEND policy and making sure that all adults working with children understand inclusive practice and also the need to work closely with parents and to seek the views of children. A SENCO may, for example, take time during the induction process to talk through policies with a new member of the team.

Taking a lead

SENCOs need to be able to lead, motivate and inform other members of staff in matters relating to SEN. This may mean working alongside colleagues to devise strategies to support a child, organising training or finding out further information and cascading it back. Most SENCOs find that they become more skilled at suggesting strategies as they gain experience and build up contacts with other professionals.

Graduated approach

Supporting and meeting children's needs by adapting provision and also using the graduated approach are essential parts of the Code of Practice. The SENCO must make sure that once children are identified as having SEN, that plans are drawn up in association with the parents to support the child. There are several different types of plans that early years settings can use (see page 89). Paragraph 5.45 states that the process of Assess, Plan, Do and Review should be led and co-ordinated by the SENCO in conjunction with parents and practitioners.

Liaising with others

The liaison role is essential. SENCOs need to be able to work with parents, children, and other professionals such as SEN advisers, social workers, health visitors and specialists such as teachers from the Speech and Language team. As well as meetings, SENCOs may also have to write reports to assist other professionals. The liaison role means that SENCOs need to have good communication skills.

Record keeping

Most SENCOs will have responsibility for the maintenance of records in the setting relating to children with SEN and disabilities. The records have to be accurate and up to date, which may mean checking the information that is being stored. It is important for SENCOs to be aware of the Data Protection Act and to have good systems in place to review the records.

Tips for good practice

SENCOs

- Form or join a network of other SENCOs in your area so that you can share good practice and ideas.
- Create a contact book so that phone numbers and email addresses of other professionals and local organisations are to hand.
- Subscribe to organisations offering support for SENCOs, such as the National Association for Special Educational Needs (NASEN).
- Look out for training opportunities for you and staff members.
- Look for ways of making contact with parents when their child first joins the setting so that a link has already been established.
- Make sure that parents are aware of the role of the SENCO as part of the inclusive practice that your setting offers children.
- Devise a brief information sheet for new members of staff to help them understand your role in the setting.
- Ask for a regular 'slot' for SEN at staff meetings to update colleagues.
- Consider setting up a resource shelf for colleagues, e.g. of books, articles, blank plans and forms.
- Develop a file of resources relating to areas of need, e.g. ideas for activities to support communication, etc.
- Make sure that other members of staff understand how and where records are stored so that they can easily be accessed in your absence.
- Look for ways of recognising and valuing colleagues' work in supporting children – a word of reassurance goes a long way.
- Keep a diary that highlights when reviews or updates are needed and remind staff if necessary.

Chapter 4

Identifying children who may need extra support

▶ Introduction

Early identification of children who may need additional support is a key principle and also a requirement of both the EYFS and the Code of Practice. This is because there is evidence to suggest that early identification can improve outcomes for children. This is partly because it means provision and practice are changed earlier to meet and support children's needs and also because children benefit from earlier interventions and targeted support. The need for early identification is the reason why it is a statutory requirement for early years settings to carry out the two-year-old progress check.

In this section we look at:

- The importance of building a picture of the whole child, including factors that might be affecting the child.
- Types of observation methods.
- What to observe.
- Analysing information from observations.

▶ Starting points

There are a few important starting points that everyone should understand when it comes to early identification.

▶ Early identification is not about 'sorting' children

Early identification is not about sorting children into groups of 'less able' and 'more able', nor is it about labelling children. Early identification should be about considering how we can best meet each child's needs. A child whose needs have not been noticed may not be able to access the curriculum fully and so is effectively being discriminated against.

In some cases, it is the parents who may bring their concerns to us, hoping that we will listen to them and look out for their child. In other instances, it is an early years practitioner who notices or has a 'hunch' about a child. The observation of children is therefore important as it is not uncommon for a child's impairment or delay to be thought of as part of their 'personality' by their immediate family or as 'something that they have always done', as the example below shows.

I wasn't picking up that he wasn't fully hearing. I just thought that his speech was quite sweet and because I was at home, I knew what he wanted as I was very much tuned in to his speech. I was amazed when I was told that he couldn't hear properly.

Gail, mother of Hugh, who had conductive hearing loss

❭ Understanding your limits

While it is important to observe children and consider the needs of particular children, it is essential that we understand the limits of our professional training and responsibility. Our role is not to 'diagnose', as this is what other professionals such as paediatricians, speech and language therapists and physiotherapists will do. Speculating or making inaccurate diagnoses can cause considerable anxiety for parents and may actually do more harm than good. Instead, our role is to notice, observe and flag up concerns to parents and if necessary to seek further advice or referrals.

❭ Building a picture of the child

Most practitioners are quick to notice children who do not appear to show the same behaviour, progress or development as other children. When this happens, it is important to begin to look more closely, not only at the child, but also at other factors that might be influencing the child's development. To get a better understanding of the child, it will be important to talk to the child's parents.

Here are some factors to take into consideration when looking at children's progress:

- **Prematurity:** Was the child born prematurely?
- How early was the child born?
- **Health conditions:** Does the child have a health condition?
- Does any medication taken affect concentration or make the child drowsy?
- Has the child had frequent absences because of their health condition?
- **Home circumstances:** Has anything changed at home recently that might have impacted on the child, e.g. family breakdown, new partner, bereavement, difficulty with sibling relationships?

- **Sleep:** How much does the child sleep?
- Do parents find sleep an issue at home?
- **Parenting:** Are there any areas of care that parents are finding difficult, e.g. mealtimes, general behaviour?
- **Settling in and key person relationship:** Is this the first time that the child has been separated from their parents?
- Mix of children.
- **Home-based and sessional care:** Are there certain days when the child is very different to others?
- Can you see a pattern to this?
- Could this be linked to the mix of children that are coming to your setting on these days?
- Is it the child or is it your setting?

The key to good identification of children's needs is to be as objective as possible. Your starting point should be to consider whether or not the environment, activities or system of deploying adults in the setting is 'disabling' a child. This is particularly important where a child is perceived as having behavioural difficulties or is reluctant to communicate.

At the same time, you should also have a clear idea of the 'normal' ranges of children's development. In some cases, by standing back and considering what is being provided, and also by referring to normative development charts, you may find that a child does not have any particular needs, but that the setting needs to consider its approach. This may well be the case if you are taking younger children into your setting than before. Many settings have found taking two year olds into their group care quite a challenge if they have not reviewed their routines and expectations.

What this means in practice

The following questions can be used to help you think about the effectiveness of your setting.

- Are there any periods of time when children are 'waiting', e.g. registration, snack time, lining up?
- Are group sizes during adult-led activities small enough to encourage children to talk and participate?
- Are adult-led activities carefully linked to children's interests and stage of development?
- Do children have a key person who spends some time with them each day?
- Does the key person greet the child at the start of the day?

- What opportunities are there for children to get individual attention in each session?
- Is a range of sensory activities available during each session, e.g. sand, water, dough?
- How attractive are the activities and equipment?
- Are there sufficient activities and equipment available to prevent squabbles?
- Are children encouraged to choose their own resources and play activities?
- Is the environment calm, with smaller spaces?
- Do children have the option to be outdoors?

❱ The child at home

How children act and react with us and how they are at home can be different. It is important to find out from parents how they perceive their child. If there is a huge difference between their perceptions and yours, it will be important to explore this further.

It may be that a child who is chatty and happy at home, but easily distressed or lacking concentration in the setting, needs more key person time or a different environment. If the child has siblings at home, it is also important to find out about these relationships as a child who happily plays with their siblings should in theory be able to play with other children in the setting.

By gaining information from parents, we might understand how best to adapt our provision or routines to meet the child's needs.

Information that might be useful to gain from parents

Can you tell me about...?

- How much physical contact, e.g. cuddles, hand holding, your child needs at home.
- The situations where your child needs more reassurance.
- How your child reacts in the company of family and friends.
- The type of things your child can do independently.
- How your child copes with new challenges.
- How your child shows frustration.
- How chatty your child is at home.
- How outgoing you think your child is.
- What your child enjoys doing at home.
- When your child plays.
- Situations that hold your child's attention and concentration.
- Your child's behaviour at home.
- Your child's play with other children outside of the setting, for example with siblings.

Case study

Harry had been in our provision for six weeks. He was just two years old when he joined us. At first he seemed to settle in well. He engaged with the play activities, although once we started to observe him, we noticed that he tended not to make eye contact or interact with other children or adults. We decided to talk to Harry's parents. It soon became clear that Harry was actually quite a sociable child when he was with children he knew well. He was also a little chatterbox. His parents brought in a film clip of him on holiday with another family. The Harry we saw there was very different to the Harry that we saw when he was with us. It made us realise that we needed to re-think our provision. We started off by re-assigning a key person for Harry. The key person was far more proactive and engaged well with Harry. They developed a strong bond and soon after, Harry was communicating well and also making eye contact with her. We also changed the environment so that there were smaller, more intimate spaces both inside and outdoors. This seemed to change the dynamics within the group and benefited other children too. Finally, we also planned more adult-guided activities with the younger children, such as cooking, and capped the adult ratio for these at 1:4. This seemed to help Harry connect with the other children.

I think from this, we have learnt to start off by reviewing our provision and also to really think about what parents say about their children at home. It is too easy to assume that it is the child with the problem rather than to reflect on how the provision is working.

Zainab, SENCO Pre-School

◗ Observing the child further

Once the routine, layout, etc., of your setting has been considered, especially in light of parents' contributions, it will then be important to carry out some observations and to gain a fuller picture of the child in question. In some situations it can be better to ask another member of staff who is not closely involved with the child (or the SENCO) to observe the child, as the key is to be as objective as possible. It is well known in research that pre-conceptions about children can influence what we perceive and see.

◗ Ways to observe children

There is a range of methods that can be used in order to collect more information about children. The type of observation method that is used will depend very much on personal preference but also on what area needs to be considered. Confidence is often the key to observation, so be prepared to adapt a method to suit your observing needs.

Event sample

Event samples are very useful as they can be used to gain a more accurate picture of how frequently any kind of behaviour is being shown. This means that they can be used to look at how often a child interacts with other children, how often they play in groups, as well as how often a child shows unwanted behaviour. Event samples can be used to monitor the effectiveness of any plans that you have in place, for example a target may be to increase the number of times a child interacts with other children and an event sample could be used to see if the number has increased.

Method

A sheet is prepared and each time the child shows the behaviour or action that is being monitored, the sheet is filled in. The number of columns is dictated by the type of information that is sought.

- Prepare the sheet beforehand.
- Add a column for each piece of information that you want to collect, e.g. the time, what happened, who the child was with.
- Make sure that everyone in the setting knows what behaviour is being monitored and where the sheet is being kept. This is important as you may be out of the room or not available when the action or behaviour occurs.
- Repeat the event sample in other sessions to build up a picture of what is happening.

Checklists

Checklists are quick to complete and many settings use them to assess children's development. A checklist is literally a list of skills and/or behaviours that can be ticked off when the observer has seen them. Checklists are useful because they focus the observer on particular things, for example whether or not a child uses plurals, or can stand on one foot. Ideally, checklists should be completed when the child is absorbed in an activity and not aware of being observed. This is because children may not always 'perform' when they know that they are being watched, especially when an adult directs them to do something. This means that in order to look out for some skills, the adult may have to think about setting up a play environment or resources that might prompt the child to show the behaviours that are being looked for.

Method

- Use a commercial checklist or create your own based on the skills that you wish to look for.
- Have the checklist to hand and tick off the skill when you see it.
- If you are not sure about how competent or confident the child is, you might make a comment.

Example of a checklist

Child's name: Date of birth:	Date: Observer:		
Developmental checklist			
By 12 months can:	Yes	No	Sometimes
Walk with some help			
Pick up objects with finger and thumb			
Transfer items from one hand to the other			
Look for an object hidden under a beaker			
Look at a person who is speaking to them			
Make tuneful babbling sounds, such as 'da-da'			
Respond to different sounds, e.g. drum, bell			
Imitate gestures, such as 'pat-a-cake' or 'bye-bye'			
Hold a beaker using two hands			
Use fingers to eat finger foods, such as squares of bread or toast			
Pick up dropped toys			
React to the word 'no'			
React to their name			

Target child observation

Target child observations are used to track individual children during a session or part of a session. They are useful because they can give a fuller picture of how a child spends his or her time and can be designed to look at several aspects of a child's development.

Method

- Prepare a sheet in advance of the observation. A column is needed for each piece of information that is required.
- The observer needs to be aware of the time, as this is a minute-by-minute recording system.
- Codes are often useful as more information can be jotted down, and it is useful if you develop your own 'shorthand' or code.

Example of a completed target child observation

Target child

Child's name: Annie	Age: 3 years 4 months		Date: 22/03/17		
Time	Activity	Language		Task	Social group
1 min	TC scooping sand with hands	TC directing herself		Sand	Sol
2 min	TC scooping with beaker			Sand	Sol
3 min	TC patting down sand in beaker	A to TC: 'Are you going to make a sandcastle?'		Sand	A
4 min	TC turning beaker over	TC to A: 'It won't come out.'		Sand	A + 1C
5 min	TC protects sandcastle	TC to C: 'Don't, it's mine.'		Sand	A + 1C

Key: TC = target child, A = adult, C = child, Sol = solitary

Time sample

The time sample method allows an observer to record comfortably for longer periods of time. Instead of continuously observing the child, the recording takes place at regular intervals, such as every 5 or 10 minutes. Some observers prefer to use a time sample in a general way and simply write down what a child is doing; others use columns to focus on particular skills and areas of development that a child is showing during each 'time slot'.

Example of a completed time sample

Time	Location	Social grouping	Activity
10.05	Home corner	Pair	Knocking on door, going in and out
10.15	Home corner	Pair	Lying down, pretending to be a baby, eye contact and interaction with Ciara
10.25	Home corner	Pair	Pushing pram with both hands, steers around objects, talks to Ciara
10.35	Book area	Solitary	Sitting on mat, looking at *The Rainbow Fish*, turning pages one by one
10.45	Book area	Pair	Showing book to Ciara, pointing to pictures and explaining

Method

- Prepare a sheet, with the timings running vertically.
- Add in a column for each type of information required, e.g. language, social grouping.
- Use a watch during the recording to help record time accurately.
- At the appointed times, note down what the child is doing.
- Remember that this is not a continuous observation.

Free description

This method is used to provide detailed information about a skill or situation that a child is involved in. This type of observation does not have to be planned ahead, as only paper and a pen are required. Note, however, that this method only provides 'snapshots' of the child and sometimes other methods need to be used alongside it.

Method

- This method can be compared to taking 'written photographs' of children.
- Spend two or three minutes observing a child, and write down as much as possible.
- The present tense is normally used.
- Write up the observation immediately afterwards as it can be difficult to decipher what has been written at a later date.

Example of a free description

Robbie is standing up in front of Sofina, who is sitting on a chair. Robbie seems to be looking down at Sofina. She is saying, 'Shall we dress up?' Sofina nods and smiles. Robbie smiles too and they both walk over to the dressing-up corner. Robbie takes a green dress, grasping it in her right hand, and places it on the floor. She pulls the back of the dress open with both hands. She steps into the dress using her right foot first and pulls up the dress gradually to a standing position, placing her right arm into the dress and then her left. Robbie walks over to the nursery and looks up. She asks, 'Can you do my buttons up?' and turns around.

Digital recording

Digital recording has been made very easy with the arrival of low-cost cameras, phones and MP3 players. Digital recording can be helpful to show how children move, talk and interact with others. One of its key advantages is that you can replay the recordings and show them to parents, colleagues or other professionals. Some parents may be keen to show you film clips of their child with them and this might also be useful. Another advantage of using digital technology is that children enjoy looking at the recordings and commenting on them. As with other observations, it is important that security measures are in place and that you have parental permission.

Method

- Decide what you wish to focus on.
- To focus on language and speech, it is worth using a sound recording and then noting the context separately. With small handheld recording devices, you can play or chat with the child and switch on the record function without the child particularly noticing.
- To focus on other areas of activity, it is worth using a camera so that you can see what a child is doing.
- When recording film clips, it is worth looking for a place where you can be unobtrusive and where you can catch the action without children 'playing up' for the camera. It is also worth using the zoom function if you are focusing on hand movements or specific physical skills.

❱ What to observe

There are some signs that can indicate a child may need additional support. While conditions and impairments that are likely to seriously affect a child's development are noticed during routine health visits, slight impairments can go undetected. It is therefore useful to hone in on the following as you observe a child, bearing in mind the normative development for the age of the child, such as that it is typical for children under three years to find sharing difficult.

❱ Physical and sensory development

- How controlled and co-ordinated are a child's movements?
- Does the child bump into objects or fall over frequently?
- Does the child have difficulty holding and manipulating objects?
- Does the child have a dislike of messy play, e.g. dough, sand?
- Has the child begun to show a hand preference?
- How confident is the child at using tricycles, climbing and balancing?
- Is the child aware of his or her body in relation to the space around them?

❱ Sight

- Does the child need to be very close to books, pictures and posters?
- Does the child ever peer or frown?
- Does the child appear to be 'accident prone'?

- Is the child sometimes frustrated when using small toys and equipment, such as puzzles or farm animals?
- Is the child uninterested in watching DVDs and television?
- Does the child look at objects in an unusual way, e.g. holding things very closely to the eyes?

▶ Hearing

- Is speech muffled or unclear?
- Do adults who are unfamiliar with the child have difficulty in understanding what is being said?
- Does the child mispronounce words that other children of his or her age manage easily?
- Does the child appear to stare intently at adults and other children's faces when they are talking?
- Does the child at times appear to be unsure as to what is happening, e.g. after some instructions have been given?
- Does the child look at and copy what other children are doing?
- Does the child appear to be in a world of his or her own, especially at story time?
- Does the child respond immediately to his or her name or to a loud sound?
- Is the child prone to runny colds?
- Does the child often 'shout' rather than talk at a normal volume without realising it?
- Does the child show aggressive or frustrated behaviour?

▶ Speech and communication

- Does the child make eye contact with adults and other children?
- How often does the child interact with adults or children?
- Does the child have difficulty in understanding what is being said?
- Does their intonation sound monotone and flat?
- Does the child often keep repeating nonsense words or phrases?
- Are the child's responses not in keeping with what would normally be expected?
- Does the child stutter or stammer or have difficulty pronouncing words?
- Does the child repeat words or phrases spoken by the adult in inappropriate contexts?
- Can the child follow simple instructions, e.g. 'put your apron on the peg'?

By listening and watching carefully, the adult can assess this child's speech and communication skills

Social and emotional development

- Is the child aware of other children, e.g. watching others, copying their play?
- To what extent does the child interact and play with other children?
- Is the child able to take turns and show some awareness of others' needs (over three years)?
- Is the child aggressive towards others for no apparent reason?
- Is the child constantly restless and does he or she find it hard to concentrate, even on self-chosen activities with adult support?
- Is the child aware of the routine of the setting?
- Does the child have great difficulties adapting to changes in routines or new members of staff?
- Is the child clingy towards adults and does he or she seek their attention?
- Does the child play in a ritualistic way, e.g. always using the same pieces of equipment in a repetitive way (over three years)?
- Does the child avoid imaginative play, e.g. dressing up, home corner?
- Does the child become distressed for no apparent reason?

Normative development charts

| Language development

Stage	Age	Development
Pre-linguistic	0–3 months	• Cries to show hunger, tiredness and distress • Recognises different tones of voice • Coos and gurgles when content • By three months can recognise carer's voice and is soothed • Smiles in response to others' faces
	3–6 months	• Still cries to show distress, but is more easily soothed • Babbles and coos • Babbles consist of short sounds: 'ma, ma, da, da' • Laughs, chuckles and even squeals
	6–12 months	• Babbling makes up half of baby's non-crying sounds • Strings vowels and consonants together to make repetitive sounds: 'mememememe, dadadadada' • Babbling becomes more tuneful and inventive and by nine months most of the sounds used are the ones needed for the language being learnt • At ten months understands about 17 words, such as 'bye bye' • Uses gestures to ask for things – points hand and whines to show adult what he or she wants • Enjoys games such as pat-a-cake
Linguistic	12–18 months	• First words appear at around 12 months, although will only be recognisable as a word to carer, e.g. 'dede' to mean drink • Words are used to mean more than one thing depending on the intonation the baby uses, e.g. 'dede' is used to mean 'I want a drink', 'my drink is finished' or 'I want more drink' • By 15 months may have about ten words that carers can understand
	18–24 months	• At 18 months, uses 15 or more words • Understands basic everyday instructions, e.g. 'where is your shoe?'/'show me your nose' • Responds to own name
	2–2½ years	• Using a minimum of 50 words • Beginning to use two word combinations • Using early action words • Shows and names body parts • Understands single words and most simple two word level commands (objects and actions)

Language development contd.

Stage	Age	Development
Linguistic	2½–3 years	• Has approx. 300 words • Asks simple questions • Links words together • Uses action words • Stammering is common • Uses own name • Understands more complex instructions (2–3 word level) • Understands simple stories
	3–4 years	• Imitates adult speech patterns accurately, e.g. 'We liked that, didn't we?' • Speech is understood by strangers • Sentences contain four or more words and are grammatical • Vocabulary is large; knows parts of the body, names of household objects, animals • Errors are still made, especially when using past tense, e.g. 'I taked it' • Knows and understands nursery rhymes • Enjoys asking questions
	4–8 years	• From four years, language is developed and refined • Mistakes become fewer – starts to enjoy using language as a means of socialising with others, expressing needs and recounting what they have done • By five years vocabulary is about 5,000 words • Uses complex sentences correctly • Enjoys telling and hearing jokes • Understands that language can be written with symbols • By eight years most children are fluent speakers, readers and developing writers of their language

Physical development

Age	Fine manipulative skills	Gross manipulative skills
12 months	• Picks up objects with thumb and forefinger • Picks up toys, such as rattles • Holds cup with help • Puts small objects in a container	• Mobile; either crawling or shuffling (some children may be walking) • Sits up unsupported for long periods • Walks with assistance • Tries to crawl up stairs

Physical development contd.

Age	Fine manipulative skills	Gross manipulative skills
15 months	• Holds/drinks from cup with two hands • Builds tower of two blocks • Makes marks with crayons • Tries to turn pages in books	• Crawls down stairs feet first • Walks independently • Seats self in small chair
18 months	• Strings four large beads • Turns door knobs and handles • Pulls off shoes	• Bends down from the waist to pick up shoes • Squats down to look at toys • Rolls and throws a ball • Walks down stairs with adult to help • Pushes and pulls toys while walking
2 years	• Uses a spoon to feed themselves • Zips and unzips large zippers • Places five rings on a stick • Puts on shoes • Draws circles and dots • Builds a tower of five or six bricks • Begins to use a preferred hand	• Kicks a ball that is not moving • Climbs on furniture • Puts together and pulls apart snap-together toys • Walks up and down stairs confidently
3 years	• Turns pages in a book one by one • Holds a crayon and can draw a face • Uses a spoon without spilling • Washes and dries hands without help • Puts on and takes off coat	• Walks and runs forward • Walks on tiptoes • Throws large ball • Kicks ball forward • Jumps from low steps • Pedals and steers a tricycle
4 years	• Buttons and unbuttons own clothing • Cuts out simple shapes • Draws a person with head, trunk and legs • Puts together 12-piece puzzle	• Walks on a line • Aims and throws ball • Bounces and catches large ball • Runs, changing direction • Hops on one foot • Pedals and steers a tricycle confidently
5 years	• Forms letters, writes own name • Draws recognisable pictures of trees, houses, people and animals • Colours pictures in neatly • Dresses and undresses easily • Completes 20-piece jigsaw puzzle • Cuts shapes with scissors accurately • Draws around a template	• Skips with rope • Runs quickly and able to avoid obstacles • Is able to use a variety of large equipment, e.g. swings, slides • Throws large ball to a partner and catches it • Hits ball with bat or stick

Physical development contd.

Age	Fine manipulative skills	Gross manipulative skills
6–7 years	• Is able to sew simple stitches • Cuts out shapes accurately and neatly • Handwriting is evenly spaced and may be joined • Drawings are detailed and representative • Makes a simple sandwich • Ties and unties laces	• Rides a bicycle without stabilisers • Runs • Chases and dodges others • Hops, skips and jumps confidently • Kicks a ball with direction • Balances on a beam or wall

Emotional and social development

Age	Development
Birth–1 year	
1 month	Watches primary carer's face
3 months	Smiles and coos Enjoys being handled and cuddled
6 months	Laughs and enjoys being played with
8 months	Fears strangers
9 months	Plays peek-a-boo Discriminates between strangers and familiar adults
12 months	Is affectionate towards family and primary carers Plays simple games such as pat-a-cake
1–2 years	
15 months	Begins to explore environment if familiar adult is close by Begins to use words to communicate Has a stronger feeling of being an individual
18 months	Language increases Points to objects to show familiar adults Explores environment and shows some independence but still needs familiar adults Strong emotions, e.g. anger, fear and joy, are shown
2 years	Plays near other children – parallel play Begins to talk when playing – pretend play Imitates adults' actions Strong emotions, e.g. anger, fear and joy, are shown

|Emotional and social development contd.

Age	Development
2–3 years	Has a strong sense of their identity, including their gender and age Is happy to leave their primary carer for short periods Starts taking an interest in other children and playing with them Shows concern for other children, e.g. telling primary carer if baby is crying Starts to wait for their needs to be met
3–4 years	Affectionate towards family, friends and carers Wants to help and please primary carers and other familiar adults During play, imitates actions seen, e.g. puts teddy to bed, feeds dolls Shares playthings Plays with other children – mostly pretend play Shows concern for other people, e.g. rubs back of crying baby

▶ Using observations to create assessments

There is little point in carrying out observations if the information gained is not effectively used. It is therefore important to spend some time analysing your information. This is the 'assessment' part of the observation process. A good starting point in the assessment process is to use sources of information about normative development, as it may be that the child's development is pretty much typical of what might be expected for their age (see pages 52–6 for normative development charts). This is important as otherwise it can be easy to base assessments on the development of other children in the setting, who in some cases may be older or may have development beyond that which is expected for their age group.

When analysing the information and drawing conclusions, it is worth considering:

- Do you feel that the observations are a good reflection of the child's usual responses, play and behaviours?
- Do you need any further observations?
- Was the provision, routine and staffing of the setting creating barriers for the child?
- Are there any immediate actions that might be taken to change the provision, routine or staffing, which in turn might change the child?
- How did the child's responses, play and behaviours correspond to those reported by the parents at home?
- Which aspects of the child's responses, play and behaviours correlate to typical development for this child's age group?
- Which aspects of the child's responses, play and behaviours do not seem to correlate with what might be expected of their age?
- How much impact is this having on the child?

❯ Raising concerns and next steps

You are required by the EYFS to flag up any developmental concerns that you have about a child with the child's parents. Ideally, you should have already been in conversation about the child so will have already talked to the parents about their child's development. (See also Chapter 5 in relation to working with parents.)

For some children, the next steps following the assessment will be to employ the graduated approach as outlined by the Code of Practice. This may help the child to make progress without any outside interventions. For some children, the next step will be to encourage the parents to seek further advice via their GP, health visitor or through the inclusion team. This should happen alongside taking the graduated approach. It is important that at this stage we do not speculate about the outcome of any referral, as our role is not to diagnose. For other children, providing there is evidence of a significant need, the next step will be to request the local authority to carry out an assessment for an Education, Health and Care plan.

❯ Education, Health and Care plan

When a child has significant needs and these cannot be met as part of the reasonable steps that settings should take to comply with the Equality Act 2010 and other legislation, an assessment can be carried out to see if the child qualifies for an Education, Health and Care (EHC) plan. An EHC plan is designed to support a child or young person to achieve the best outcomes possible. It is also meant to be very person- or child-centred and so the needs and interests of children are meant to be reflected in the document. The plan records what support and provision is needed to help the child achieve the desired outcomes. This includes social care, as well as health and education needs. Once drawn up, the plan is legally binding.

❯ Assessment process

The assessment process has many statutory components. It is important to understand the process and also how to support parents during it. The flow chart on the following page, taken from the Code of Practice, shows the process.

Request for an EHC plan

The first step in the process is a request that is sent to your local authority. Your local authority should have information about how to do this which will probably include a form to fill in.

If you think that a child needs an assessment for an EHC plan, you should talk to the parents and together decide who will make the request. Once the request goes to the local authority, they have six weeks to decide whether or not to carry out an assessment based on what has been written in the request. In practice, I suspect, this means that requests that are well written and have good evidence are more likely to go forward for an assessment. If parents decide that they will make the request, they will need evidence from you. It is important to make sure that parents know that a request for an assessment may not automatically result in an EHC plan for the child. They also need to know what must be included in a request for an assessment.

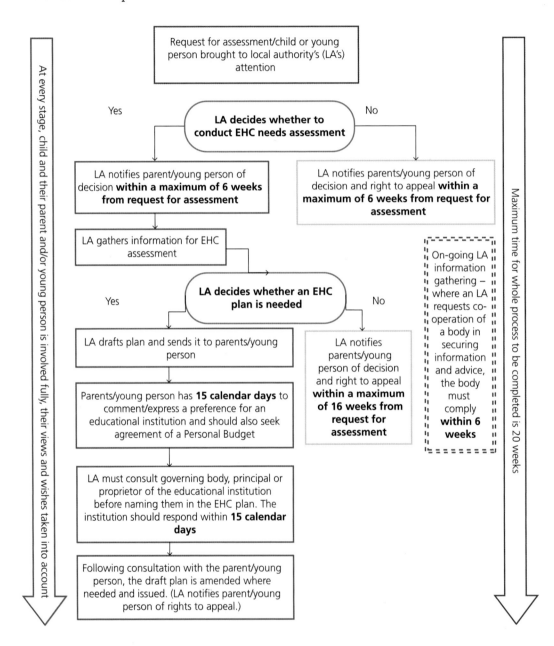

Statutory timescales for EHC needs assessment and EHC plan development

Every local authority has a slightly different format, but the basis of the information is similar and is likely to include:

- Description of the child's need in detail – a case must be made as to why the child's needs are exceptional and cannot be met without additional support, e.g. rate of progress, developmental milestones.
- Explanation and evidence of the support and interventions that have already been tried, e.g. support plans, provision plans.
- Reports and evidence from other professionals, along with how any suggested interventions have been acted on, e.g. letter from Area SENCO, paediatrician's report, educational psychologist.
- Views and feelings of the child and parents.

What this means in practice

You will need to keep very accurate and detailed plans and records. You will also need to show that you have implemented the graduated approach and evaluated your interventions. It will also be important to work closely with parents so that if they have any copies of reports from other professionals, etc., these can be included.

It will be important to ask any other professionals who visit the setting to see the child to record their professional comments. If interventions are suggested by other professionals, you will need to show that you have implemented them.

When a request is refused

If the local authority has stated that it will not assess a child, it is required to state the reasons for its decision. At this point, parents are able to either talk this through with the local authority, attend mediation or appeal to the SEN and disability tribunal. The local authority is required to tell parents about how to do this in their area.

What happens if the local authority agrees to an assessment?

If the local authority team believes that an EHC assessment is necessary, they will contact the child's parents early on so that information and also their views can be taken into consideration. The local authority will contact your setting as well. They will also inform any other service which has involvement with the child, e.g. the health service.

During the assessment, information is gathered about the child from a range of professionals, and the parents and the child, in order to reach a conclusion about whether an EHC plan is required.

How long does this process take?

The Code of Practice requires that the whole process from request through to issuing an EHC plan has to be completed within a 20-week timescale, although there are some exceptions. If the local authority decides not to issue an EHC, parents have to be told within 16 weeks and they must be given a reason why. As with the refusal to carry out an assessment, parents also have to be given information so that they can appeal if they wish.

Draft plan

Once the local authority agrees that an EHC plan is necessary, it will quickly draw up a draft plan and consult with the child's parents. The draft plan will contain the information listed in the table below, although the order may vary from local authority to local authority. Each section within the EHC plan is statutory.

Draft plan contents

Section	Content
Section A	The views, interests and aspirations of the child and his or her parents.
Section B	The child or young person's special educational needs.
Section C	The child or young person's health needs which are related to their SEN.
Section D	The child or young person's social care needs which are related to their SEN or to a disability.
Section E	The outcomes sought for the child, including outcomes for adult life. Arrangements for the setting of shorter-term targets by the early years provider, school or other education provision.
Section F	The special educational provision required by the child or young person.
Section G	Any health provision required by the learning difficulties or disabilities which result in the child or young person having SEN.
Section H1	Any social care provision which must be made for the child.
Section H2	Any other social care provision reasonably required by the learning difficulties or disabilities which result in the child or young person having SEN.
Section I	The type and/or name of the school, maintained nursery school or other institution to be attended by the child.
Section J	Where there is a Personal Budget, the details of how the Personal Budget will support particular outcomes and the provision it will be used for.

In addition, there is a final section where the advice and information gathered during the EHC needs assessment has to be listed. The actual documents are then put into the appendices.

The parents have 15 days to respond to the draft plan and express their views. In terms of education provision, parents can make alternative suggestions. There are legal obligations on the local authority to work in partnership with parents and to agree the plan together.

Final plan

Once consultation has taken place, a final plan is issued. Parents at this point still have the right to appeal if they are not happy with the contents.

Chapter 5

Working alongside parents

❙ Introduction

It is good practice and a requirement of the EYFS for early years settings to work closely with parents. There are huge benefits when parents and practitioners can develop strong relationships based on trust and respect. One of the key principles of the Code of Practice is that parents should play a key role in decisions made about their children. In this chapter we look at the Code of Practice in relation to parents and at practical strategies that will support clear communication and the development of effective parent–practitioner relationships.

There were many wonderful things about Sophie's nursery. On a personal level, I felt that for the first time, I was properly listened to and that the staff were trying to see things not only from Sophie's perspective, but also from mine.

Sophie's mum

❙ Defining parents

The definition of 'parent' is quite wide as the term includes anyone with parental responsibility. In general, all mothers have parental responsibility, as well as fathers married to the mothers at the time of birth and those unmarried parents who both sign the birth certificate. Parental responsibility can be sought by fathers afterwards, but can also be granted to others in some circumstances by a court. This means that a guardian, grandparent or social services department may have parental responsibility if they are responsible for the child and a court order has been granted.

❙ Understanding the legal requirements of the EYFS and the Code of Practice in relation to parents

Both the EYFS and the Code of Practice have clear stipulations which should be reflected in the way that we work. It is worth highlighting them as they are key to complying with the Code of Practice.

❱ Principles of the Code of Practice

Emanating from the Children and Families Act 2014, the Code of Practice reiterates the following as being the key principles underpinning the Code of Practice:

- 'The views, wishes and feelings of the child or young person, and the child's parents.'
- 'The importance of the child or young person, and the child's parents, participating as fully as possible in decisions, and being provided with the information and support necessary to enable participation in those decisions.'
- 'The need to support the child or young person, and the child's parents, in order to facilitate the development of the child or young person and to help them achieve the best possible educational and other outcomes, preparing them effectively for adulthood.'

❱ Putting the principles into practice

There are many practical ways in which the principles from the Code of Practice and the EYFS should be put into practice. These are illustrated in the figure below.

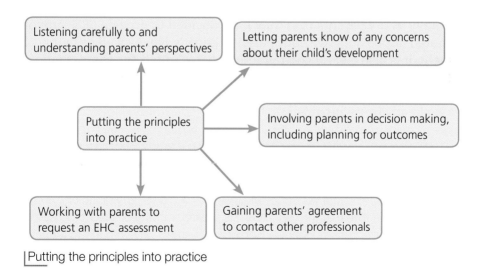

Putting the principles into practice

Listening carefully to and understanding parents' perspectives

One of the key ways in which the Code of Practice and the EYFS is put into practice is by literally listening to and trying to understand parents' perspectives. Many a time parents will say that they had voiced concerns about their child's development, but that these were not taken on board by others. If this happens repeatedly, many parents are likely to lose faith in the system and also be prevented from engaging further. It is important therefore to make a note of what parents say about their child and to follow this up. It is also important to recognise, as we will see later on in the chapter, that parents may have views and priorities that are different to ours. Being able to listen to and take on board these will be particularly important when planning for children, if this is to be a genuine collaboration.

Letting parents know of any concerns about their child's development

As well as listening carefully to parents, we also have a legal requirement to flag up straightaway any concerns that we may have in terms of children's development. This is a requirement of the Code of Practice and also the EYFS. Early years settings will not comply with this if they continue to carry out observations and assessments without telling parents why these are taking place. In addition, paragraph 5.40 of the Code of Practice states that settings must formally notify parents that they have decided to provide SEN support and so this should not be done without parents' knowledge. As well as being a legal requirement, it is also clearly good practice as it is unfair for parents who may think that their child is developing typically to suddenly be told after a period of time that the setting thinks that there may be underlying needs and that support is already being provided.

The process of identifying children who may have SEN and working with parents begins during the settling in period. We will often chat to parents about their child as part of working through our 'All about you' booklet. This provides a starting point for the child's development. If we notice that the way a child is playing, moving or interacting seems unusual, we simply ask parents about it. Sometimes parents have not thought about it or noticed it. Sometimes it turns out that at home their child is different. This early dialogue is very helpful as our next step is often to say to parents that we will be carrying out some observations in respect of that area of development and that we will share these observations once they are completed. We find that parents are usually pleased that we are so proactive.

Julie, nursery manager

Involving parents in the decision making, including planning for outcomes

One of the key features of the Code of Practice is the identification of outcomes that need to be decided with parents, also taking into consideration the views of the child. This is one of the keys to planning support for the child and

Parents need to feel welcome and valued

how well it has been done may also affect whether a request for an EHC assessment is considered. While parents may not be experts in the stages and sequences of development, they will know what has been tried so far, what their child enjoys doing and what strategies are most likely to work. They may also have clear priorities that they feel will impact on their child. Working with parents in the planning process is not optional as it is a legal requirement.

Gaining parents' agreement to contact other professionals

There is a requirement that parental agreement is sought before involving other professionals. There is no guidance in the Code of Practice as to what should happen if a parent denies this, even though it might be in the child's best interest. The need for parental agreement means that without this, referrals to the Area SENCO or for other professionals to work with the child cannot go ahead. This is a clear example of why it is essential that there is a strong focus in early years settings on working with parents from day one.

Working with parents to request an EHC assessment

One of the ways that we may work with parents is to help them request an EHC assessment where children have significant needs. This process is quite time consuming and parents may well need our support.

▶ Supporting parents during their journey

One of the most useful things for parents whose children have SEN and/or disabilities is that their journey feels as if it is being shared. Many parents will need the support of early years settings to meet their children's needs, especially if EHC plans are being considered. It is therefore important that we know about the services that are available to parents. The Code of Practice looks at four important services that are available to parents:

- parent partnership services
- disagreement resolution services
- mediation
- SEN and disability tribunals.

▶ Information, advice and support services (parent partnership services)

The previous Code of Practice required local authorities to arrange parent partnership services. The aim of these services was to ensure that parents had access to support and information. The current Code of Practice requires local authorities to build further on these services so that parents are able to access information, advice and support. They are now currently rebranded as Independent Information, Advice and Support services, although in different areas the name can vary. The type of advice and support includes information about the law on SEN and disability, as well as how to navigate the local processes and procedures, including how to appeal. The current Code of Practice also requires that these services can be accessed in a range of formats, including electronically, as well as face to face and by telephone.

What this means in practice

Your local authority should have provided your setting with information about their service and details of the variety of ways parents can access it. You should make sure that parents know about the service so that they have additional support, if they want it. If you are not sure about the name of your local service, you can find this out by visiting www.iassnetwork.org.uk and clicking on the tab 'Find your local IAS service'.

▶ Disagreement resolution services

The Code of Practice requires local authorities to commission an independent organisation which parents can choose to use if they have any disagreement or dispute relating to SEN. Disagreement resolution services can only be used if the local authority, early years provider or school also agrees to use them. The idea behind the disagreement resolution service is that it may prevent disputes from escalating and that it will provide a neutral environment in which the difficulties can be pinpointed and together the varying parties can work through a solution.

What this means in practice

You will need to find out about how this service is run in your local area so that you can provide parents with information about it. It may also be a service that you agree to use with parents if there is some level of disagreement that you cannot work through together and where you feel additional support would be helpful.

❱ Mediation

A significant part of the current Code of Practice deals with the role of mediation services. It is compulsory for local authorities to offer mediation to parents who are in dispute over a child's EHC where education or social care is involved. (Where parents wish to appeal in respect of only the health element of a plan, it is the duty of the health commissioning body to offer mediation, which may be run by a different mediating service.) While parents do not have to attend mediation, they will need a certificate to prove that it has been offered to them before they can attend a tribunal.

What this means in practice

It is important that parents who are in dispute in relation to an EHC know that mediation will be offered to them and that it is up to them whether or not they wish to try it. It is also helpful for parents to know that they will not be penalised for refusing mediation and that, even after mediation, they can still take their concerns further. It is important though that parents know that they will need to obtain a certificate showing either that they did not accept mediation or that mediation was tried.

❱ First tier SEN and disability tribunals

For parents who are unhappy about the outcomes of the local authority decision making, there is the possibility of taking their case to an SEN and disability tribunal. The tribunal can only make judgments in respect of the education and social care parts of the child's needs.

Parents and young people can appeal to the tribunal about:

- a decision by a local authority not to carry out an EHC needs assessment or re-assessment
- a decision by a local authority that it is not necessary to issue an EHC plan following an assessment
- the description of a child or young person's SEN specified in an EHC plan, the special educational provision specified, the school or other institution or type of school or other institution (such as a mainstream school/college) specified in the plan, or that no school or other institution is specified
- an amendment to these elements of the EHC plan
- a decision by a local authority not to amend an EHC plan following a review or re-assessment
- a decision by a local authority to cease to maintain an EHC plan.

What this means in practice

It is helpful for parents to understand that there are different appeals and dispute processes. It is also important that parents understand that there is a timescale in place and that they have to register their appeal within the timescale set out in the Code of Practice (within two months of the decision being sent to them by the local authority or within a month from the certificate following mediation).

▶ Other sources of information for parents

As well as the services that are provided as part of the Code of Practice, there is a range of independent and voluntary organisations that can help parents. It is worth having a list of both national and also local ones. In Part 3 of this book, we look at meeting children's specific needs and provide a list of national organisations that provide support for specific conditions and disabilities. Here are some additional examples of sources of advice on a national scale.

Independent Parental Special Education Advice 2015 (IPSEA)

IPSEA is a charity that provides advice and guidance for parents who are navigating their way through the SEND process, including statutory assessment. Its website is www.ipsea.org.uk.

Contact-A-Family

This is a charity that provides information and support for parents of disabled children. It helps families to get in touch with each other on a local level, as well as providing information and support. Its website is www.cafamily.org.uk.

Special Needs Jungle

This is a parent-led website that provides information for parents of children with special educational needs. It provides opinions and blogs, as well as information that might be of interest to parents. The website is www.specialneedsjungle.com.

Parent–carer forums

Many local areas have parent–carer forums. These are groups of parents and carers who play an important role in providing information and feedback to local authorities, commissioning groups and health services. Local authorities are encouraged to work with such groups as part of the commissioning of services and organising the Local Offer. While these forums may not provide advice, they do give parents opportunities to influence what might be available locally and so some parents may be interested in joining them.

Every parent and every family is different

Although obvious, a good starting point when looking at how best to work with parents is to remember that every parent and every family is different. Two parents may have children of the same age, but the context in which they live, their lifestyle and experiences to date, will be different. It is important that this is recognised in our policies and interactions with parents. With parents who have children with SEN and/or disabilities, there may be many more differences as a result of the individual needs of their child and also of the journey that the parents have taken so far. It is worth being aware of some of the factors that might affect parents' responses and views in order to recognise the importance of sensitive communication and working.

Acceptance

Learning that aspects of your child's development are different to what you were expecting can be hard. For some parents, this journey begins before or shortly after birth when health professionals are involved. For other parents, their journey is just unfolding and they may have many questions and anxieties as well as mixed emotions, including anger, guilt and blame. Some parents early on in the journey also talk about a sense of loss, as well as denial that this is happening to them. As parents are individuals and therefore unique, no two parents will respond in the same way. This means that parents of the same child may have very different approaches and responses, which can in itself cause tensions.

Experiences

While some parents may have had great support and experiences on their journey, others may not have been so lucky. They may have been ignored or patronised. They may have had to plead or fight to get their child's needs met. Some parents may also have been promised support that has never materialised or been constantly moved around from one professional to another. Negative experiences, especially where parents feel that they have been let down by the system, can of course affect their enthusiasm and this in turn may affect their ability to engage with us.

Financial hardship

While there are financial benefits available to families, many parents still find themselves in a worse position financially than had they been able to return to full-time work. Returning to full-time work is often difficult when children have significant needs because fewer options for childcare are available and these are more expensive. This means that money can be tight and we should always be aware of this. Asking a parent to attend a meeting might seem straightforward, but if this requires taking the bus to come into the setting or taking time off from work, this is a cost to the parents.

Principles of effective working

One of the most important skills that all practitioners need to learn is how to communicate and work effectively with parents. Where practitioners are good at this, outcomes for everyone are usually positive.

The previous Code of Practice outlined seven key principles that you should adopt when working with parents. These remain essential for delivering the current Code of Practice, in which parents are viewed as central and are meant to be properly involved in all decision making. Following these principles and linking them to our day-to-day practice will provide a good template for creating strong parent–setting relationships.

Each of the principles emphasises the vested interest that parents have in their children's lives and also the knowledge and contribution that parents are able to give to practitioners.

1 Acknowledge and draw on parental knowledge and expertise in relation to their child

Parents usually have a great deal of background knowledge about their own child and may have tried out a range of strategies and equipment or have contacts with different professionals and support groups. Using this parental knowledge will be helpful both when drawing up support plans and when agreeing outcomes. It will also be helpful as part of the 'review' process when reflecting on what has and has not worked well and analysing the reasons why.

What this means in practice

Think about how you engage with parents and the systems that you use to record and help parents to communicate their knowledge about their child. Many settings have an initial 'all about me' sheet that is used to help parents and the practitioner learn more. It is also worth reflecting on how this information is actively used to help everyone working with the child to understand their interests, needs and strengths from the parents' perspective.

❱ 2 Focus on the child's strengths as well as areas of additional need

This principle is particularly relevant in terms of both working with parents and also delivering elements of the Code of Practice. One of changes to the Code of Practice is the requirement for practitioners to see the child more holistically, which includes their strengths and interests. In relation to parents, this is particularly important. Parents can become frustrated by practitioners who focus on the 'problem' or the 'condition' and seem to forget that their child is a wonderful and unique individual. Sharing and talking about a child's interests, pleasures and personality helps to open up communication as well as ensuring that the child's needs can be properly met.

❱ 3 Recognise the personal and emotional investment of parents and be aware of their feelings

The emotional tie between parent and child is a powerful one. Parents do not see their children in terms of 'key learning intentions' and 'normative development'! Most parents' focus is for their child to be happy and reach their potential. It is therefore essential that you are thoughtful and consider the effect of your words, especially when talking about a child's area of need. It is also important to be looking forward as this is a more helpful construct and one that is emphasised by the Code of Practice.

❱ 4 Ensure that parents understand procedures, are aware of how to access support in preparing their contributions, and are given documents to be discussed well before the meetings

The current Code of Practice requires local authorities, but also settings, to involve parents in the process at all times. It also states that in order for parents to be involved in the process, they will need to be provided with sufficient information. While they may be experts on their own child, they may need some help in familiarising themselves with how the graduated approach works in your setting and how they can be involved in this. Parents will also need information about how the process of requesting an EHC plan works and again how they can be involved.

What this means in practice

You will need to reflect on how and what information you provide for parents. You will need to consider whether parents have sufficient information in order for them to fully understand the processes, including planning in your setting. You should also consider asking parents how they would prefer to receive different types of information, e.g. face to face, by email or hard copy.

▶ 5 Respect the validity of differing perspectives and seek constructive ways to reconcile different viewpoints

In an ideal world, practitioners and parents would share the same views and perspectives. The reality is that this may not always happen and we will have to find a way to navigate a consensus. Gaining parental agreement is important in the current Code of Practice, as without it you cannot refer the child or organise for other professionals to help the child. Many practitioners view any disagreement with parents as a challenge to their authority or expertise. This can create very negative meetings and can be a significant barrier to working through the issues. Our starting point, therefore, has to be to accept and respect that parents may have a very different view of what will be best for their child. This will be based on knowledge of their child and their experiences to date. It will also be based on the information that they have gained from a variety of sources.

In some cases this information may be misleading, but without understanding that parents have a right to their own viewpoint, a dialogue cannot begin.

What this means in practice

Learning how to show respect, provide for open communication and find ways of mediating through potentially difficult situations requires many skills. For some settings, it might be worth organising additional staff training so that these skills can be learnt and practised in a safe environment.

▶ 6 Respect the differing needs that parents themselves may have, such as a disability or communication and linguistic barriers

Some parents may have particular needs which, if we are not sensitive to them, may create a barrier to effective communication and information sharing. It is not uncommon for some parents to find reading and writing difficult and if we are not sensitive to this, we may unintentionally create a situation in which parents feel they cannot participate. To overcome potential barriers, we may need to be flexible in our approach. A parent may wish to bring along an interpreter or advocate or we may need to translate or record documents. The key is to find out sensitively from the parents how best we can meet their needs in order that they can participate fully in the process.

◗ 7 Recognise the need for flexibility in the timing and structure of meetings

To achieve true involvement with parents, you will need to make sure that you are 'user friendly'. It can be very difficult for some parents to take time off work or to find alternative care if they have younger children. This in itself can be a barrier to parents' participation.

What this means in practice

It is a good idea to think about where and how you organise meetings. Consider how it might feel for a parent who is new to your setting or this situation. You should also think about whether some parents who are very busy might prefer alternative means of holding a meeting, e.g. by video call or conference call.

Tips for good practice

- Recognise that parents may have a different perspective on their child's development and may have different priorities from you.
- Acknowledge that while you may be an expert on your setting, parents are the experts on their children.
- Do not make comparisons between children in the setting.
- Remember that trust can be shattered by breaches of confidentiality and thoughtless words.

◗ Confidentiality

If you have developed a good relationship with parents, it is likely that they may provide you with personal information, both about the child and themselves. It is essential to regard all information that is passed to you as confidential, unless you are told otherwise.

❯ Data Protection Act

While it is good practice for all records to be 'open' so that parents feel part of the process, you should also be aware that any written personal information that you hold will be subject to the Data Protection Act, whether it has been processed on a computer or by hand. The Act is designed to protect everyone's right to know what has been written about them and to safeguard information being given out without consent. Some settings will need to register with the Information Commissioner's Office. To find out more about how to comply with the Data Protection Act and also whether you need to register, visit http://ico.org.uk.

Tips for good practice

- Check whether your setting needs to register with the Information Commissioner's Office.
- Make sure that your records are secure as well as being accurate and relevant.
- Invite parents to check written information as part of your open communications strategy.

❯ Communicating with parents

We have looked at the key principles involved in working with parents. While the principles are important, they do require good communication skills. There are no magic 'tricks' needed to communicate with parents. You will, however, need to be a good listener, to be supportive and to create environments and situations that help parents feel at ease. You will also need to show empathy for parents. Note that empathy is not sympathy, but reflects concern, care and warmth towards another person.

Parents have unique insights about their child's needs and interests

❯ Listening to parents

Many parents comment that some practitioners do not listen to them. This perception is more likely to occur when parents feel that they are being hurried or that the environment in which conversations are taking place is hectic or noisy. In these conditions, a practitioner's attention might be divided or time may be so short that instead of listening to a parent's perspective, the practitioner concentrates only on what he or she wishes to say. It is therefore essential to find quiet areas and times in which to talk to parents. It is also important to show parents that you are actively trying to understand their viewpoint and are listening to their messages. There are many ways in which we can do this. First, show through your body language that you are keen to listen. Take the time to sit down with the parent, nod and make eye contact. Remember to avoid interrupting what a parent is saying.

Clarification

Good listeners also check that they are receiving the message by clarifying points; for example, 'So if I have understood you correctly, you are finding that Jo points rather than using words at home.' Clarification is particularly useful when parents' views and perspectives are different to ours. By clarifying what the parent is saying, we can be sure that we have understood their point of view, which reduces the danger of misunderstandings.

As well as checking that you are receiving the message well, you can show parents that you really are listening to them by reflecting back their words; for example, 'So Jo was very frustrated yesterday.' This can help parents to keep talking as they feel that they are being listened to.

▶ Talking to parents

It is easy to forget that our words can be very powerful. They can destroy the trust and confidence that a parent has in a setting or a person. Words can also make parents feel guilty and defensive or make them feel that their child is 'not good enough'. This means that while you are talking to parents, you will need to be aware of the effect of your words and notice parents' body language and responses. It also means that you should prepare for meetings carefully. Look again at the child. Notice the strengths of the child. Consider what this child can bring to the setting. It can also be a good idea to think about what the child now needs from the adults in the setting. In this way, you are more likely to show that you care and have the child's best interests at heart.

Tips for good practice

- Do not focus on what the child can or cannot do.
- Focus on what adults need to do to help the child.
- Monitor parents' body language as you talk.
- Consider the effects of your words.
- Make sure that you talk about the child in positive ways.

▶ Understanding that parents may have strong emotions

Many parents will have strong emotions when they talk about their children. This is perfectly natural as the emotional bond between parent and child is, after all, what makes parents parents! So understanding that this is essential, and allowing parents to express their emotions without feeling embarrassed, will be a cornerstone to building a good relationship.

As well as emotions linked to parents' attachments, parents may also experience a wide range of other emotions. Some parents may feel angry for a variety of reasons. It may be that they feel let down by other organisations, professionals or even by your setting. In some cases, parents also say that they feel both fear and anger. The fear can come from not knowing what in the long term will happen to their child and the anger can come from feeling that they lack the power to change the situation. It is important to recognise that anger and fear can change the typical way in which parents may communicate. Talking about their child and their child's needs may evoke uncomfortable emotions and so parents may react in quite strong ways. It is important to be calm in these situations and to be non-judgemental. This can be difficult and is another reason why training can be helpful.

What this means in practice

- Find a quiet and private space for conversations.
- Consider using a 'Do not disturb' sign on the door.
- Make sure that you are really listening to parents.
- Check that you have understood what a parent is saying by asking if you can summarise and invite them to correct you.
- Do not show embarrassment or surprise if a parent openly cries; have tissues to hand and make sure that the parent does not feel rushed.
- Reassure parents that their emotions and feelings are important.
- Consider whether a parent's anger is based on frustration; have you really been listening to and acknowledging his or her viewpoint?
- Consider whether you would benefit from some training in basic counselling to help develop your listening skills.

▶ Parents as an invaluable source of information

Parents can usually provide information, not just about their child, but also about the strategies, equipment and resources that they use to 'enable' the child to live happily in the home environment. This is worth remembering because often a child who appears to be 'disabled' in some way in a setting may well be 'abled' in their own home. It can therefore be a good idea to visit a child at home, especially if you are worried about managing a medical condition or making sure that your setting is accessible.

Some parents also become 'experts' on their child's condition and can provide up-to-date information and also contacts with other professionals. Tapping into this information can therefore be helpful in finding effective ways to support and enable the child.

What should I do if I notice that a child's behaviour or development is giving me cause for concern?

Early identification of children with additional needs is essential in order for children to gain any support that they might need. It is also a legal requirement in the EYFS. Hopefully, you will already have developed a good working relationship with the parents as this forms the basis of good practice within all early years settings. This should mean that you will feel able to raise your thoughts before you start to observe and assess the child in more depth. Parents who feel the most dissatisfied with settings are often those whose first contact with staff is when they are called in to talk about a 'problem'. When approaching parents with your concerns, it will be important to listen to their thoughts. It is worth pointing out to parents that children under five years old often show a wide range of development and that additional intervention can make a significant difference. It is also important to explain what the potential next steps might be and to agree with the parents how you will move forward together.

Tips for good practice

Raising a concern with parents
- Find out when parents are able to come in to talk.
- Begin any meeting by explaining that you are hoping to help the child and that it would be helpful to exchange as much information as possible about the child.
- Talk through the child's overall progress in the setting, emphasising the strengths of the child in order for parents to understand your perspective on the child.
- Ask for their perspective; emphasise that they will have a more global view of their child.
- Make sure that any meeting ends with everyone involved having a clear idea of what the next steps might be.

What should I do if I am concerned about a child's progress and the parent does not seem to accept that there is a developmental delay?

If, when talking to parents, you sense that they do not share your view of the child's progress, it will be important to acknowledge this. The child they see at home may be very different to the one you see in your setting, especially in terms of behaviour and language. The starting point is therefore to find out more about the child and to keep in contact with the parents. You may consider jointly carrying out some observations so that the areas of concern can be more accurately assessed. It is also important to check normative development from a range of sources so that you can be sure these assessments are accurate. It is essential to remember that a parent's concerns may be different to your own.

A parent may focus on the happiness of their child rather than having an educational perspective. You must take care to consider the 'whole' child and not just to focus on the child's weaknesses. Parents will also need to feel that you are on the child's side and that any concern you may have does not reflect badly on either the child or the parent. Some practitioners who are concerned that parents are not taking on board the message that they are trying to give can make the situation worse by almost building a case against the child. This makes parents defensive as it can feel as if the child is being blamed and victimised. You should be clearly reflecting the idea that, by considering the child's needs, your aim is to 'enable' the child by changing your approach, resources or strategies.

It is also worth recognising that some parents may be at the start of a potentially emotional journey. Some parents are afraid that their child will be labelled or treated less favourably than others and so they may distrust any attempt to record the child's needs. This is a natural reaction in view of how children with additional needs have been treated in the past. It is therefore essential to reassure parents that you will be working closely with them and that their views and perspectives will always be taken into consideration.

In other cases, parents may need some time to consider your perspective and to adjust to this other view of their child. This may mean arranging further meetings so that parents can come back and ask further questions and gain more information.

I was presented one day with a list of everything that was 'wrong'. I was so angry that in the end I tore the paper up and asked them who they thought they were.

Lesley, parent of Robert, aged 5

What this means in practice

- Make sure that your assessments of the child are accurate.
- Remember to focus on the child's strengths as well as on areas causing concern.
- Listen to and acknowledge any differing perspectives that parents may have.
- Avoid making meetings 'adversarial'; parents should feel that you are on their child's side.
- Remember that parents want the best for their child and that being protective is normal.
- Consider whether it is your setting that is 'disabling' the child.
- Talk to parents about any fears they may have.
- Give parents information about the Parent Partnership Service in your area.

Chapter 6

The graduated approach – Assess, Plan, Do and Review

▶ Introduction

The past few years have seen many ways of planning for the needs of children. The current Code of Practice states that SEN support in the early years should consist of a 'graduated approach' whereby support to children is implemented in a consistent and also considered way. The Code of Practice states that this should be delivered through an Assess, Plan, Do and Review cycle of interventions. In this chapter we look at what is meant by the graduated approach and ways in which it might be implemented in your setting.

▶ Who will need the graduated approach?

The key test to indicate if you need to use a graduated approach with a child is whether or not you will need to provide very different or extra support to help the child. A child with a medical condition such as diabetes or asthma is unlikely to need this approach because these types of conditions do not usually affect children's learning and overall development. In the same way, a child who uses a wheelchair will not need a graduated approach, as once adjustments are made to the environment to 'enable' the child, he or she will be able to enjoy the same play, activities and learning experiences as other children. It is important to recognise which children need this approach because it is time consuming.

▶ Who will be involved in the graduated approach?

The 'Assess, Plan, Do and Review' approach draws on expertise and information from a range of people, depending on the needs of the child and how far on in the process they are. For children who have just been identified as needing additional provision, it will be the child's parents, the setting's SENCO and the key person or practitioner who will have responsibility for the child. If the child already has involvement with other professionals, their input will also be included.

❯ Involving parents

The 'graduated approach' as outlined by the Code of Practice involves parents. Their insights into their child and the strategies that they may have already been using at home need to be recognised and valued through the process. While this was already recognised in the previous Code of Practice, there is now significantly more emphasis on parental involvement. This is why creating strong relationships and models of communication, as we looked at in the previous chapter, becomes so important.

❯ Involving children

The Code of Practice has as one of its key features the involvement of children in their own education. While very young children will not necessarily understand the process of drawing up plans, they can still be involved, as working from children's interests is likely to make more impact. This means that before a plan is drawn up, the child's parents or key person can ask the child about what they enjoy doing most in the setting and who they like being with. It is also possible to use observations and film clips of children to help build a plan that reflects their interests as well as meeting their needs.

This child expressed an interest in playing football

▶ Starting points for planning interventions using the graduated approach

A good starting point when you have identified children who may need additional support is to read Chapter 5 of the Code of Practice and the section entitled 'SEN support in the early years', and also to find out if your local authority has provided you with paperwork to plan for SEN support. This is important because the evidence from such plans is needed in order to support applications for an EHC assessment. There is a range of different formats being used and different titles for these formats. Some local authorities use the term 'Support plans', others 'Individual provision planning', but regardless of their title, they are all likely follow the process of Assess, Plan, Do and Review set out in the Code of Practice. To find out more, it is worth contacting your Area SENCO or your advisory team.

 Can we carry on using Individual Education Plans (IEPs)?

 Individual Education Plans were a focus of the previous Code of Practice and they were quite prescriptive. You can continue to use them if you wish to provide more detailing in planning, but they may need modification to accommodate some of the features of the new Code of Practice, which includes the need to work with parents and also take into consideration children's views.

▶ Assess

The starting point for the graduated approach is always about assessment. While assessment should be a constant feature of your work with children, the graduated approach begins when you identify that children may need additional support beyond that which you would ordinarily offer to help children learn and develop. At this point, you should have already been talking to parents about your concerns, but if you have not for any reason, it is now essential as the Code of Practice requires it.

> 'Where a setting makes special educational provision for a child with SEN, they should inform the parents.'
>
> Code of Practice 5.38

The Code of Practice is clear that the assessment stage of the process should also involve your setting's SENCO, as well as the parents.

◗ Type of information required in the 'Assess' section

While the format changes in the Assess phase, most local authorities' paperwork for early years settings is similar in approach to that used in drawing up EHC plans. The focus is to provide a holistic view of the child, including their strengths and interests, as well as to focus on areas of need. In the Code of Practice, four areas of need are stated:

- communication and interaction
- cognition and learning
- social, emotional and mental health
- sensory and/or physical needs.

With the exception of cognition and learning, these areas of need fit very well with the three prime areas of learning and development within the EYFS, namely:

1. communication and language
2. personal, social and emotional development
3. physical development.

This means easy links can be made to the assessment that you have already carried out. Some children's needs will fall across the four areas of need and this should be made clear in the assessment. In addition, the 'Assess' section may also include relevant information about who else is supporting the child and family, for example other professionals who may be involved.

What this means in practice

You will need to revisit with the parents any information that was provided when the child started at the setting in order to check that it is still up to date and relevant. You will also need to talk to the parents about the child's interests and strengths at home, as well as areas of developmental need.

◗ Plan

◗ Type of information required in the 'Plan' section

The next step in the process is to agree a plan with the parents and your setting's SENCO. The plan should include the following, as specified by the Code of Practice:

- Outcomes agreed with parents.
- Interventions and support to be put in place.

- Expected impact on progress, development or behaviour.
- Date for review.

Outcomes agreed with parents

It may take some time and discussion to agree outcomes with parents, who may have different priorities. It is possible to have some outcomes that are about the child at home, as well as the child in the setting. When agreeing outcomes, it is important that they should be realistic and based on the child's current stage of development. They should also be short term and an explanation should be provided as to why they are needed. Many local authorities suggest that it is best to focus on three or four outcomes at a time and that these should have a tight focus.

This parent is showing a photograph of their child playing at home

Using SMART to help the 'Plan' process

Setting outcomes allows us to focus on developing or improving children's particular skills. The acronym SMART is often used when doing this to help practitioners and parents think carefully about the outcomes that they are setting. The approach of using SMART has been shown to be very successful and so is worth considering.

SMART is an acronym standing for:

S = Specific
M = Measurable
A = Achievable
R = Relevant
T = Time bound

Specific

This is about making sure that the outcomes or targets in the plan are very tight and specific. Working out 'tiny' next steps for children is a skill, and experience definitely helps. Many teams, when thinking about outcomes or targets, will use a range of materials such as those produced by their local occupational therapy teams or their speech and language teams.

Measurable

As we have seen, there is a requirement in the Code of Practice for the plan to show the impact that it is likely to have on children. It is worth thinking about what this will look like in practice. Here are some questions that might help to shape this part of your plan.

- How many times will we need to see the child demonstrating that they can achieve the target/outcome?
- How confidently or easily must the child be able to achieve the target/outcome?
- In what type of situation does the child need to achieve the target/outcome, e.g. during adult-directed activities, with support of another adult, at home as well as in the setting?

Achievable and Relevant

By thinking about how the outcomes/targets are going to be measured, it is more likely that you will choose achievable outcomes/targets for the child. Choosing targets that are relevant is also important. Relevant targets or outcomes are focused on meeting children's needs and interests. Do think about whether outcomes are being set that are more about the smooth running of your setting's organisation, e.g. 'Jamie to sit still during registration'!

Time bound

SMART targets or outcomes always have specified dates and time built in for review. Ideally, if the outcomes/targets chosen are specific and realistic, it is possible for them to be completed fairly swiftly. The need for a time frame is, of course, why there is a requirement in the Code of Practice for a review date to be put on to the plan.

Interventions and support to be put in place

Information should be recorded about how the outcomes are to be achieved. This should include the strategies that are to be used, who will be working directly with the child and the frequency of the interventions. It may also be important to record the resources to be used. It is also worth noting that the Code of Practice states that the interventions must be carried out by practitioners who have the necessary skills and knowledge.

In the interventions and support section, there may also be space to record what parents would like, if anything, to do at home. It is worth noting that this is something that the Code of Practice mentions.

'Parents should be involved in planning support and, where appropriate, in reinforcing the provision or contributing to progress at home.'

Code of Practice 5.41

When planning interventions and strategies, you may need to use a range of information to ensure that the interventions and strategies that you are choosing are the best ones to support the child. It can be worth talking to your local Area SENCO or to other professionals in your area. Some occupational therapy and speech and language teams provide resources to help parents and practitioners. You can also look at what is available digitally as many specialist teams supply leaflets online.

Expected impact on progress, development or behaviour

You will also need, with the parents, to consider and record the difference that the interventions are expected to have on the child's progress, development or behaviour. These are sometimes called 'success criteria'. It is worth thinking about this in detail and aiming to give measurable or tangible examples; for example, 'Harry will be able to concentrate on a four-piece jigsaw while being supported by an adult for five minutes.'

Date for review

You should also agree with the parents when you are going to review how the approaches are working. There is no set time limit and this may be tricky to judge. On the one hand, there needs to be enough time for the interventions to take place; but on the other hand, if the interventions are not working, additional support will need to be sought. Most settings have plans that last between four and eight weeks.

What this means in practice

It is important when drawing up the plan that careful thought is given to it so as not to create a plan that cannot be fully implemented. This is particularly important when considering interventions and strategies in relation to who will be responsible for carrying them out. It also means that some settings may need to organise further training for their staff so that they have the skills to work effectively with the child.

Views of the child

There is also a requirement that plans should take account of the views of the child and so, together with the parents, you should think about how best to gain these. It might be that the child will have a favourite toy, interest or place where they enjoy being and this might inform the plan. It might be also that we can ask children directly what they would like to be able to do and incorporate their ideas into the plan.

What this means in practice

Many settings are concerned that they will not be able to show that they have taken into consideration the views of the child. It is possible to do this through watching children carefully, talking to the child's parents about the child's interests and reactions at home. It is also important to use visual prompts such as photographs to help children communicate their thoughts.

▶ Carrying out the 'Do' phase of the plan

While the 'Plan' stage of the process provides outcomes and strategies to implement the 'Do' stage of the process, it is likely that you will need more detailed implementation plans. There are many ways of creating such plans and we look at these in the next section in this chapter. During the 'Do' phase, it is useful to keep careful notes of how well the interventions are working, how the child is responding and what seems to be of interest to them. These can then be used when reviewing the plan later. It is also important during the 'Do' phase to think about when the plan needs to be re-shaped and whether the review needs to be brought forward.

> One of the things that I would recommend to anyone new to this is not to treat the plan as an inflexible tool. It is meant to be a working document and you can put in additional sheets of paper or, if you are doing this electronically, create new versions. We have had to do this with one or two children when it became obvious that the strategies we were using were not really effective. Of course, you need to involve parents and make sure that they are of the same mind. There is also a balance to be struck in giving interventions sufficient time.
>
> *Julie, nursery manager*

What this means in practice

It is important that the interventions and strategies are implemented in the way that has been outlined in the plan. If the interventions and strategies are not working well, the plan can be changed but this should be evidenced. For children who may go on to need an EHC, there has to be evidence that interventions and strategies have been used first, and this is another reason why good notes should be kept.

▶ Review

The final stage of the process is for a review meeting to take place. At the review meeting, an update on the child's progress should be recorded. The different interventions and strategies should be discussed and analysed. Thought should be given to what is working well. There should also be an attempt to discuss what has not worked so well and why. This in turn should inform the next round of planning. 'Assess, Plan, Do and Review' is repeated, with the progress that the child has made being recorded in the 'Assess' section.

'This cycle of action should be revisited in increasing detail and with increasing frequency, to identify the best way of securing good progress. At each stage, parents should be engaged with the setting, contributing their insights to assessment and planning. Intended outcomes should be shared with parents and reviewed with them, along with action taken by the setting, at agreed times.'

Code of Practice 5.44

If the child is clearly not making sufficient progress despite a range of interventions, the next step is to involve specialist services such as speech and language therapists or educational psychologists. If a referral is successful, the interventions suggested by the specialist services will then need to be included in the next round of 'Assess, Plan, Do and Review'. In cases where the child continues to need additional support that cannot be met without further significant interventions, the next step is to request an EHC plan.

What this means in practice

The review process needs to be carefully documented and time needs to be spent on analysing what is, and in some cases what is not, working so well. This is important as it is linked to the success of getting a request for an EHC plan accepted by the local authority.

▶ Evidence

As the 'Assess, Plan, Do and Review' process is used as evidence to support the application for a request for an EHC or in some areas to gain a referral to specialist teams, it is essential that this process is carefully recorded. You should also keep detailed records of how the plan has been implemented and detailed assessments. As these records can make a significant difference to the child and their family, it is worth talking to your Area SENCO about how best to complete any forms that they have produced and also what level of detail is required.

 Do we need to undertake 'Assess, Plan, Do and Review' in addition to what we are doing for two year olds?

 Following the two-year-old progress check, you are required to produce a targeted plan for those two year olds who are showing developmental delay. The 'Assess, Plan, Do and Review' should dovetail well with the requirements of this so there is no need to have separate paperwork unless you choose to do so.

▶ Examples of plans and monitoring sheets to support the 'Do' phase

The 'Do' phase of the graduated response is of course the one that is likely to make a significant difference to children's progress. While the interventions and strategies need to be outlined, many settings then find it helpful to draw up more detailed plans to help the key person and others on a day-to-day basis. These plans can also be used to record evidence of implementation and children's responses. There are many formats that you can use, although it is always worth starting by seeing if your Area SENCO has drawn up any tools that you might find useful.

Following are some examples of plans from different settings that might be useful to consider. In addition, some plans might also be useful to support children who do not need SEN provision, but still need some level of intervention.

Name:		Key worker:
Date of Birth:		SENCO:
School:	Photo of child	Start date:
Parent/carer name:		Specific Area of Need:
Parent/carer consent and signature:		Other agencies involved:

A little bit about: What people like and admire about me	What's important to me:	How best support me:

First targets:	Strategies:	Review – date
•	•	Achieved Partially achieved Not achieved
Agreed home actions:	Further actions required:	

Name:

Second targets: date	Strategies:	Review – date
		Achieved Partially achieved Not achieved
Agreed home actions:	Further actions required:	
Third targets: date	Strategies:	Review – date
		Achieved Partially achieved Not achieved
Agreed home actions:	Further actions required:	

Example of a Support Plan that can be used as part of Assess, Plan, Do and Review

Individual Support Plan			
Setting name:			
Name:	DOB:	SEN Co-ordinator: Keyworker/person:	Date:
What I can do now?	Areas of concern and what works/doesn't work for me:	Parent(s)/carer(s) views/future aspirations:	
Long-term outcomes:	Other Professionals involved consulted:		
	Paediatrician		
	Health Visitor		
	Speech and Language		
	Physiotherapist		
	Occupational Therapist		
	Portage		
	Advisory/Outreach teacher		
	Educational Psychologist		
	Improvement Advisor (EYCS)		

Example of an Individual Support Plan

Individual Provision Plan for:		
Early years setting	Sessions attended	Group size ratio (adult:child)

Support needed	Intervention		Positive outcome for child
	How?	Who?	
Outline what support is needed and when	What specific action will be taken? What will the adult/carers do with/for the child?	Which adults will be involved in supporting the child or taking responsibility?	What will this support do for the child? What are the positive benefits for the child? (These should be agreed with parents)

Example of a plan to support individual children during sessions

Support monitoring plan

Setting: Date:

Name:

Key person: Support worker.

The things my key person and I agree that I can do well are:

My next targets are to:

I shall try to achieve my targets by (methods/strategies):

Everyone will know I have succeeded because (success criteria):

My parents/carers can help me by:

Parent/carer comments and signature(s)

Evaluation

We will get together to talk about my progress and set new targets on/by (date):

Example of a parent-friendly planning sheet

Review sheet

Name of child

Date of review

	Setting	Parent/Child
What we have tried		
What we are pleased about		
What we have learned		
What we have concerns about		
What we need to do next (Agreed actions)		
Date of next review		

Signed (Parent)...

Signed (Setting)...

Example of a review sheet

Chapter 7

Sources of information and support

▶ Introduction

While many children's needs can be met within the setting and through working closely with parents, some children will need additional support from other professionals. What is available and how to access it will vary from area to area. This reflects the current legal framework that provides for each local authority to publish their 'Local Offer'. In this chapter we look at what is likely to be available in your area, the role of other professionals and also other useful sources of information.

▶ The need for consent

An important starting point when considering gaining further support or advice about a child is to understand that you need parental consent. While some professionals will be happy to talk in general terms about a specific difficulty such as how to encourage pencil grip, you must not refer to or talk about a particular child without parental consent. The only exception to this would be where there is a safeguarding issue in which case you would need to follow the child protection procedures that are in place in your setting.

▶ Sources of support and information

It is very difficult to write with any precision about the different types of support that will be available in any given area. This is because not only are teams and structures different in each area, but also the level of access and the processes for referrals are different. While one service will accept direct referrals in one area where a child does not necessarily have SEN, but does have a specific difficulty, another may have a triage approach where all referrals are dealt with centrally. It is therefore useful to develop your own directory and network of contacts so that you can easily find help or advise parents whom to contact. It is worth noting that many of the services outlined in this chapter offer training courses and workshops. Attending these can help you learn more about how the services in your area are organised, including the process of referring children.

As well as gaining support from specialist professionals, remember, in your local area there will be other SENCOs working in early years settings. By exchanging phone numbers and emails, you can potentially pool ideas and suggestions.

It will be important to work closely with other professionals to support children with SEND

▶ SEND and inclusion team

These are sometimes referred to as inclusion support teams or SENCO area teams. Most local authorities have a service to support teachers and early years professionals who are working with children who have special educational needs in mainstream settings. The exact title of the teams can vary and so it will be important to find out the name of the service in your area, as well as how it operates. Following the Code of Practice's emphasis on mainstream education, many teams are now offering advice and training. In some areas, there are both advisory SEN teachers who specialise in early years, as well as Area SENCOs. In other areas, there may just be Area SENCOs. Contacting the SEND and inclusion team for your area will help you to find out about other services in your region. You may also be able to arrange for either an Area SENCO or an advisory teacher to visit your setting to give further advice, either about a particular child or about how to improve your provision to make it more inclusive.

▶ Early years advisory teams

In some areas, early years advisors are part of the school improvement team. Early years advisory teachers can be very helpful in ensuring that the routines, resources and activities in your setting are working well. They can be a good first step when you have concerns about a child, as you should always begin by aiming to adapt your provision.

▶ Speech and language teams

Every area will have a speech and language service or team. Technically, this service is provided by the health service but there is a range of delivery models and sometimes schools and education settings will 'buy' in their services. In some areas, speech and language therapists work in children's centres or have drop-in sessions in local libraries or community centres. Referral processes vary, but in many areas parents can ask for a referral and an assessment directly. In other areas, settings with parental consent can refer children to the speech and language service. Speech and language therapists work to optimise speech, communication and language, but they can also be involved in helping a child to swallow and feed. They work closely with parents, early years professionals and teachers. The type of support that a child receives will depend on his or her need and also age, but usually exercises and strategies are shared with everyone involved in the child's care and education, especially parents. Many speech and language teams are also involved in delivering training.

Case study

My role as a speech and language therapist

My name is Anne-Marie and I work for the NHS in a paediatric clinic as well as in schools and nurseries. I enjoy my work immensely. It's great to see a child who could not communicate before therapy being able to communicate with their family. Communication is not just about being able to make your needs known – it's about being able to share a joke with someone, make friends with your peers and have a conversation about your interests. My job satisfaction comes when I see a child who I've worked with being able to do this. Working with parents and staff in settings to achieve this is crucial. While I can see a child for a therapy block of 4–6 sessions, they see the child every day. If they can carry on the speech and language therapy work on a daily basis, the child will make great progress.

▶ Educational psychologist service

Every education service or department will have an educational psychologist service. Educational psychologists are trained to look at children's development and learning. They assess and identify children's learning and developmental needs and provide advice and guidance to parents and professionals.

Educational psychologists are likely to be involved in the drawing up of EHC plans. They may also be involved in the annual review of EHC plans. Referrals to the educational psychologist service can usually be made directly by parents or by settings with parental consent. In most areas the demand on the service is high, so many early years settings usually involve the SEN advisory teacher or Area SENCO as a starting point where a child's needs are moderate rather than complex. Educational psychologists usually observe a child in the setting, as well as talking to the parents and the child, in order to build up a picture of how the child behaves and learns. Following an assessment, an educational psychologist may provide the parents and the SENCO with advice and may arrange to see the child again at a later date.

Sensory impairment team

Many education services have a team dedicated to helping children who have visual and/or hearing impairment. While the title of this service can vary from area to area, the role of the team is similar. Most teams employ specialist teachers, who visit families to work directly with the child and their parents. They also visit settings to advise them on the effects of the child's impairment and to give them practical suggestions as to how best to meet the child's needs. This service can also become involved in the drawing up of plans as the teacher will be assessing and monitoring a child's progress. Most sensory impairment teams also have strong links with the speech and language service. If you are aware that a child is coming to you with a sensory impairment, it may be possible to contact this service for some advice before the child starts.

Health visiting service

Health visitors are trained health professionals who have undertaken specialist training in health promotion. Their role is to promote health across all age groups in the local community, although many health visiting teams divide their work to focus on particular groups. The health visiting service can be organised in a variety of ways. In some areas, health visitors are attached to clinics, while in others they are attached to GP surgeries. Health visitors who are involved with parents and their children carry out routine health checks, including the two-year-old check. They are also able to provide support by giving advice about childcare and development. It can be very useful to talk to a child's health visitor, but it is essential that the parent gives permission for you to do so. Health visitors can refer children to further services and are usually good at giving advice. It is important to remember that they are not education specialists nor will they necessarily have a grounding in the EYFS.

▶ Paediatric occupational therapy service

Paediatric occupational therapists work with children to maximise their physical movements and development so that they can become as independent as possible. They work with a range of children including those who may have a physical impairment, perceptual disorder or difficulties with hand–eye function. As well as working directly with children, they also tend to work closely with the child's family. In early years settings, they will advise how best to make a setting accessible and some services are able to lend equipment and resources. Paediatric occupational therapists may also ask settings to become involved with the programme that they have devised for the child.

Case study

My role as an occupational therapist

My name is Sharon and I work as a paediatric occupational therapist. I enjoy my work because of the variety of experiences that every day brings. I work in collaboration with school staff, families and the other networks supporting the child or young person and their family. The focus of my work is to find strategies, techniques and equipment, small or large, to enable the child or young person to complete a task they wish to be proficient at. It is satisfying to see a child or young person's smile when they realise 'they can' do something such as cut their food up or write their name, and when the child/young person's family or carers see what their child can do and the potential they have.

▶ Portage

Portage is a home-based teaching service for children under five years and is provided for children whose needs have already been identified. The portage system relies heavily on parents, as it is recognised that the child is likely to make more progress if parents are involved in the teaching of skills. The portage teacher, or volunteer in some cases, visits the home regularly and works with the parents to devise a structured programme to build on a child's skills. If you have a child in your setting who is receiving portage, it will be helpful for you to talk to the parents about how the child is doing at home as you may be able to incorporate and reinforce the skills in your planning. Developing a contact with the portage service can be extremely helpful as it may be able to give informal advice on how to 'break down' skills into small steps.

❭ Physiotherapists

Physiotherapy is usually provided by the health service. Children who may need physiotherapy include those with medical conditions such as cystic fibrosis, children who have injured themselves and children who have a physical condition. As well as directly treating children, physiotherapists will provide advice and guidance to parents and settings about exercises and movements that will help the child. Referral to physiotherapy is likely to occur via a GP or a paediatrician.

❭ Social services

By law, local authorities have a duty to provide services for 'children in need'. This means that most children who have complex and severe needs are likely to have a social worker involved with their families. Assessments will be carried out regularly to see how the local authority can support the child and the family. A social worker is likely to be involved in the annual review of a child's EHC plan, especially if social care is involved.

❭ Support groups and voluntary organisations

Local and national support groups and voluntary organisations can provide settings with advice, fact sheets and, in some cases, resources. Many organisations hold awareness training or workshops for professionals and so it is useful to develop contacts locally in your area. It is very easy to find out the contact details of groups using the internet, although details of a range of national support organisations are provided in Part 3 of this book.

❭ Toy libraries and resources

While at one time there was a strong network of toy libraries, this service is now no longer available in many areas. In some areas, it has been taken over by other organisations including Children's Centres. It is worth looking to see if there are any local lending schemes in your area. There is nothing to stop groups of early years settings including childminders coming together and sharing resources such as sensory toys, which may be expensive for each setting to buy individually.

❭ Internet

The internet is not a perfect tool, but it can be an extremely useful source of information, particularly if you are trying to track down contact details of organisations or are looking out for ideas and up-to-date information. It is important to be aware that anyone can set up a website and this means that there is always a danger of gaining inaccurate information. You should also think about whom the website is designed for and also the country in which it was set up. This is because approaches can vary from country to country. There are some very good websites set up by professionals that provide free ideas for activities. The following are worth considering.

Useful websites

Website address	Comments
www.speech-language-therapy.com	Good if you need to support a child with communication difficulties.
Afasic www.afasic.org.uk	Useful information on this website, particularly the glossary pages that explain varying communication difficulties.
I CAN www.ican.org.uk	Gives a wide range of information about children's speech and language generally, as well as tips for how to support children.
OTplan www.otplan.com	Useful ideas for activities for fine motor control and also sensory difficulties.
Therapy Street for Kids www.therapystreetforkids.com	Useful ideas for fine motor activities but also an explanation as to why the varying skills are important.
National Portage Association www.npa.org.uk	Find out more about portage.

PART 2

Working with children

It is sometimes thought that to work with children who have been identified as having special needs or disabilities requires new skills. This is not really the case. All children require adults to be patient, thoughtful and flexible in their approach. They also need adults to give them time and respect. Armed with these requirements, sensitive adults should be able to help all children. Having said that, most practitioners find it helpful to have an understanding of child development, a knowledge of how to support the child's needs, as well as examples of strategies that they can use in order to help specific children. This section is divided into five chapters. The first chapter looks at the importance of building good relationships with children and involving them in decision making. This is, as we have seen, a significant requirement of the Code of Practice. The remaining four chapters consider each of the 'areas of need' that are referred to the Code of Practice:

- Communication and interaction
- Cognition and learning
- Social, emotional and mental health
- Sensory and/or physical needs.

In each chapter we look at strategies that might be used to support children and also give examples of activities that might be helpful.

Chapter 8

Valuing and empowering children

▶ Introduction

The starting point for working effectively with any child is to respect and value the child for being him or herself. A common criticism of practitioners is the tendency to focus so much on the area of development, the impairment or condition, that the child becomes a problem that has to be solved. This can lead to low self-esteem and underachievement, which is one reason why the Code of Practice stresses the importance of children having an active voice and involvement in their care and education. This chapter looks at the importance of building strong relationships with children, but also of finding ways to empower and involve them in their own care and education.

▶ The Code of Practice

A good starting point is to look at the Code of Practice and its requirements in relation to involving children. The Code states as one of its principles that local authorities must have regard to 'the views, wishes and feelings of the child or young person, and the child's parents'.

In addition, the Code states that this principle is designed to support 'the participation of children, their parents and young children in decision-making'.

As well as the Code of Practice, there is also other legislation in place, notably that related to the United Nations Convention of the Rights of the Child (UNCRC), which gives children a right to have their views considered when decisions are being made that will impact on them.

> 'Children have a right to receive and impart information, to express an opinion and to have that opinion taken into account in any matters affecting them from the early years. Their views should be given due weight according to their age, maturity and capability.'
>
> Articles 12 and 13 of the United Nations Convention on the Rights of the Child

What this means in practice

The requirement for children to be involved in decision making means that you should always be looking for ways of helping children to express their ideas and interests. This may mean giving simple choices to young children, while explaining a situation and outlining varying options for older children. The skill is to judge what level of information and choice is appropriate given the child's age and maturity. It is also important to recognise that young children may have changing interests and that we will need to be flexible when planning to accommodate this.

▶ The role of the key person

It is a statutory requirement of the EYFS that all children should have a key person. A key person is someone who can develop a strong relationship with an individual child and their family. This supports the child's emotional well-being and so allows them to settle and learn. This role is particularly important in relation to children who have SEN and disabilities and as such is recognised in the Code of Practice.

'The early years practitioner, usually the child's key person, remains responsible for working with the child on a daily basis. With support from the SENCO, they should oversee the implementation of the interventions or programmes agreed as part of SEN support.'

Code of Practice 5.24

▶ Developing a bond with a child

The basis of a strong key person relationship is that the child develops a bond with a practitioner. This does take time, especially if a child has never been separated from their parents before or has had an 'unsuccessful' separation which has left the child unsettled. It is worth finding out as much as you can about a child's temperament, interests and previous experiences from a parent, preferably before meeting the child. This way you can gain an insight into how best to respond to the child and how you might build the child's trust. Unless there are exceptional circumstances, you should ensure that you have made a bond with a child before any separation takes place and parents leave. This is because young children can quickly show separation anxiety and their distress can prevent them from being able to form a relationship.

▶ Working with parents to build a bond

The involvement of parents in the process of building a relationship with a child is critical. Children often follow their parents' cues as to whom they can trust. This means that spending as much time as possible talking to parents while settling in children can be very helpful. We also need to find out from parents some of the strategies that they use to reassure their child or, in the case of a child with care or medical needs, how they manage these.

Tips for good practice

Settling children in

An effective way to settle children in is to follow a five-step process. Each of the steps is practised and repeated until the child is relaxed and shows no anxiety.

Step 1 Key person, parent and child play together.

By the end of this step, the child is able to carrying on playing or interacting with the key person without the encouragement or support of the parent.

Step 2 Key person and child play together while the parent moves slightly away.

By the end of this step, the child is happy to interact with the key person while the parent moves slightly away and then comes back.

Step 3 Key person and child play together while parent moves in and out of sight.

By the end of this step, the child is comfortable with the key person as the parent bobs in and out of sight, e.g. gets something from a cupboard within the room.

Step 4 Key person and child play together when parent leaves the room for one minute.

By the end of this step, the parent is able to tell the child that they are popping out of the room for one minute to collect an item, e.g. a sticker. The child is relaxed and able to continue playing with the key person.

Step 5 Key person and child play together when parent leaves the room for 20 minutes.

By the end of this step, the parent is able to tell the child that they are leaving and that the time spent out of the room has been built up to 20 minutes.

▶ Transitions

The term 'transition' is often used to describe any change that takes place that affects the child. Transitions that involve the transfer of care to a different person can be particularly difficult for children and it is important that we find ways of making these as smooth as possible. The best way of ensuring this is to make sure that the child has developed a relationship with the 'new' adult before the transition takes place. In some ways these transitions need to be seen as 'mini settling-ins', with the child having a chance to build a relationship before the transition takes place.

What this means in practice

Adults often underestimate the number of transitions that can occur fairly regularly. Make a list of transitions that children you work with may experience. These might include lunchtimes, staff breaks and also training days. Think about whether the child has sufficiently strong relationships with the adults who will be with them during these transitions.

Tips for good practice

Supporting children during transitions
- Use pictures and photographs to aid understanding.
- Make sure that a relationship is in place before the transition takes place.
- Talk to children so that they know what is going to happen and can ask questions.
- Encourage children to think about what they may need to help them make a transition, e.g. a comforter.
- Communicate carefully with other adults so that the child's needs and interests can be met.

▶ Empowerment

The model behind the Code of Practice and working effectively with children with SEN and disability is about empowerment. To empower children means to consider their feelings and rights and to look for ways of making them independent and assertive. This is highly effective because it means that children are more likely to have positive outcomes, as they see themselves as being strong and having some control over their destiny. Children who are not empowered from their earliest years are more likely to develop 'learned helplessness'. They may grow up seeing themselves as not capable and this can seriously prevent them from fulfilling their potential. Adults play a huge role in preventing this from happening. The first step in the journey of empowering children is to ensure that children develop strong self-esteem.

Developing independence is important for children's self-esteem

▶ Self-esteem

Self-esteem is sometimes referred to as having 'confidence'. Children who have additional needs are vulnerable to developing low self-esteem. It is important to avoid this because low self-esteem can limit children's expectations of themselves and others. This means that a child may not feel confident enough to try a new activity, take the initiative or see him or herself as worthy of respect. In short, low self-esteem limits children's ability to fulfil their potential. Low self-esteem is also linked to behaviour. Some children quickly learn that in order to avoid being in a situation they are unsure about, they should 'misbehave'. By doing this, they may be taken away from the activity or be given extra adult attention.

We are not born with low or high self-esteem. Our levels of inner confidence are the result of an ongoing process. This begins in the early years of children's lives when they develop a self-image or a view of themselves. As children get older, they begin to consider whether their view of themselves matches up with what they want to be like: their ideal self. If a child views him or herself as being very different to the child he or she wants to be, the result will be low self-esteem.

❯ Understanding how a child develops a self-image

We come into the world knowing nothing about ourselves, not even our names. The first step for children is to find out about themselves. They do this mainly by listening to and noticing others' responses to them, especially key adults in their lives. This is sometimes referred to as the 'looking glass' effect. The responses from others towards the child is as if they are seeing themselves in a mirror.

❯ How children can learn about themselves from listening

Children will listen to the comments that adults make about them and to them. They are quick to pick up on the tone of voice and over time will interpret the words to come to an understanding of what adults think about them. This all feeds into their self-image.

A phrase, such as 'Good girl, Sam, you were very kind', may give this young child four messages:

- I am good, the adult is pleased with me.
- I am a girl.
- My name is Sam.
- I am kind.

If we look at another comment, such as 'I really wish you would try harder, Samantha. This isn't really that difficult', we can see that the child may gain some other information:

- The adult is not happy with me.
- I am not trying hard enough.
- When this adult is not pleased with me, my full name is used.
- The adult thinks this is easy, so therefore I cannot be that clever.

As well as the actual words, children are also good at tuning in to the intonation of the voice used. Research has shown that most babies are able to distinguish an angry-sounding voice from a relaxed voice, even when the language is unfamiliar to them. The ability for children to interpret tone of voice also means that children can tell when adults are being insincere, e.g. when adults give them false praise.

❯ What children learn from non-verbal responses

As well as learning through words and signs, children also notice our non-verbal behaviour towards them. Children can sense whether someone is happy to see them and genuinely enjoys being with them. They are also able to notice when adults are irritated, disappointed or frustrated with them. Children notice our eye movements, facial expression and overall body language. As with tone of voice, children can distinguish between an adult smiling with sincerity or putting a smile on. When children regularly see non-verbal responses that are not positive, they are likely to internalise this and come to the conclusion that they are unlovable.

▶ Why children need a positive self-image

Children need to be gaining positive responses from us if they are to develop a strong self-image. If a child constantly hears that he or she is 'naughty', 'lazy' or 'difficult', he or she will begin to believe that this is the way he or she has been 'made'. This in turn creates situations where the child acts in line with the adults' expectations. By contrast, children who hear and sense positive things about themselves develop a strong and healthy view of themselves. A strong, positive self-image needs to be developed when children are young, as the pressure on their self-image can increase once children become older.

▶ Becoming aware of others

The pressure on children increases as they become more aware of others. This shows often in the way that they begin to look at what others are doing and then compare it to what they are doing. For many children, this will happen in their primary school years from around five or six years old, although for some children this may happen earlier and for others not at all. Children who become aware of others are likely to compare themselves, and in some cases this may make them feel that they are 'lacking' in some way. This can have serious implications. A child who becomes aware that he or she is not fast at running may decide not to bother any more, even though the child previously enjoyed running. While it is impossible to create an environment which will prevent children from noticing what others are doing, it is important that adults reinforce messages about how we are all different and will do things in a range of ways.

▶ The development of an ideal self

As well as comparing themselves to others, many children will go on from this to develop an 'ideal self'. This is an imaginary picture of what they would like to be. Children gain this ideal self by working out what others around them value, i.e. what seems to impress their teachers, their parents and their friends. Children can also be influenced by what the media portray as being important. Low self-esteem is often seen as resulting from the difference between the child's ideal self and his or her own self-image or picture of themselves. While confident children may wish that they were a little different to how they see themselves, children who have low self-esteem will see themselves as being nothing like the 'perfect' child.

Helping children to develop a positive self-image

There are many ways in which we can help children to develop and maintain a positive self-image. It is important to remember that as practitioners, we should be doing this to help all the children that we are working with, regardless of any additional or special needs.

What messages are children receiving from adults' interactions and body language?

We have seen that children learn about themselves by noticing the reactions and interactions of adults towards them. This has strong implications as it means that we should consider carefully what messages we are sending out to children. When we are working with children whose behaviour is challenging, we need to make sure that a child is not receiving so many negative signals that he or she comes to believe he or she has been born 'naughty'. It is important to remember that children will need more positive signals to counteract any negative ones they have received.

How is this adult's body language showing this child that they are valued?

Most practitioners do not realise that they are sending out negative messages. Be careful of signals that focus on what the child cannot do or is not doing. Always try to turn negative messages into positive messages. Look at the examples in the box below.

What this means in practice

If we understand that what children see and hear affects their self-image, we may need to reflect on the ways that we promote self-image within the setting.

Try monitoring the number of positive interactions that a child in your setting receives in a session. Keep a simple tally sheet. Has the child gained more positives or negatives by the end of the session?

- Consider the ways in which children are greeted and made to feel welcome.
- Look for opportunities to positively recognise children's special attributes and skills.
- Make sure that you signal to children when you are working with them that you enjoy being with them, e.g. using eye contact, smiles, touch.
- Remember that children respond to adults who have a sense of humour and are fun.
- Be very clear when managing behaviour that you are not unhappy with the child, but with the behaviour that he or she is showing.
- Consider carrying out a simple observation to check that interactions are positive.

❭ Praise and recognition

When and how to praise and recognise children is a complex issue. It is very important that children learn that adults care for and cherish them for themselves, not only for what they can do. This means that while it is important to praise children when they achieve, you also need to strike a balance so that children do not feel that praise is conditional only on performance. You should also be careful that love is not associated with pleasing the adult. Phrases such as 'Be a good boy and do that for me' will give children the message that in order to be a 'good boy', you have to please the adult. This is a dangerous message as a child might worry about not being liked if they are not 'good enough'.

In addition, it is helpful to understand that the type of praise and recognition that children need may change according to their age and stage of development. While praise is important for younger children, over time we need to help children learn to be reflective and to recognise for themselves their efforts and achievements. This model is very effective in helping children to gain inner motivation and to cope with setbacks. It also means that over time children start to learn more self-regulation skills and so can become emotionally less reliant on adults.

What this means in practice

It is worth as a team working out the role of praise and recognition in your setting and how best to use it for individual children. It is worth thinking about whether praise and recognition is 'achievement' orientated or whether the children's qualities are also being recognised. It is also worth considering whether some children are becoming over-reliant on praise and are only doing things to get adults' attention and praise, rather than for their own sake.

▶ Avoiding competitive environments

Where children are at the stage of comparing themselves to others, it will be important to consider if the environment is structured to negatively reinforce 'differences' between children, i.e. through competitions with prizes for some children but not for others. If so you may consider encouraging everyone to share an individual's achievement. For example, 'Today, everyone is getting a sticker so that we can all celebrate Marty's success. Let's all have a clap.' This type of approach helps children to be recognised, but also makes everyone in the setting feel good.

▶ Have fair but high expectations of the child

Children are quickly able to sense whether adults believe in them. Having too low expectations of children can mean that they too do not believe that they are capable of certain things. Phrases such as, 'Never mind, you have done your best' can actually give children a signal that the adult does not believe that they are capable of any more.

The path between encouraging children and putting them into situations where they might fail is therefore a sensitive one. Too many apparent 'failures' can result in children losing confidence, while not being challenged can deny children the opportunity to develop their skills further. In the past, there was a tendency to underestimate what children were capable of. This resulted in many children missing out on opportunities to learn new skills and have a wide range of experiences. This effectively discriminated against children. The key is always to observe children carefully so as to get a feeling of what will be challenging but within their reach. Considering what children really can do, and working out what they may be capable of, will help children in the longer term to achieve their potential. It is also important to vocalise your expectations so that children know that you believe in their potential. For example, saying, 'Why don't you have another go at pouring the drinks out. It is tricky and it takes a little practice, but you can do it' will be far better than saying to a child, 'Never mind, you have done your best', and doing it for them.

❱ Provide opportunities for children to be independent and to take on responsibility

The more children can do for themselves, the stronger their confidence can grow. It is often easy for adults working with children to 'take over' rather than give children the time and encouragement to master a skill or finish a task. Children in this way can be disempowered because they learn to rely on an adult rather than on themselves.

There are many ways in which we can help children to take on some responsibility and have some control over their care and education. Children can be involved in their own self-care, choice of clothes, food and activities. The key is to adapt the routine or the way we work to allow for choices and for children to take control. A child may not be able to manage to pour a drink from a large jug, but may be able to do so if he or she is provided with a much smaller jug. It is always worth asking yourself why a child cannot do something for themselves. The solution may be to break down the task into much smaller and more manageable steps. It may also be to provide different resources, provide instructions one by one or to find an alternative system of communication.

Sometimes, you may find that a child resists being independent. Children may become so used to someone else tidying up that they refuse to do so. Many adults find it helpful in these situations to look for ways of turning the activity into a game or by asking the child to do just part of it at first. A child who does not want to tidy up may be given the box to hold while the adult puts the objects in it. In this way, children learn to be involved and can see for themselves that they are capable.

❱ Enabling environments are empowering

The term 'enabling environment' is one that is associated with EYFS. It is a very positive term and if we can take it on board in practice it can be very empowering for children. An enabling environment allows plenty of opportunities for children to show independence, make choices and show their interests. An enabling environment is by its very nature inclusive. To create an enabling environment for a child that you work with, consider firstly the needs of the child and the limitations that the current environment places on them. Then think about the resources, equipment and layout that may help the child to show more levels of independence. In some cases this can be very small things such as changing door handles so that they are easier to grip, changing the heights of tables so that they suit a child who may be using a standing frame, or looking out for pens that are ball shaped for a child who has fine motor needs.

❯ Provide a range of resources and activities that reflect positive images of disability, ethnicity and gender

It is important for children to see positive images of disability, as well as gender, ethnicity and culture, in order to learn that everyone has differences and that these should be valued. Being different does not mean that you are less important or worthy and this must be the message that all children learn. It is important that this message is embedded into the books, resources and images that you present to children. A child who wears spectacles or is in a wheelchair will need to feel that he or she is not alone or 'different'. This is especially important when children become aware of others and start to compare themselves. You should also look for some activities that encourage children to talk about differences and see differences in a positive way; for example, we may all have different food preferences or enjoy wearing different clothes. It is also a good idea to encourage all children to talk and ask questions about differences. This allows misconceptions to be put straight and prevents children from acquiring stereotypes and potential prejudices.

▶ Suggested activities

There is no single activity that can work on children's self-esteem or work to empower a child, but here are some suggestions of activities that might be worth considering.

Activity 1 Sense of pride

Aim

To help children gain a sense of pride in their own choices and differences.

Resources

Any group of objects that have some dissimilarity, e.g. buttons, shells, small boxes, labels with children's names.

Activity

Put the collection of objects on to a tray. Encourage children to handle and touch them. Talk about which ones they prefer. Do they have favourites? Give each of the children their own small box and ask them to put their favourite item inside. This box can then be labelled with the child's name. Display the children's favourites on a table. As the children are sorting out their favourite objects, notice carefully any children who seem particularly keen to change their favourites to fit in.

Possible adaptations

- Encourage children to talk about what makes the object their favourite.
- Repeat this activity with a variety of different objects.

Activity 2 All about me

Children need to develop a strong sense of self-image and identity. Creating a photo book or a slide show that children can watch can help children feel valued.

Aims

To help children value themselves.
To encourage children to talk about their identity. This book can also be helpful to show to new adults in the child's life.

Resources

Photographs of the child, paper, glue, pens, etc. to make a book.

Activity

Show the child the photographs. Ask the child about the photographs. Does the child have a favourite? Talk to the child about the photographs and why you particularly like them. Together make a book about the child based on what they want to use. Anything can be put into the book that will help the child learn and think about themselves. What does the child enjoy doing? Who are the special people in the child's life? What does the child enjoy eating?

Possible adaptations

- Create an electronic slide show with the child so that it can be shared with the child's parents.
- Create an 'all about me' box that has items that are important to the child, as well as photographs.

Activity 3 Positive recognition

Positive recognition is important for all children but especially for children who feel different in some way. Positive recognition is about saying something sincere to another person that is positive.

Aim

To help children to learn to use positive recognition.

Activity

This activity will work best with small groups of children whose language is developing well.
Begin by teaching children the phrase, 'I like the way you…' (this could be sung). Go around the group and say to each child, 'I like the way you…' and then add in something special about each child; for example, 'I like the way you smile when you hear that it is snack time.' Ask the children to turn to the person next to them and to think about something that they like about the child using the phrase, 'I like the way you…' When all the children have positively recognised each other, the whole group can give themselves a clap.

Possible adaptions

- Make this an activity that is done to a tune or song.
- Repeat this activity and see if children can positively recognise themselves using the altered phrase, 'I like the way I…'

Chapter 9

Communication and interaction

▶ Introduction

A large proportion of children with special educational needs have difficulties with communication and interaction. For some children, difficulties in communicating their needs, or in not being able to understand what is happening, can create feelings of frustration and isolation. The ability to understand how to support children's communication and interaction is therefore important when working with them. In this chapter we look at why communication is important, the components of interaction and potential barriers, as well as ways of supporting communication and interaction.

▶ Why communication is an important skill

Communication is an essential part of most people's daily lives. It is used in a variety of ways, for example to help people express their needs and to build and maintain relationships. It is a skill that is often taken for granted, but it actually plays an important part in children's overall development, as the spider diagram below shows. For most children, communication begins shortly after birth when they engage in eye gazing with their parent before language is used. Later, when language is developed, children can finally begin the journey of learning to read and write.

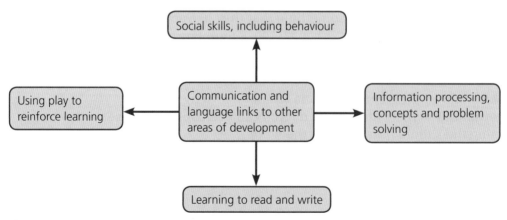

Communication and language links to other areas of development

◗ Communication, social skills and behaviour

There is a significant correlation between difficulty in communicating and in modifying behaviours in response to social situations. Some children with communication needs may show behaviours that are linked to their frustration, such as tantrums and even biting. Others may withdraw and opt out of activities. This means that while strategies that work only on behaviour may have some success, the key for adults is to identify the nature of the child's communication difficulty and work to support the child.

◗ Links between language and thought

Language is also important because it is linked to thought. Language allows us to organise our thoughts as it is used as a way of classifying and storing information in our memories. Language is also needed for children to acquire strong concepts and to engage in problem solving and reasoning. Children who have difficulties in communicating and using language may therefore sometimes find it harder to retain information and may not be able to process and organise their thoughts easily. This can place children at a significant disadvantage and so finding ways of helping children's language to develop is essential.

◗ Learning to read and write

Reading and writing are ways of encoding spoken language. This means that children without fairly fluent language find it very difficult to learn to read and to write. Interestingly, children who have lower levels of vocabulary may also find learning to read difficult as even though they may be able to work out what a word says, they may not be able to understand its meaning. Children may also have difficulties in terms of writing as in order to write you need to have something to say.

◗ Communication, language and play

As children's language and communication skills develop, it is usual to see a change in the way that they play. This means that by three years, most children with typically developing communication and language are likely to engage in role play with their peers. This is a significant shift from parallel play or solitary play which is more likely to be physical in its nature. Imaginative play and role play often help children to further develop their social skills, as well as help them to explore concepts. It is therefore worth observing children's play and considering how it is linked to their communication and language.

◗ Early identification and specialist support

The role of communication, interaction and language in children's overall development is so important that it is essential for children whose development is atypical to be identified early on. In some cases, by being aware that children need additional support, strategies can be used within the setting to boost the amount of opportunity for interaction. Other children may need to be referred for professional assessment by a speech and language therapist. Such specialist intervention in children's early years can be extremely helpful as there appears to be a 'critical period' in children's lives when it is easier for them to acquire language. Sometimes following a referral, parents and a setting will be given ideas for supporting further a child or even a tailored programme to follow. Some children, however, may be offered a block of therapy, usually of around six weeks at a time, although the speech and language therapist is likely to involve parents and settings in this so that the strategies that are being used can also be repeated between sessions.

What this means in practice

As early identification of need is important in supporting children's long-term outcomes, it is a good idea to know how to refer a child for support in your area and also what training and programmes are offered locally. Many speech and language teams also produce information sheets that explain when a referral is needed.

◗ Understanding the components of interaction

It is useful to have an understanding of what is involved in interaction. Children may have difficulties that link to one or more components.

◗ Non-verbal communication

It is thought that around 60 per cent of communication is non-verbal. Children need to learn to interpret and respond to others' gestures, facial expressions and body movements. They also need to become aware of their own expressions and use them appropriately. Some children with autism spectrum conditions may have difficulties in understanding the non-verbal signs that people send out, while some children with a visual impairment may have limited experience of using and seeing non-verbal communication.

❱ Language

Using and understanding language is complex as it is divided into several components.

Syntax

Language is rule based, although the communicator can be quite creative once the rules are learnt. The rules of language are important because language is a two-way process and other people have to be able to understand what is being said. Some children find it difficult to acquire and understand the rules. This can affect their understanding and also their ability to use language.

Semantics

As well as being based on rules, language is also based on meaning and thoughts. Children have to know what the words mean in order to be able to understand what is being said. It is also important to understand that written and spoken language is abstract. The collection of sounds or symbols is used to represent something and children have to learn the link between the sound or symbol and the object or idea. Some children with cognition difficulties may find it difficult to process their thoughts into words and thus require visual cues alongside spoken ones.

Phonology

For spoken language, children need to be able to recognise, store and produce the sounds that are required in the language they are using. Some children have particular physical difficulties in producing sounds, while others may not be able to hear them properly, thus making it difficult to understand what is being said and hard to reproduce the sounds accurately.

Pragmatics (use)

Children also have to learn about the purpose of language and what type of language is appropriate in different situations. Being able to alter the way in which we use language allows us to communicate more effectively. Some children with communication difficulties may need guidance to use language appropriately, for example not constantly changing subjects as this confuses the listener.

Understanding interaction as a process

As well as understanding the individual components that make up language, it is important to understand that interaction is a two-way process that can be represented as a cycle. When thinking about children who have difficulties in communicating, it can be worth considering where this difficulty happens within the communication cycle.

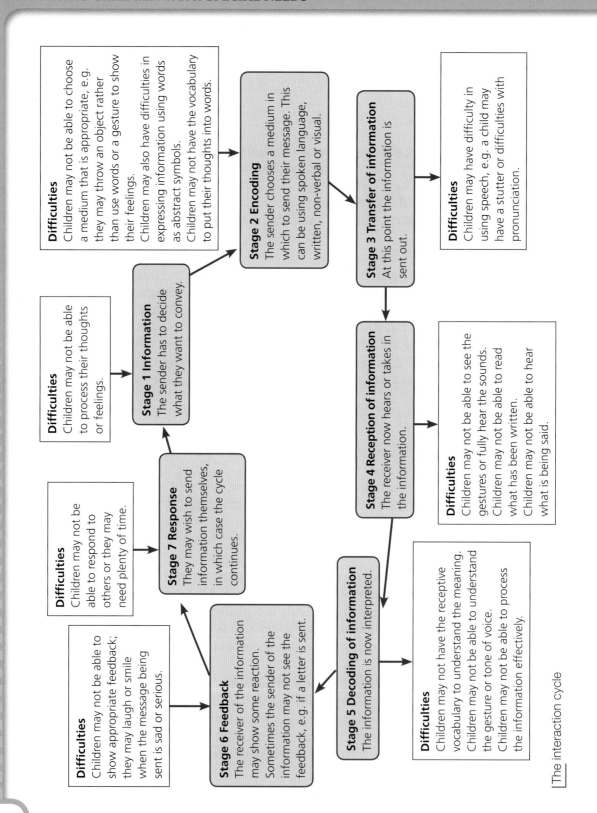

Stage 1 Information
The sender has to decide what they want to convey.

Difficulties
Children may not be able to process their thoughts or feelings.

Stage 2 Encoding
The sender chooses a medium in which to send their message. This can be using spoken language, written, non-verbal or visual.

Difficulties
Children may not be able to choose a medium that is appropriate, e.g. they may throw an object rather than use words or a gesture to show their feelings.
Children may also have difficulties in expressing information using words as abstract symbols.
Children may not have the vocabulary to put their thoughts into words.

Stage 3 Transfer of information
At this point the information is sent out.

Difficulties
Children may have difficulty in using speech, e.g. a child may have a stutter or difficulties with pronunciation.

Stage 4 Reception of information
The receiver now hears or takes in the information.

Difficulties
Children may not be able to see the gestures or fully hear the sounds.
Children may not be able to read what has been written.
Children may not be able to hear what is being said.

Stage 5 Decoding of information
The information is now interpreted.

Difficulties
Children may not have the receptive vocabulary to understand the meaning.
Children may not be able to understand the gesture or tone of voice.
Children may not be able to process the information effectively.

Stage 6 Feedback
The receiver of the information may show some reaction.
Sometimes the sender of the information may not see the feedback, e.g. if a letter is sent.

Difficulties
Children may not be able to show appropriate feedback; they may laugh or smile when the message being sent is sad or serious.

Stage 7 Response
They may wish to send information themselves, in which case the cycle continues.

Difficulties
Children may not be able to respond to others or they may need plenty of time.

The interaction cycle

◗ Common difficulties for children

Some common difficulties can affect children's speech and language.

◗ Background noise

Background noise can restrict children's progress in communication and interaction for a variety of reasons. Babies, for example, need to tune in to the human voice that is directly interacting with them. Radios, television or music being played can interfere with this process. Also, both babies and toddlers have very quiet voices when they are babbling and talking. Adults may therefore not always notice or respond if the child is competing with other sounds. Background noise can mean that children cannot hear themselves talk. This can affect the amount of interaction that they engage in and also they may not engage in self-directed talk. Self-directed talk is where babies babble to themselves or when toddlers and young children talk as they play and think.

What this means in practice

Think about the level of background noise in your setting. Consider if there any areas which are particularly noisy. It is also worth listening to check that children are engaged in self-directed talk. A good strategy to cut down on background noise is to position furniture so that it is adjacent to walls – this cuts the flow of sound down. You can also buy sound-proofing foam, which is worth considering if you work in a large space which echoes.

◗ Frequency and quality of interactions

Over the past few years, there have been concerns that some children are not getting the frequency and quality of interactions from adults that will support language acquisition. There have been many suggestions as to why this is happening, ranging from the introduction of forward-facing buggies, the arrival of social media which distracts adults, or the lack of time given that many families lead quite hectic lives. Whatever the truth of these theories, the reality is that babies and young children do need plenty of opportunities to be involved in interactions. The interactions that seem to be the most powerful are those where the child has a strong relationship with the adult. This is another reason why the key person relationship in settings is so important.

What this means in practice

Consider the number of opportunities available in your setting for children who need additional support with their communication and interaction. Adults often overestimate these, particularly in group settings where it is easy to be distracted by other children or the demands of a routine. It can be worth creating a monitoring sheet to check just how many interactions individual children in need of support are actually getting. Think also about how many interactions take place between the key person and the child.

▶ Hearing problems

When looking at a child's communication skills, it is always worth considering whether or not the child is hearing properly. It has been estimated that as many as one in four children in a Reception class at any time may have mild or slight hearing loss caused by otitis media, a conductive type of hearing loss. Otitis media occurs when fluid collects in the Eustachian tube and results in the child receiving distorted sounds. This type of hearing loss can fluctuate, as the fluid in the ear may drain away, but may build up again if the child has a cold. The fluctuating and sometimes slight nature of this type of hearing loss can make it harder for adults to identify. It does, however, have an enormous impact on a child's ability to hear, store and say sounds correctly, as well as to respond to others. Children who are not hearing the full range of sounds are also likely to find it hard to pick up the phonic programmes currently used as a way of teaching reading. If you suspect that a child is not fully hearing, it is essential to encourage the parents to visit their doctor or health visitor. It is worth explaining to parents that the nature of otitis media means that on one day a child could be hearing well, but on another day the child's hearing may be restricted. Therefore, just because their child has 'passed' a hearing test in the past, it does not necessarily mean that the child is hearing at that level all the time.

Checklist for hearing

- Does the child have frequent coughs and colds?
- Does the child often fail to respond to his or her name or instructions when engaged in an activity?
- Does the child find it hard to follow simple instructions?
- Does the child watch other children when instructions are given?
- Does the child appear to study a speaker's face intently?
- Is the child withdrawn or does he or she appear to be in his or her own world?
- Is the child's speech muffled or very unclear?

- Does the child appear to lack concentration during group activities such as story time?
- Do parents report a lack of interest or the need to increase the volume when engaged in activities such as watching DVDs or using other media?

What this means in practice

If you are aware that a child is not fully hearing because he or she has a cold or ear infection, you will need to take extra steps to help the child understand what is happening.

- Always turn to the child so that he or she can clearly see your face.
- Make sure the lighting allows your face to be seen.
- Do not cover your mouth with your hands, hair, etc.
- Make sure that children understand the subject of a conversation early on.
- Emphasise key words in a sentence.
- Use props, gestures and facial expressions to help the child follow what is happening.

▶ Sight

As well as considering whether children are fully hearing, it is also worth considering whether a child is seeing well. A child who cannot see the expression on other children's faces or pick up clues from their body language may find it hard to act appropriately, especially as children rely heavily on non-verbal communication. Look out for children whose own facial expressions and gestures are limited or who appear not to understand what is happening. (See page 185 for a checklist for visual impairment.)

▶ Stammering

Stammering affects children's fluency in speech and is therefore also known as dysfluency. Stammering is not unusual in young children's speech between the ages of two and three years, and for most children this is simply a phase which, if handled sensitively, they will move on from. Stammering in young children often reflects their thoughts not always being as fluent as their language. They may therefore stumble over initial sounds of words, particularly if they are feeling under pressure to speak quickly. Stammering is likely to increase when children are tired, excited or nervous. If you hear that a child is stammering, it is essential that all members of staff look for ways of reducing the pressure on the child.

Seeking help for dysfluency

It can be difficult to assess at what point 'natural' dysfluency has become a habit, but there are several indicators that a referral should be considered. Firstly, it is important to consider the effects of the stammer on the child. Once children become aware of and frustrated by their stammer, they are more likely to put themselves under pressure. This leads to the child being less relaxed, resulting in a further increase in stammering. Secondly, it is also worth referring if a parent indicates that they are becoming anxious and/or there is a family history of dysfluency. It is important to gain advice from a speech and language therapist if the dysfluency continues once a child has turned three as if left untreated, stammers can become permanent.

Tips for good practice

- Avoid situations where the child has to compete to say anything, e.g. first child to put up a hand or shout out an answer.
- Avoid asking too many direct questions. Answering questions can increase children's stress levels.
- Allow lots of time for the child to answer to reduce pressure.
- Avoid finishing off the sentence or letting other children interrupt the child.
- Reduce the speed at which you talk. This can help the child to relax and to speak more slowly to you.
- Make sure that you are on the same level and are making eye contact with the child.
- If a child is stressed and stammering because of feeling emotional, talk to the child about the emotion that he or she is feeling, e.g. 'You are upset because you can't find your picture.'

▶ Attention and listening

One of the difficulties that some children have is that their levels of attention and listening are limited. This is important as it underpins other aspects of interaction. Children cannot tune in to the speech sounds of language or develop vocabulary if they are not able to concentrate and listen carefully. It also means that children cannot pick up cues from others and carry on with an interaction if these skills are not in place. Children with limited attention and listening also find it hard to engage with some of the activities that are routinely used to support language and communication, such as sharing books.

What this means in practice

It is important that settings foster opportunities for children to be able to attend and listen. Often the starting point is having opportunities to be with adults who carefully model attention and listening, e.g. making eye contact, getting down to the child's level. It also means thinking about how to create opportunities to reduce distractions at some point, as well as planning specific opportunities to build children's attention and listening skills. (See the end of this chapter for activities relating to this.)

❱ Reluctant talkers

Some children choose not to talk in settings. There is a language difficulty called 'selective mutism'; this is quite rare but it might need to be thought about. The starting point with reluctant talkers to is to consider what level of relationship they have with their key person and also to think about how easily the transition is being made between home and the setting. Children may often not be able to talk when they are feeling stressed and so beginning by assessing the quality of the key person–child relationship is important. It is also important to look at whether the child is communicating with other children in the setting. If this is so, it would probably indicate that the difficulty lies with the quality of the adult–child relationship. It is also important to find out about the child's language use at home. Does the child interact at home and have the parents noticed any reluctance?

Tips for good practice

Helping reluctant talkers
- Play alongside the child without talking, copying their play and actions.
- Encourage the child to take part in one-to-one routines, e.g. feeding the fish with their key person.
- Reduce the amount of questions that are being used.
- Avoid putting pressure on the child, e.g. at group times.
- Acknowledge any form of communication, including non-verbal communication such as shaking of the head.
- Consider introducing a new key person if the relationship is not improving.

Seeking help

If a child is not communicating with either adults or other children in the setting after four weeks and strategies to work on the key person relationship and environment have been tried, it will be important to seek a referral.

❱ Principles of supporting children's communication and interaction

We have seen that there are many skills that children need to master in order to be able to communicate and interact effectively. While many children appear to be able to 'pick up' language effortlessly, children who have difficulties in communicating and interacting need optimum conditions for language learning and interaction.

▶ Be a language partner rather than a teacher

Children can learn about communication and language from responsive adults. If children enjoy being with an adult, they are likely to want to interact with the adult and will learn about the process of shared communication. This means thinking about your role as being that of a partner rather than an instructor, and thus concentrating on building a good relationship with the child. This approach seems to have more success as it gives opportunities for children to hear language being modelled in context and also seems to encourage children to interact more.

What this means in practice

Being a language partner requires an adult to relax and to let children interact at their own speed. It also means allowing conversations to develop naturally and to follow the child's lead and interests. For toddlers and children who are not using much verbal interaction, it may mean copying their movements or playing alongside them and then narrating what they are doing rather than using questions. Here are some tips that are useful to remember when attempting to use this style of working:

- Make good eye contact with the child.
- Avoid being distracted by other children or ongoing situations.
- Smile and express genuine pleasure when the child tries to involve you.
- Avoid interrogating the child and use a chatty style of language with them.
- Acknowledge the child's vocalisations, language or gestures by reflecting back rather than giving praise.
- Allow plenty of time for a child to vocalise or use language – don't feel the need to keep talking.
- Value children's non-verbal communication.

▶ Provide opportunities for one-to-one and small group work

Children who have difficulties in communicating will require one-to-one or small group work. It is important that they are not just 'left to get on with it'. This does not necessarily mean 'teaching' language, but actually making sure that children have adequate opportunities to interact. A child playing alone and silently, however happily, is not gaining any new language or communication skills. Playing alongside children or involving them in small group activities where their language 'output' can be monitored is therefore essential. Targeting children in this way for extra language support can also be beneficial in terms of reducing unwanted behaviour and encouraging the acquisition of social skills.

Interestingly, some children enjoy being involved in adult activities such as tidying and cleaning, as well as experiences such as cooking.

❱ Rhymes, songs and books

One of the features of a language-rich environment is that children have plenty of access to rhymes, songs and books. This allows children to explore sounds, patterns and intonation and also to develop new vocabulary. Sharing books with children seems to be particularly powerful, especially where children have one-to-one experiences with an adult. This allows them to look carefully at the images, repeat phrases or engage in conversation about the story or the pictures. The advantage of a one-to-one shared book is that children also can process the information at their own speed, which in practice means children looking back at previous pages.

What this means in practice

Think about adopting a planned approach to rhymes and songs so that new ones are regularly introduced to children. This can help the acquisition of speech sounds, as well as helping children to distinguish between individual sounds. It is also a good idea to look for ways of planning opportunities when children can have one-to-one shared books with their key person.

❱ Prompts to encourage interaction

We also have to make sure that the environment has enough stimulation within it to motivate children to want to communicate. Interestingly, children often choose to interact more when they are experiencing something new or seeing something for the first time. A child who spots that there are three teddy bears hanging from a tree outdoors is likely to point and want to communicate this.

What this means in practice

It is worth being very objective about how your environment supports children's language, especially for children who spend many hours within it. Some children will spend over 2,000 hours a year in full-day care, for example, and so it is important to think about what new experiences, objects and activities they will have access to. While routines and familiarity are important, things that are different can act as prompts for interaction.

▶ Integrate language into children's play

Play is pleasurable and thus provides a perfect backdrop to learning language. Children who are relaxed are more likely to acquire and use language and so using games and providing for imaginative play can be very effective. Adults can play alongside children and thus introduce new language, but can take a backseat at times if children are communicating with their peers.

What this means in practice

If you are working with children who enjoy role play, it is worth thinking about how you can plan opportunities to extend vocabulary and opportunities to talk further. Consider creating a list of role-play opportunities that can be resourced and regularly changed over. Good resourcing helps children acquire more specific words that they can link to the actions inherent in the situation, e.g. a tea towel in the kitchen is more likely to encourage the child to learn and use the verbs 'wipe' or 'dry' as they wash up.

This activity helps children to practise the letter sound 'b'

❱ Make language meaningful

Adults communicate for a purpose and the same is true for children. Children will learn language more effectively when it has some meaning for them. This means that we need to check that we make the most of everyday situations and link language to play and activities. Taking children away from an activity that they are enjoying to 'do' some language may therefore not always be the best approach. It may be better to incorporate the language into the activity.

❱ Adjust language and groupings to suit the child

To help children gain the most from play activities, story times and conversations, it is essential that the language being used matches the child's level of comprehension. It is therefore crucial when we talk to children that we monitor their responses and check that our language and gestures are being understood. In some settings, the routine of the day includes several group times. These can be effective, but only if children's language levels are carefully considered. A child who cannot understand or is slower to process language than another child is likely to become frustrated or even disruptive. Mismatched groups can also reduce an individual child's motivation to contribute as other children may be quicker to answer questions and make comments.

What this means in practice

Think about how you structure group times and whether they are matched to meet children's needs. Carefully monitor children's responses and be objective about how much they have gained from the time spent. Think also about whether the length of time that children are expected to attend and listen matches their developmental level.

❱ Using 'parentese'

Parentese or 'motherese' is the style of speech that most adults naturally use with babies. This style of language is special because it encourages the child to focus on one or two key words in a sentence as they are emphasised and repeated by the adult. Sentences tend to be short and simplified. The child is able to work out the meaning of the sentences because the adult talks about something that is actually taking place. Adults will point to objects to draw the child's attention to them. Interestingly, adults check first that the child is paying attention before talking. This style of language is also characterised by exaggerated facial expressions including the lifting of eyebrows. Using this style of speech can be particularly helpful for children who are in the early stages of learning language. It is also helpful when working with children who are new to English. The example shows how speech is simplified and key words are drawn to the child's attention.

An adult is alongside a child who is playing with a farm set. The adult picks up a cow.

Adult: '**Look**! Can you see the **cow**? There's the **cow**. Let's see if the **cow** can jump. Whoosh! **Look**, the **cow** is jumping! **Look**, the **cow** is coming to see you.'

▶ Strategies to develop children's language

▶ Modelling language

Before children are able to use words or make specific speech sounds, they will need to become familiar with them. Modelling language is a technique where children hear words and sounds in context. The key to good modelling is creating a relaxed situation where the child can concentrate and so focus on what is said. Children will, of course, listen more actively if the activity is of interest to them. The example below shows how an adult models language to help a child talk about size and also to help the child hear speech sounds.

Modelling what children are doing can create opportunities for language

Child: [*Pointing to the smallest fish in a tank*] Dat one is the baby.

Adult: Yes, that one is the smallest fish in the tank. It is tiny, isn't it?

▶ Recasting and expanding children's language

Recasting and expanding is a technique which helps children to hear a grammatically correct and fuller version of what they were trying to say. This technique can be used with all children as it is a subtle way of helping children to hear a fuller and more grammatically correct version of their language. This technique also encourages children to communicate more as it shows them that the adult has been listening and has understood what they are trying to say. This means that this technique is particularly useful with children who have limited speech. The example below shows how an adult recasts the child's speech while also extending it.

Child: [*Letting a car go down a slide*] Brrrm, down go.

Adult: The car went down the slide, didn't it? It went down the slide very quickly.

▶ Using visual means of supporting communication

Many children benefit when we present information and language to them in a visual as well as spoken code. This helps children's comprehension and can also help them to remember new language. There are many ways of supporting communication using visual means. The most simple is to point to objects as you refer to them and to allow children to take you over to show you what they are trying to talk about.

Picture representations

Some children benefit from using pictures and photographs to aid communication. You might show a picture of an apron to a child and accompany this with the words, 'Get an apron.' In the same way, pictures might allow the child to show you what he or she needs in response to your question, 'What would you like to do?'; the child might show you a picture of the type of play activity.

Photographs are also a great way of helping children to communicate, especially about events that have happened out of the setting, such as a family party. Photographs seem to help children access their memories as they provide a prompt for what has happened.

Commercial systems of picture representations are available and it may be useful to explore the possibility of using these with the speech and language therapist. One system known as PECS (Picture Exchange Communication System) has been used successfully with children who are reluctant to interact. Children give and also take pictures and thus learn about the 'exchange' nature of interaction. For more information on PECS, visit www.pecs.org.uk.

Sign representations

Some children will need to use signs alongside spoken language. Makaton is an example of a signing system that supports language. The decision to use Makaton is normally taken by speech and language therapists in conjunction with parents. The signs give the child a visual cue and thus can help them to understand and communicate their needs. Makaton is particularly helpful for children who find it hard to understand the meaning of words because of difficulties in processing abstract information. For more information on Makaton, visit www.makaton.org.

Some children benefit from using Makaton to help them communicate

Puppets

Many children respond positively to puppets and cuddly toys. They enjoy the characters and in some cases will talk more to a puppet than to us! Use puppets as a way of modelling language and also as a way of keeping children's attention.

⌐Puppets can motivate some children to vocalise

What this means in practice

It is helpful to think about increasing the amount of visual communication that we use with children as this strategy is very effective at helping children to maintain attention and also to process information. Think about what strategies you use in your setting and consider how well they work and with which children.

❱ Suggested activities

Activity 1 Hide and seek with sounds

This game can be used to help children's auditory discrimination, but it can also be adapted to encourage children who are mastering the pronunciation of particular sounds (see Possible adaptations).

Aim

To encourage children to listen to sounds.

Resources

Musical instruments, keys, rattles, plus teddy or other object to hide.

Activity

Hide the teddy or another object. Ask the child if he or she can find it. Tell the child that as he or she gets nearer, you will make louder and louder sounds with a tambourine or bunch of keys, but if he or she moves in another direction you will stop making sounds.

Possible adaptations

- Repeat the game, but ask the child to hide the objects and make the sounds.
- Ask the child to hide the object, but you have to ask the child questions as to where it is hidden.
- Ask the child to hide the object and when you are moving in the right direction to make certain sounds (these can be ones that are being worked on in speech therapy).

Activity 2 Odd one out

This is a versatile activity that can help children in a variety of ways with their language. It can also be used to help children see visual differences (see Possible adaptations).

Aims

To encourage children to look closely at familiar objects and to think about differences.
To encourage children to use the names of familiar objects and to talk about the purpose of familiar objects.

Resources

Bag or box with familiar objects in it, e.g. household objects, toys, teddy (optional, some children may not respond to imaginative play).

Activity

Put three objects in the box or bag. Choose two objects that are either the same or that would be put together and one object that is very different, e.g. spoon, fork and toy car. The child can take them out one by one. Using language appropriate to the child's understanding, talk about each object. Use the teddy as a stooge if the child responds well to imaginative play. Which ones are the same? Which ones go together? Which one is the odd one out? Ask the child to show the teddy which ones go together. Can the child tell the teddy what the objects are used for?

Possible adaptations

- Some children may benefit from a simple repeated script as they play this game.
- Play this game with pairs of children.
- Repeat this game with a new odd-one-out object, but retain the other two objects so that children already know their names and purpose.
- Encourage children to choose from a selection of objects; they can see if they can fool teddy and you.
- Adapt this activity to help children see visual differences in symbols or pictures; put three cards in a bag or box. Can the children find two that match, e.g. two cats and one dog, or two words that are the same and one that is different?

Activity 3 Fishing games

Fishing games can be used in a variety of ways to support children's communication and language (see Possible adaptations).

Aim

This game helps children to build sentences.

Resources

Cards showing pictures of boys and girls doing things, e.g. a boy reading a book, a girl kicking a ball, also paper clips, baton or small stick, string, tape, magnet.

Activity

Attach a paper clip on to each card. Attach a magnet on to the string and tie the string on to the baton or stick. Put the fish (the cards) into a pile or on to a small tray. Show the child how to fish for cards. Encourage the child to enjoy 'fishing'. Ask the child to see if he or she can fish out a card and say what is happening, e.g. 'The boy is riding a bike'. You may need to model how to construct the simple sentence.

Possible adaptations

Instead of using a fishing rod, put the cards into a box so that children with motor difficulties can pull them out instead. Other examples of how this game might be used:

- Pictures of animals or other objects can be stuck on to the fish – can children say the name of the object?
- Pairs of photographs can be put on to the cards – can children find the matching pairs?
- Individual letters or children's names can be put on to the cards – can children find their name or a specific letter shape?
- Play the game with two or more children – can they find each other's names?
- Use the game to teach other concepts, e.g. fishing for colours or sizes of fish.

Activity 4 Feely bags

Feely bags can be used in a variety of ways with children to promote a range of language and literacy skills (see Possible adaptations).

Aim

To help children use descriptive vocabulary and frame questions.

Resources

Bag with objects that will be familiar for the child, plus a teddy.

Activity

Put out all the objects that you are going to use. Check that the child knows what they are used for and their names. The teddy can be used here as the child can tell the teddy about the objects. Encourage the child to handle the objects and model descriptive words about each of the objects, e.g. 'That's quite soft, isn't it?', 'That feels quite hard.' Put one of the objects into the bag without the child seeing and remove the rest. Ask the child to guess what is inside the bag. Ask the child questions about the object, e.g. 'Does it feel hard?' Repeat the game with the aim of encouraging the child to tell you about the object.

Possible adaptations

- Use objects that all begin with the same speech sound. This can be used either to help a child who has difficulty in saying a particular speech sound (assuming that this is developmentally appropriate) or to help phonemic discrimination.
- Play the game with partners as a 'yes and no' type of game. Children have to ask each other questions about what is inside the bag.
- Encourage children to choose an object to put inside the bag to see if you can guess what it is.

- Play the game with pairs of objects, one inside and one outside the bag. For example, if a spoon is inside the bag, the child has to find a fork from among the objects that are out of the bag.
- Develop children's 'thinking' language; children have to guess what is in the bag but also say why they think this.

Activity 5 Sequencing

Most children love to look at photographs of themselves. Activities involving photographs of the child can help children to talk more freely and use the skills of recall.

Aim

To help children sequence and use the past tense.

Resources

Three photographs of the child taken during a routine event, such as hand-washing or dressing. The photographs should illustrate the beginning, middle and end of the routine.

Activity

Show the child the photographs. Ask the child if he or she knows who is in the photographs. Chat about what is happening in the photographs. Together, can you work out the sequence of the photographs?

Possible adaptations

- Increase the number of photographs, e.g. to four or five.
- Involve the child in taking photographs, e.g. the child takes pictures of you or another child engaged in an activity.
- Make the photographs into a book and put simple labels under the pictures.

Chapter 10

Supporting children's cognition and learning

❱ Introduction

Psychologists are still researching how learning takes place in children and the reasons why some children learn at a slower rate than others. This is not surprising as the brain is very complicated. This means that there is no single method of helping children to learn. Indeed most practitioners find that they need continually to try different strategies to meet the needs of the individual child. While accepting that there are several theories of learning, this chapter focuses particularly on how children process information. This approach to children's learning can generate many helpful strategies for practitioners.

❱ What is cognitive development?

In its simplest sense, cognitive development is the process by which children begin to understand the world in which they live. They learn, for example, that objects do not just disappear. They also learn to predict, reflect and reason. The notions of time, colours and being able to differentiate between objects are all examples of cognition.

The development of cognition requires that children learn to take in information, categorise it and use it to inform their thinking. As well as processing information, advanced cognition requires that children are aware of how to make the best use of their knowledge to problem solve. This aspect of cognitive development is sometimes referred to as metacognitive development.

There is much evidence to suggest that cognitive development is linked to other areas of development. Understanding how to support children in areas of development such as language can therefore also have an effect on their cognitive development.

❯ The importance of the emotional climate

A good starting point when considering children's cognitive development is to be aware of the importance of who they are with and what they are feeling when they are learning. This has been dubbed the 'emotional climate'. Children and adults alike find it easier to absorb information when they are relaxed. This in part has been explained by research that suggests that when we are under stress, less memory space is made available to us. This would account for why children sometimes 'freeze' when they feel they are being tested or why a nervous child may not remember a simple instruction.

- Remember that the emotional climate in which learning takes place is more important than the 'learning outcome'.
- Begin by building a good relationship with the child.
- Adjust activities according to the child's emotional responses.

❯ Physical development and cognitive development

There appears to be a strong link between physical and cognitive development. This is an area that is still being researched in terms of brain development, although it would appear that physical movements stimulate the brain's neural pathways. There are, for example, correlations between difficulties in assimilating and using symbols and children's early co-ordination and handedness. The importance of developing children's balance, co-ordination and range of body movements must therefore not be overlooked. As a practitioner, this means that you should ensure children are encouraged to take part in physical activities as these are seen as playing an important role in children's cognitive development. Activities that appear to be particularly beneficial include balancing, throwing and catching, along with skills that encourage the brain to sequence, such as climbing and crawling.

What this means in practice

As physical development seems to be linked to cognition, it is worth reflecting on the types of physical play opportunities available in your setting. For children who have multiple needs, this may mean adapting equipment and the environment to ensure that they can participate. It is also important to think about how much physical activity is inbuilt into your routines.

- Give children plenty of opportunities to develop their physical skills.
- Look for ways of taking 'learning' out of doors and making it physical.
- Consider adapting programmes that are designed to sequentially build children's physical skills.

▶ Sleep, tiredness and processing information

As well as the role of physical activity, it is also important to be aware of the role that sleep plays in children's cognition. It is now understood that during sleep, the brain reviews and stores information that it has been exposed to. Sleep is also needed to help children concentrate. This means that children who are under-sleeping may find it harder to learn and retain information. In addition, at different points in the day children may become tired and it is worth recognising that learning during these moments will be harder for children.

Physical activity is linked to cognitive development

What this means in practice

It is important to share with parents the importance of sleep in relation to their child's development. Some parents may not be aware of how much sleep children need, while others may be finding sleep routines hard to establish. As sleep is now recognised as being important for not only children's well-being but also for cognition, more support is available than before. It is worth finding out what is available in your local area, including sleep clinics. In addition, there is a range of online resources available. Look out for strategies and guidelines about sleep on the NHS website (www.nhs.uk/livewell). There is also an 'Early Support' leaflet about sleep written for parents of children with disabilities available on the website of the Council for Disabled Children (www.councilfordisabledchildren.org.uk/resources/early-support-information-on-sleep).

It is worth thinking about the timing of activities and adjusting these according to the tiredness levels of children, as well as the provision that is available for children to have naps.

▶ Language and thought

The acquisition of language appears to make a significant difference in the way children process information. It would appear that language allows us to categorise and store information more efficiently. Children who have not yet developed language may therefore find it harder to process information and organise their thoughts.

What this means in practice

The link between language and cognition means that early identification of language delay is important and that once identified there needs to be a plan as to how to support language as well as support cognition.

◗ Language and self-direction

Most people mutter to themselves when they are trying to think through something complex or give themselves instructions. This is an important use of language as it links to our ability to organise our thoughts and actions. As we get older, self-direction becomes mainly internal and can be thought of as an 'inner voice'. Children also self-direct and use language in this way. At first this is always done aloud, but later children are able to think their thoughts internally. Children whose language development is atypical may often carry on needing to think aloud and it is essential that this be encouraged.

What this means in practice

With some children, you may have to help them learn to self-direct as this is an important metacognitive skill. By modelling the way that you break tasks into smaller steps and saying what you are doing, some children may learn to copy this approach. A good example of this is the way that when you are trying to find something that you have lost, you may begin by asking yourself where you last used it.

● Avoid telling children who are commenting or talking aloud to be quiet; it may be their way of organising their thoughts.
● Put children who need to think aloud into small rather than large groups for activities.
● Model talking aloud behaviour to children as this helps them learn how to go about problem solving.

We have a couple of children who tend to constantly talk and make comments. This can be tricky when other children are trying to listen, but now that we understand this is helping them to process information, we are more relaxed about it. We also think more carefully about how we group children and now do many more pair and small group activities.

Theresa, Reception teacher

◗ Language for problem solving and reasoning

There are many ways in which we use language in our day-to-day life. While language is often used to communicate and maintain relationships, children also benefit from using language to help them develop thinking skills including problem solving and reasoning. This way of using language requires children to have the vocabulary and the grammatical structures to express thoughts and concepts. A good example of language for thinking might be, 'I like this one better because it is blue and blue is my favourite colour'. In this example the child is able to use language to explain his or her preference in terms of a colour.

Developing children's language for problem solving and reasoning

In order to help children use language for thinking it is essential that they have 'labels' for their thoughts and feelings and for objects and concepts. Labelling appears to draw children's attention to certain features, which in turn helps them to develop new thoughts. For example, 'Look at this leaf. It is prickly. This one is not prickly, though, it has smooth edges.' As well as making sure that children have the 'labels', it is also important to encourage children to use their language to show their thinking. This often requires practice, and children will need to see this being modelled at first. The key words to use with children when they are ready are 'why' and 'how'. For example, this may mean saying to a child who has sorted out cars, 'I would like to sort the cars like you. How do I do this?'

◗ Understanding how information is processed

It can be useful to consider how children take in and store information. Psychologists who are researching into this relatively new area talk about 'information processing'. Comparisons between the human brain and computers are often used in this field because of the idea that the brain is constantly inputting, handling, storing and then retrieving data in the same way that computers function. Some information-processing theorists suggest that differences in cognitive development may result from the speed at which children are able to process information, and that children whose cognitive development is atypical may have difficulties in one or more areas during the actual processing. One child may have difficulties in being alert enough to respond to and register information, while another child may have difficulties in retrieving and using information.

❱ Helping children to register information

In order to register information and for it to be stored, children need to be alert. They need to be able to focus on particular aspects of the information. This is a skill that adults tend to take for granted but is actually quite hard for children. Information-processing theorists have found that as children develop, they usually become better at being able to filter out information. For many children this might happen as part of the usual sequence of development but for others, such as children with attention deficit hyperactivity disorder (ADHD) (see page 204), this will be harder.

❱ Levels of arousal

In order to pay attention, children need to be sufficiently alert or aroused. This allows them to respond to the data that is being presented and so be able to concentrate. Some children's level of alertness or arousal can be too low or too high. It is often when a child's level of alertness is low that they cannot pay attention. There are many reasons why children may not be able to maintain arousal. The activity itself may not be of interest, which causes their levels of arousal to drop. Interestingly, being active seems to help children maintain arousal levels, as does using sensory materials. This is one reason why sand, water and dough and also natural materials seem to engage most children for longer. The exception to this is children who can actually find sensory materials over-arousing and therefore uncomfortable (see 'Children who are over-sensitive to touch (tactile defensive)', page 181). In extreme cases of under- or over-arousal, children may be given medication, either stimulants or depressants, although treating young children with drugs is extremely controversial.

The following diagram shows how the use of sand can help some children to maintain their arousal levels.

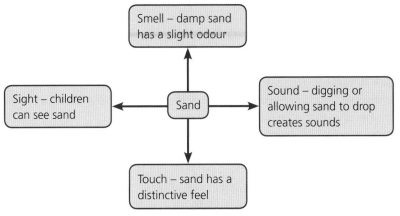

Ways in which sand can engage children's senses

❱ Attention

As well as being alert, children also need to 'ignore the irrelevant'. The brain is constantly bringing us new information from the senses. Selecting and remaining focused on the relevant information is known as selective attention. Some children find this very difficult and will, for example, turn their head to respond to a noise behind them or notice something within their reach. When this happens we may say that a child is easily distracted when, in reality, the child is having difficulty in putting aside new information that is being presented to him or her.

❱ Divided attention

There are many occasions when we need to do two or more things at the same time, for example talk and prepare a meal. This means being able to respond to and take in several sources of information at the same time. The ability to divide our attention does to a large extent depend on the tasks that we are doing. The easier we find a task, the easier it is to take on another alongside it. The ability to cope with several sources of information at once and process them is developmental. Very young children may not be able to answer a simple question while engaged in a play activity and children will often be four years old before they can engage in a conversation while doing a simple play activity. Children with atypical cognitive development often find it hard to split their attention, so this must be taken into consideration when planning activities or giving children instructions.

What this means in practice

There are no hard and fast rules about how to help children concentrate, but the following strategies may be helpful.

- Consider whether the child is actually concentrating, even though not necessarily on your learning objective!
- Go to activities that are already engaging the child and look for ways of extending learning or language there, rather than taking the child away.
- Look for activities that will engage several of the child's senses at once e.g. sand, water, dough, shaving foam, cooking. This can help arousal.
- Look at the layout of the learning environment. Are there too many sources of distraction for the child? For example, in a bustling room it may be difficult for the child to filter out the noise, movement and play of other children.
- Make sure that activities are appealing and perhaps have a surprise or interest element, e.g. 'What's in here? Look what teddy has brought in.'

- Avoid overloading children with too many tasks and instructions at once; look carefully at their divided attention skills.
- Think about the way and speed in which children are being presented with information. If children do not appear to be attending to you, change your tone of voice and if necessary slow down the pace so that children have time to register information.
- Repeat activities and once children are familiar with them, change one feature of the activity.

▶ Helping children to store information – memory

Memory is a crucial, but too often overlooked, component in children's learning. If children are limited in their ability to store and retrieve information, this will limit their learning. Research and theories about how our memories work are ongoing, but it seems that children's storage and retrieval systems are not as sophisticated as most adults' and that they gradually develop both strategies and systems. In particular, it seems that children's ability to 'boost' their short-term memories is limited. This might account for children who have apparently been listening, who then often forget simple instructions. Children whose cognitive development is atypical may have difficulties in 'holding' information or making the relevant connections in order to retrieve it.

Short-term memory

The short-term memory is an intermediate store of information and it is thought that the duration of memories stored is less than 30 seconds. Information that is not processed and moved along is usually lost. A key strategy that adults use to hold information is to rehearse it. We repeat instructions or telephone numbers over and over in order to hold them in our minds. Young children and older children with atypical cognitive development will not use this strategy. Another strategy that adults use is to group individual pieces of information together into 'chunks'. Instead of trying to remember all the items needed for breakfast, you may chunk the information into an overall heading 'breakfast'. It is thought that children who have difficulties with language are at a disadvantage because they are not using language to categorise in this way.

Memory codes

There appear to be three main ways in which information is encoded in our memory:

1 **Acoustic** – information stored in a sound code.
2 **Visual or iconic** – information stored in picture form.
3 **Semantic** – information stored using abstract symbols, e.g. writing, words.

As adults, we tend to store a lot of information using the semantic code, for example words can trigger many memories and thoughts, but young children rely heavily on their visual code. This is thought to be the reason why your first memories are likely to be visual ones. In order for children to store information semantically, it is important that they have a good level of language. This will mean that, in general, young children will find it hard to process and retain information that is 'word based', but will fare better if information is encoded visually or as sounds, for example songs and rhymes.

| Hello | Coat off | Breakfast | Play outdoors |

Visual timetables can help children understand what is about to happen

What this means in practice

There are many strategies that we need to adopt to help children retain information. It is worth looking at your current practice and then adapting it according to what seems to help individual or groups of children. Here are some tips that can often help.

- Use props or visual aids when telling stories or giving information.
- Show rather than tell children what they should be doing.
- Avoid presenting information using 'talk' as the medium.
- Look for ways of touching, feeling and seeing.
- Think about how information is being presented to children.
- Some children respond well to songs and remember these better than just 'words'.
- Encourage children to repeat important instructions, e.g. 'What do you do when you go to the toilet?'
- Play games that involve memory, such as picture lotto or Kim's game.

▶ Retrieving information

As well as storing information, children also need to be able to retrieve it or remember it. This can be tricky, especially if children are trying to retrieve information in a different situation or place from where it was encoded. This is why children often find it hard to talk about what they have done at home without a prompt such as a photograph. There are many forms of remembering and if we provide children with the right prompts, they may find it easier to retrieve information.

What this means in practice

Children have often encoded information, but they may need our help to retrieve it. Time seems to be important in this, but also providing children with photographs or putting them back in a similar context or situation can help. Here are some of the key points to remember when supporting children to retrieve information.

- Avoid creating rushed situations as stress can slow down or stop retrieval.
- Allow children plenty of processing time so that they can 'scan' their memories.
- Help children to find information by asking associated questions, such as 'What were you wearing at the time?' This helps children hook into their visual memory.
- Provide prompts or triggers for the child such as props and photographs: 'What were you doing in this photograph?'
- Repeat activities, e.g. using the same props, in the same place.

We have recently reviewed the way in which we give information to children. One of the big changes that we have made is to make things far more visual. We realised that relying on 'talk' to explain things to children or give instructions was not working. Children would often switch off or simply forget anything that had been said. Now everything is structured so that it is more active and visual than before. If we want children to get their coats, we show them one! We also repeat actions and words so that children can process them more easily. We make sure not to bombard children with too much information at a time. We go at a much slower pace. These simple strategies have really made a difference, not just to the children that we were targeting, but the others too.

Carly, Nursery teacher

▶ Helping children to use information and make connections

As well as being able to store and retrieve information, children also have to learn how best to use it to solve problems. Being aware of the information that you have and being able to transfer this knowledge are metacognition skills.

Problem solving is about being able to take the information that we have acquired and use it in new situations. This is a skill that develops gradually, but children benefit from working through various problems with adults. Problem solving is linked to many areas of the curriculum, including mathematics, but also to solving problems thrown up by everyday life, e.g. packing a bag or deciding which clothes to put on.

There are some specific steps that may be involved in problem solving:

1 Identify the nature of the problem/task.
2 Consider what knowledge and information is available.
3 Identify strategies, ideas or resources.
4 Plan how to use the strategy, idea or resource.
5 Use the strategy, resource or idea and then consider its effectiveness.
6 If the strategy, resource or idea is not effective, store this knowledge for future reference.

By solving problems alongside us, children can learn to think sequentially about a problem or task. In the EYFS, this is one of the ways that you may help children with 'sustained shared thinking'. By working with children, we can guide them through the process of problem solving so that eventually they will have developed the strategies and processes to tackle simple problems independently.

It is, of course, essential to provide opportunities for problem solving that are achievable and of interest to the child so that they are able to feel successful. Examples of ideas for everyday problem solving include the following:

● Jigsaw puzzles: Talk about how to look for and try out specific pieces.
● Snack time: Talk about checking that there are enough chairs, plates, etc.
● Getting dressed: What do you need to keep you warm?
● Construction play: What shall we make together?
● Teach children the steps in problem solving by going through each step with them.
● Try and help the child.
● Model problem solving by using running commentary.

Children need sensitive adults to guide their learning step by step

What this means in practice

Practising the skills and the thinking required to solve problems is very helpful for children, but they are likely to need an adult to coach and mentor them. It is also likely to take time and patience and adults need to be skilled at gently guiding them. It is also important that the problems or tasks are of interest to children as this is likely to help them maintain their focus.

We have started to use a 'Plan, Do and Review' approach with some of our children for child-initiated play. This is working very well for children who, with an adult, decide what they would like to play with and then work out what resources they will need. The adult who supports them also helps them to think afterwards about their play and they have a structured conversation about it which helps them evaluate what they enjoyed doing and why. It is interesting to see how some children are able to learn from what they did the day before.

SENCO, pre-school

▶ Adapting information to new situations

Many children who have difficulties with their cognition find it hard to transfer and use information and skills in new situations, e.g. applying the rules of a simple board game to another game. It may be that they find it hard to see similarities between situations. Children can be helped by sensitive prompting and also by being given tasks that have similarities.

What this means in practice

Some children will need a lot of reassurance and support to use information and see how to apply it to a new situation. Adults who find this an easy skill may not always recognise that some children find it hard. The following strategies can be helpful:

- Talk to children about the features of a situation that are similar to those they have already experienced; for example, 'This picture shows a man with a blue coat. Yesterday you wore a coat too. Can you remember that it was blue too?'
- Repeat activities, but change one feature so that while children are familiar with the core activity, they are also experiencing something that is different.

▶ Motivation

As well as looking at the ways in which we can help children to process information, it is also worth considering motivation. Children will learn better if they are motivated, with the adage 'learning is caught not taught' coming to the fore here. Relevance and expected success are two factors worth examining.

Children are more likely to attempt to problem solve and concentrate if a task meets their needs and interests. This is why it is important to build on children's interests; for example, a child who enjoys playing with toy cars and lining them up is more likely to be motivated by a task if toy cars are in some way involved.

What this means in practice

Our expectation of success is often a key factor in whether we attempt tasks. Children who have repeated failures will not be motivated to try out new tasks, and so tasks must be suited to the children's level of development and support must be offered where required.

- Make sure that children can see the purpose of what they are doing, especially if it is an adult-directed task.
- Children respond well when there is a reason involved.

- Simplify and structure the task so that children experience success.
- Break down tasks into small, manageable ones.
- Talk through the reasons why a task has not been successful and help children learn to evaluate their role or outside influences.

▶ Learning about abstract concepts

Abstract concepts such as numeracy and literacy can be hard for some children to respond to. As with many areas of working with children who have particular needs, there is no single strategy that will automatically work.

While some children may be able to grasp concepts quickly, other children will need a variety of reinforcing activities. The danger for practitioners is in assuming that just because a child appears to understand at the time, he or she has acquired the concept. Presenting too much information too quickly can make the child lose confidence. As with supporting other areas of cognition, it is always important to break down the learning of concepts into smaller steps.

▶ Mathematics

Many elements of formal mathematics are based on abstract concepts. Before children can do formal mathematical activities, they need plenty of concrete practical experiences. During these experiences, they need adults to draw their attention to the mathematical features such as numbers, shapes, sizes or patterns so that not only can children begin to understand the concepts, they can also learn the language related to the concepts.

One of the interesting features about mathematics is that children often show strengths as well as weaknesses in different areas. A child may be able to count ten objects accurately, but on the other hand not be able to recognise a simple pattern. This means that careful assessment is needed across the range of mathematical skills that children need to acquire. As many areas of mathematics build from each other, it also means that we need to be sure that children are secure in each step before moving on. A child who finds it hard to recognise a grouping of four objects is not ready to tackle division. Most children will need plenty of reinforcement activities before they become secure.

Counting dinosaurs

What this means in practice

One of the topic areas that some children find difficult is Number. This is an area that needs repeated reinforcement. Here are some strategies that can reinforce children's concept of Number:

- Make sure that children learn the relevance of number in their everyday lives, e.g. counting the number of chairs needed at a table or the number of children who want to play a game.
- Model ways in which you use number, e.g. count things aloud, talk about the number of objects. Encourage children to group materials and sort them.
- Look for opportunities for children to match items, e.g. putting a plate down where there is a place mat, putting one piece of apple on to each plate.
- Use sensory materials such as dough, sand and water for activities about number.
- Put objects into bags: can children tell if there is more than one object in the bag?

- Look for ways of 'slipping' numbers into children's play, e.g. 'Would you like any extra cups in the home corner? How many would you like?'
- Introduce written numbers in a variety of ways, but only when children have begun to grasp number, e.g. fridge magnets, numbers drawn in sand.
- Use games to help children use number, e.g. roll a dice.
- Avoid abstract recording, e.g. worksheets, as children find it easier to use, see and touch real objects.

❯ Literacy

Being able to read and write is another facet of communication. From an early age, children begin to find out about this type of communication and gain some of the underlying skills that are required. It is important to emphasise that formal reading and writing programmes are unnecessary and can also be unhelpful before Reception class. Providing naturalistic and playful opportunities in which to learn about reading and writing tends to have greater success in motivating and encouraging children. To be able to read and write, children need to acquire a range of skills. Some children with special educational needs will need greater support to master these.

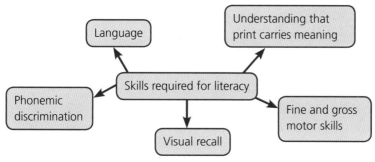

Skills required for literacy

Language

Most children need to have a strong grasp of a language before they can master reading and writing. This means that unless otherwise advised, you should aim to work on children's speech or sign language before focusing on reading and writing.

Understand that print carries meaning

Children need to be aware of the purpose of print and understand that print has meaning. For some children, this realisation begins with enjoying stories and picture books, while other children may become interested in trying to write.

Tips for good practice

Supporting the understanding that print carries meaning
- Make sure that children see you reading and writing.
- Share books with children.
- Run your finger underneath words as you are reading and writing them.
- Use opportunities to write the child's name in front of the child.
- Provide a range of writing materials and role-play situations where writing is used.
- Play games where children find words that have particular meaning for them, e.g. treasure hunt names.

Visual recall

Reading and writing letters requires children to have good visual recall of symbols. Reading requires recognising the symbols and remembering their meaning or sounds. Writing requires children to be able to actively remember the shape of symbols. Children who cannot recognise and remember images will need support before they are ready to look at letters as these are more abstract.

Tips for good practice

Helping children with visual recall
- Encourage children to play with jigsaw puzzles, shape sorters and other resources that encourage children to observe shapes.
- Play games that encourage children to notice differences or similarities.
- Play games such as snap and picture lotto as these require children to remember pictures.
- Encourage children to physically handle letter shapes.

Auditory discrimination

Children need to be able to hear the individual sounds (phonemes) that make up the components in words. This is important because as part of the reading programme, they will then connect the sounds to letter shapes. Children need plenty of opportunities to hear clear speech, but also to hear rhyming patterns. Traditionally, nursery rhymes have helped children to develop this skill, as well as games such as I Spy and musical games. Interestingly, there is a link between attention and listening and learning to read because the same skills are needed.

What this means in practice

Consider how many different nursery rhymes a child will know before they move to the Reception class. Do you have a planned programme for introducing them to children? It is also important to play games that will help children focus on individual sounds, such as encouraging children to stop moving if they hear a certain sound.

Gross and fine motor skills

Physical development plays an important part in the development of writing. Children need to have developed gross motor co-ordination as well as fine motor skills. Children who have not acquired sufficient co-ordination may find it hard to use and control a pencil or pen. This can lead to poor handwriting habits and postures. Children can also become frustrated by their inability to control their movements.

▶ Suggested activities

Activity 1 Letter shapes

This is a physical activity that can help children to recognise the shape and form of letters and can be used as a precursor to children's writing.

Aim

To help children develop visual and sensory 'maps' of letters.

Resource

Scarves or ribbons.

Activity

Begin by encouraging the children to enjoy feeling, touching and waving the scarves. You could use music for children to move and dance to. Show children particular arm movements with the scarves that link to letter shapes, i.e. a vertical movement downwards or an anti-clockwise round movement.

Possible adaptations

- Encourage children to make repeated movements such as several 'O' shapes in the air.
- Ask children who have some awareness of letters to make the letter shape of the initial letter in their name.
- Use cards with names or letters on them as cues.

Activity 2 Same and different

This activity helps children to discriminate between objects and also encourages them to use language to express their thoughts. This activity can be used with a variety of objects.

Aims

To encourage children to use language to think about and notice similarities and differences. This activity also helps children to sort and categorise.

Resources

Pairs of objects that have shared characteristics but are also different in some way, e.g. a blue pen and a red pen of a different size, and a teddy, puppet or other type of stooge.

Activity

Begin by using a teddy or puppet to bring out the two objects that you have chosen. Does the child know what they are and what they are for?

Tell the child that teddy finds it hard to tell the objects apart. Can we find a way of helping him to remember what makes them different?

If the child cannot see the difference or does not have the language, model the language for the child and then ask the child to repeat it back to teddy, e.g. 'We could tell teddy that this one is much bigger. Would you like to tell teddy that this one is bigger? Here, take it to teddy and tell him, "This one is much bigger".'

Possible adaptations

- Choose objects that will focus children's attention on particular concepts, e.g. size, shape, colour, purpose.
- Repeat the activity with the same objects later in the day. Can the child remember some of the language that has been modelled?
- Ask the child to choose two objects: 'Can you or teddy talk about them?'
- Use objects that are unfamiliar to the child.

Activity 3 Kim's game

Kim's game is a traditional game that can help children's visual recall.

Aim

To help children's memory and categorisation skills.

Resources

Tray, six assorted objects that can be grouped in some way, e.g. two toy dinosaurs, two cars and two small world people.

Activity

Show the objects on the tray to the child. Encourage the child to hold and touch them. Encourage the child to describe them. You may need to model language for the child. Ask the child to put them into groups or pairs. Take one object away. Can the child now work out what is missing?

Possible adaptations

- Show the child through questions how to guide his or her thoughts, e.g. 'There were two cars; are there two cars now?' 'There were some spoons; are there any spoons now?'
- Draw outlines of the objects first so that the child has a visual cue as to the shape of what is missing.
- Encourage the child to categorise objects before playing the game.

Activity 4 What is hidden in the sand tray?

Many children respond well to things being hidden. Sand is also a sensory activity and so carrying out this activity in this way can help children to maintain attention.

Aims

To encourage children to find a finite number of objects.
To encourage children to do some one-to-one matching.

Resources

Small tray filled with damp sand (a cat litter tray is ideal!), three spoons and three bowls.

Activity

Ask the child to put his or her hands in the sand tray. Can the child find anything that has been hidden? As the child takes out the spoons, count them one by one. Ask the child to put a spoon in each of the bowls.

Potential adaptations

- Ask the child to hide the spoons for you to find.
- Hide other objects such as buttons and cars in the sand tray; these can build upon a child's favourite playthings.
- Hide objects that can afterwards be sorted according to size, e.g. a teaspoon, a dessert spoon, a tablespoon.
- Hide pairs of objects, e.g. two teaspoons, two buttons, two keys.

Activity 5 Find teddy

This activity is a variation of the traditional game of hide and seek and can be adapted to provide a variety of learning outcomes.

Aim

This type of activity can help develop children's problem-solving skills.

Resources

A little teddy or other object that will captivate the child's imagination or interest.

Activity

Tell the child that little teddy is playing hide and seek. Can you together work out where teddy is hiding? This activity requires the adult to show the child how to problem solve, e.g. by asking questions: 'Now, where would a teddy like to hide?'

It is also important that children hear the adult's thought processes, e.g. 'I have already looked under here and he is not here, but I have not looked here.' Once the teddy has been found, the activity can be repeated again.

Possible adaptations

- Encourage the child to hide the teddy. You can then ask the child questions as to where he is hidden and comment on why you are looking in certain places.
- Encourage the child to think about what he or she knows about the teddy and to use this knowledge to work out where teddy might hide.
- Use other objects that will help children to problem solve, such as hiding a large object and encouraging children to eliminate smaller places from the search.

Chapter 11

Social, emotional and mental health

▶ Introduction

Being able to socialise, feel part of a community and have a strong sense of self are important for children. Children whose social and emotional development needs are atypical are in danger of being 'excluded' by adults and other children. Understanding ways in which we can foster children's emotional and social development and support their mental health is therefore essential. This chapter focuses on ways in which we can help children to develop these social and emotional skills. We also consider strategies for guiding and promoting positive behaviour.

▶ Starting points

In Chapter 8, we looked at the importance of how we work with children. The themes of self-esteem and empowerment were considered. Children also have a basic emotional need to be loved and accepted by others. This forms the basis of social interaction and also positively supports mental health. It is therefore important to read this chapter alongside Chapter 8. Children's ability to learn as well as to achieve their potential is closely tied to their social, emotional and mental health needs being met. Sadly, there is evidence to show that where children's needs are not met in childhood, there is a higher likelihood of mental illness including depression in later lives.

▶ Ways of supporting children's social and emotional development

Adults play a key role in helping children to socialise and engage with others. We need to start by making sure that we create the optimum conditions for children to socialise. There are many ways of doing this within a setting, depending on the age, stage and needs of the children who you work with.

▶ Creating a feeling of belonging for all children

All children need to feel that they belong in a setting. This begins with the way that we settle children in, which we looked at in Chapter 8. Children who are comfortable in a setting when they first start are more likely to develop a sense of belonging. The key person therefore plays an important role in helping children feel that they belong. In addition, there are other tangible ways to help children feel that they belong and are part of a community. These include children being greeted by adults and also by each other as they come into the setting. Small things such as children having an assigned drawer, coat peg or cubby hole can all contribute to a sense of belonging.

What this means in practice

Think about what it might be like for a child to come into your setting. Consider what they will see and hear first. You might also like think about the following:

- Do children know each other's names?
- Are children encouraged to help each other?
- Are opportunities available for children to play in a range of group sizes?
- Do you have a 'group' song?
- Are children encouraged to greet each other?
- Are there opportunities such as parties for children to celebrate together?

◗ Routines

Routines that help children to make the transition into your setting at the start of the session can be helpful. Routines are very important for children whose home lives are inconsistent and where no two days ever feel the same. The sense of security offered by a routine can therefore help individual children to feel calmer and to relax. Routines to help transition do not necessarily have to involve all children in the setting doing the same thing at once. They can be individualised and this is often more effective as it means that the individual child may get more attention than if they were sitting down as part of a large group.

We used to get all the children to come in and sit down first thing in the morning. It tended to be quite difficult though as some children wanted to get on and explore the resources while others seemed to look quite lost and bewildered. We started then to explore what individual children were gaining from this approach and in doing so realised that it was not working that well. We now work quite differently. We identify which children need to have more adult support at the start of the session and we set up routines for them. One boy, for example, always begins his day by saying hello to our guinea pig with his key person. Another begins by going over to the dough table each day and making her key person a 'cake'.

Wendy, Children's Centre manager

❯ Snack and mealtimes

Food has traditionally been a social event. Through careful use of snack and mealtimes, it can be possible to help support children's social development. Snack and mealtimes are great ways of children coming together and learning to share, sit and enjoy something together. A good start when thinking about how to structure snack and mealtimes is to be aware that some children may not have had opportunities to sit and socialise with others. They may need to be guided by sensitive adults and might benefit at first from just taking snacks with one or two other children. It is also worth recognising that large scale snack and mealtimes can not only be daunting, but they may not achieve good social interaction between children.

What this means in practice

Think what skills and needs each individual child has when constructing snack and mealtimes. How much adult support might each child need? What experiences have they already had in relation to taking meals and snacks with others? It is also worth thinking about pairing children for snack and mealtimes alongside an adult who can guide them. Many children also enjoy being involved in preparing for snack and mealtimes and this can act as a good learning experience at the same time.

❯ Creating a community environment

Ideally, we need to work in ways that will help children feel that they are part of a community or small family, if they are in small or home-based settings. The way we talk to children and acknowledge them will influence how other children relate to them. Some children quickly become labelled by other children based on how they perceive adults relating towards them. A child who is seen as 'naughty' is more likely to be excluded from the play of others, while a child who is frequently positively acknowledged is more likely to be included. The way in which children pick up cues from adults means that sometimes children become scapegoated by other children. They may come and tell us that another children is not behaving well, hoping to gain some credit from us.

In addition, we may need to think about whether withdrawing children from a room to work individually therefore always meets children's needs in this context. While children may benefit from individual attention, it is worth considering whether this is sending out a negative signal to the child or other children. While younger children are often positive about being singled out for special attention, older children may be reluctant as they do not wish for their peers to pick up on their needs.

| Adults play a role in helping children to play alongside each other

▶ The role of play in supporting children's social and emotional needs and mental health

Play is a wonderful way for children to explore their emotions and to develop social skills. It is also thought to be important for children's mental health as it reduces their stress levels. Through play, children can legitimately and safely show anger, be destructive and release a range of emotions. They can also use play to explore social situations and to develop some important social skills such as learning to interpret others' emotions. In Chapter 9 we looked at the importance of role play in helping children to try out different roles and also act out what they have experienced. This is just one of many types of play that can help children and is worth considering when planning for children's emotional and social skills. The table below shows some types of activities grouped into play types and looks at examples of how they may support children's emotional and social needs.

Types of play, examples and benefits

Type of play	Examples	Emotional and social benefits
Sensory materials	Water, gloop, sand, mud kitchens	• Relaxation through repeated movements and feel of materials • Allows children to show anger and be destructive • Children may model each other's movements • Children can play by themselves, in parallel or co-operatively • Provides rich experiences which do not have to lead to an end product
Imaginative play	Role play, dressing up, small world play with farm animals, play people	• Children can play out their experiences and so express their feelings • Children can take on a range of roles, including feelings of being powerful and in control • Children can choose to play alone or with others
Construction	Building blocks, Meccano-type kits, large-scale junk modelling	• Making things can help children to feel in control and powerful • Children can feel purposeful and also have a sense of achievement • Children may choose to create and then destruct • Construction can help children to work with others as they share a project together • Children can choose to play alone or with others
Physical play	Climbing opportunities, using a ball to kick or throw, swings, balancing games, obstacle courses	• Physical activity can help children to express anger and frustration • Physical activity can help children to feel calmer afterwards and less stressed • Children can play alone, with others or in parallel
Creative play	Painting, dough, cutting and pasting, collage, drawing	• This type of play can help children to express ideas and emotions using a range of media • Children can feel a sense of achievement • Children can use creative play to represent their feelings or to represent a situation • Children can play alone or in parallel with others

What this means in practice

It is important to consider how the play opportunities that you provide support individual children's emotional and social needs. As well as observing and supporting children as they choose different play opportunities, it is also worth thinking about introducing a child to a type of play that might benefit their needs.

◗ Teaching children the skills of play

We often take play for granted, but some children need support to learn how to play alongside others. It can therefore be helpful for children to learn to play at first with an adult. Look for games where children have to take turns or co-operate as part of the enjoyment. Something as simple as 'roll a ball back' can help children make eye contact and encourage turn taking. Give children feedback as to why they are playing well; for example, 'When you waited for your turn, it made me enjoy the game more.' Introduce other children into any game and, where possible, gradually take a step back.

Adults can model how to take turns

Helping children to join others' play

Some children need to learn how to join in or approach other children. This is a sensitive area and in the first instance it can be worth modelling how they might do this. When children are playing, join in by at first observing them and then playing alongside them, but not disrupting or taking over their game. Use phrases, such as 'May I use this, if you have finished?', rather than taking materials. These modelled behaviours are important for children to learn. Quite often children try to 'take over' a game or become aggressive rather than trying quietly to blend in. Children may also need to learn how to positively recognise others' ideas and play, for example, 'That's a good idea' or 'Your tower is going to be really big.'

Some settings have successfully adopted a slogan within their setting of 'We all play, we don't turn away' and have reinforced it with all the children. This can help very young children learn to let others play alongside them.

What this means in practice

Think about whether you need to help some children learn the skills of playing with others. Consider play activities and resources that already seem to be popular in your setting. Think also whether you might need to build up children's play skills through modelling, structured support or feedback.

Create opportunities for group co-operation

The toys, equipment and style of activities can be important in helping children to play. Certain activities such as role play, construction and cooking can foster co-operative or parallel play. It is also important to check that there are sufficient resources, as children often become predatory and competitive when materials are scarce.

Think about the activities that are available; will they encourage parallel or co-operative play?

- Use parachute games with children.
- Sing rhymes and action songs so that children feel part of the group.
- Plan parties or activities with children so that they can all make suggestions.
- Play party games, but change the focus so that they are not competitive, e.g. hunt the thimble – one child has to look for it, but the other children help by telling the child if he or she is 'hot' or 'cold'.

❯ The role of physical activity in supporting children's social and emotional needs and mental health

Physical activity seems to be important for all of us, but particularly for children. Not only does it give health benefits, it is also important in helping to reduce stress and anxiety. This is because 'feel good' hormones called endorphins are produced during physical activity. These lessen the effects of stress and also create a sense of well-being. Physical activity also has other benefits including helping us to sleep better, which in turn helps to regulate other hormones associated with mood and self-regulation.

❯ How much physical activity?

Many adults underestimate how much physical activity children need. The latest guidelines suggest that children under five years should be engaged in three hours of physical activity a day. Meanwhile, older children and young people will need a minimum of an hour a day of moderate to vigorous exercise, but ideally should be engaged in several hours.

❯ Additional benefits of outdoor activity

Outdoor activity seems to be particularly helpful in providing opportunities for exercise and play. Interestingly, many children when they are engaged outdoors in some type of activity seem to show fewer incidences of unwanted behaviours. The reasons for this are unclear, but perhaps it is because children have more space, a wider range of opportunities and also the environment may allow children to be louder and show more boisterous behaviours.

❯ Planning for physical activity

While we often talk about exercise in relation to physical activity, for children it is important that this is translated into play and enjoyable activities. This might include going for walks, as well as games involving throwing, catching and running. We may also need to think about whether children need to be helped with the skills that may make physical activity more enjoyable, such as throwing, catching and balancing. We look at these in the next chapter.

What this means in practice

Consider how much physical activity is planned in your daily routines and whether this meets the minimum requirements for physical activity. (If you are unsure about the type and variety of activities, download the 'UK physical activity guidelines' factsheets from the Department of Health, produced in 2011, see www.gov.uk/government/publications/uk-physical-activity-guidelines.) It is also worth being aware that some children are not used to playing outdoors for a range of reasons, including living in flats with no outdoor space available. This might mean that some children may need additional support to help them enjoy being outdoors.

▶ Identifying children who may be at risk of mental health issues

It is important that we are proactive in recognising whether children may need additional support. In terms of mental health, there are some factors to consider that may suggest that some children are more at risk. Being aware of these may help to influence our practice with these children, but may also help us to recognise when children and their families need the support of other professionals. As well as risk factors, there are also some protective factors that also need to be considered. The protective factors may in some cases help us to focus our practice, e.g. the importance of secure attachments, encouraging children to have control and also the importance of encouraging communication. The table shows some of the risks and also the protective factors based on information from the charity Young Minds (www.youngminds.org.uk).

Risks and protective factors for children's mental health

Predisposing factors in children	Protective factors in children
• Attachment difficulties to primary carers • Learning difficulties, specific developmental delay • Communication difficulties • Difficult temperament • Physical illness, especially long-term conditions • Low self-esteem	• Secure attachment experience • Outgoing temperament as an infant • Good communication skills, sociability • Being a planner and having a belief in control • Humour • Problem-solving skills and a positive attitude • Experiences of success and achievement • Capacity to reflect

Risks and protective factors for children's mental health contd.

Predisposing factors in families	Protective factors in families
• Inter-parent conflicts, including domestic abuse • Family breakdown • Inconsistent or unclear discipline • Hostile or rejecting relationships • Parents failing to adapt to children's changing needs • Parental psychiatric illness • Parental criminality, alcohol or drug abuse • Frequent moves, meaning that children lose friends • Bereavement	• At least one good parent–child relationship (or one supportive adult) • Affection • Clear, consistent discipline • Support for education • Supportive long-term relationship or the absence of severe discord

What this means in practice

We can see that children who have SEN or a disability are more likely to be at risk of developing mental health difficulties and so it is important to be vigilant and thoughtful about this. It also means that we need to have good referral mechanisms in place to help parents and to refer them to other services. Finally, some of the protective factors, such as children learning to reflect and also having consistent boundaries, need to be built into the way we work.

▶ Strategies to promote positive behaviour

Learning and showing appropriate behaviour is a part of children's social development. Unfortunately, children who for a range of reasons struggle to show socially appropriate behaviours often find it harder to connect to other children. They may have fewer friends and may miss out on learning opportunities that can be gained from being with others. We also know that in relation to mental health, children are likely to benefit from consistent boundaries and an expectation of positive behaviours. In this section we look at strategies to promote positive behaviour and also reasons why children's behaviour may take a while to change.

▶ Factors affecting behaviour

There is a range of factors that can affect children's ability to show positive behaviours. It is important to understand these in order to know how best to guide children.

Developmental factors

There are some facets of positive behaviour that are linked to children's development. A good example of this is being able to take turns or wait for some equipment or resources to become free. This is typically shown from three years, but for children with developmental delay it may take longer and children may need support. The reason this is stage-linked is that self-regulation, the skill that enables waiting and turn-taking to happen, is linked to language and cognitive development.

What this means in practice

It is important to recognise and have fair expectations of children whose development is delayed, especially if they have cognition or communication needs. Strategies to promote positive behaviour for these children will need to tie in with their level of development.

Parenting styles

Some children's home lives may not help them to show positive behaviour in line with their age/stage of development. There are many reasons for this including inconsistent parenting, lack of expectations or aggression shown towards them. Some children may also be coping with conflicting expectations if, for example, they spend part of the week with one parent and the rest with the other.

What this means in practice

Children who are experiencing inconsistent or unreasonable parenting are at a disadvantage as they have no clear and consistent guidance as to how to manage their behaviour. They may need us to help them with consistent routines and boundaries. We may also, if appropriate, signpost parenting classes to support parents further.

Emotional factors

Stress, whatever its origin, can impact on children's behaviour. While it is said that children are adaptable, this is not quite true. Children can find it hard to cope with change and will often show behaviours that are linked to stress. These can include attention seeking and withdrawal, as well as frustrated outbursts.

Children benefit from simple routines and praise

Sleep

Tiredness and lack of sleep can have a significant impact on children's behaviour. Lack of sleep can have a variety of causes, including the impact of medical conditions, as well as difficulties in parenting. It is important to be aware of how tired children are and if necessary to adjust our expectations of their behaviour accordingly. Common characteristics of tiredness in relation to behaviour include difficulty with self-regulation, irritability and also emotional outburst.

▶ Being proactive

One of the key strategies to support positive behaviour is for adults to be proactive in their approach rather than constantly reacting to children's unwanted behaviour. A good starting point when taking a proactive approach is to stand back and consider what is happening and why.

Observing children

In many cases, observation of a child's behaviour will provide a good understanding of what is happening and why. It is also likely to provide some clues as to how best to support the child. Observations can also provide us with a way of seeing the effectiveness of any strategies that have been put into place. There is no one standard way of observing children. Different types of observation simply provide different types of information. This means that you need to start by thinking about the information that you need. In some cases, an informal observation may suffice, as by simply spending time closely watching a child, you learn more about the child's needs. The questions below may help to focus your thoughts when observing a child.

- How well does the child appear?
- Does the child seem tired?
- Does the child appear to be seeking adult attention?
- Are adults unwittingly reinforcing unwanted behaviours, e.g. giving attention instead of ignoring behaviours or waiting until the child is showing positive behaviour?
- Does the child respond well to any particular adults or children?
- What activities and equipment does the child appear interested in?
- Are there any areas of the child's development that appear to be delayed?
- Is the structure and routine of the setting causing periods of inactivity for children?

The types of observation methods have been described in Chapter 4 (page XX) and include event samples and target child observations. Once observations have been carried out, it is essential that staff and perhaps parents consider what information has been gathered. Settings that are good at guiding and modifying children's behaviour are able to be objective and analytical about the way in which staff are meeting children's needs, as well as focusing on the child themselves.

What this means in practice

Observations may reveal that part of the difficulty lies in the way the child is responding to the curriculum, routine or environment. This means that you will need to consider how best to change these elements in order to meet the child's needs. This can be hard as it requires being objective, but it can provide immediate answers and therefore strategies. Some behaviours, such as wandering, lack of concentration or spoiling other children's play, can result from a child being either over-stimulated or under-stimulated. Consider these questions if you think that this could be the case:

- What play activities or resources engage and interest the child, and are these available?
- Are the activities suitable for the child's stage of development?
- Are the activities enjoyable and achievable for the child?
- Is the length of an activity 'fixed' or can a child finish when he or she has lost interest?
- Are the activities and equipment accessible and sufficient?
- Are there periods in the routine when children are expected to wait?
- Does the child need frequent changes of activities or resources, and does this happen?
- Does the child need a strong routine in order to feel secure, and if so does the child need reminding of the routine?
- How can the layout be changed, e.g. can furniture be moved if children are running?
- Does the child need quiet areas if he or she is sensitive to noise and over-excitement?

Giving children clear guidance

Another proactive approach to supporting children's behaviour is to give them clear guidance. Children may need to be reminded or told what they should do before they start an activity. This should be done in a positive way, for example 'Can you remember where the apron goes when you have finished painting?' Guidance needs to be given in ways that the child can understand and process. For some children, guidance needs to be given in small pieces, as too much information at the same time is hard for them to process. Where appropriate, reasons for the guidance should be clearly explained: 'If you put the apron away, other children will find it easily.' With children who find it hard to process the spoken word, visual guidance might be helpful, i.e. actually showing the child where the apron goes. Some children may also need visual timetables to help them know what they need to do during and after an activity.

Giving children feedback

Feedback helps children to learn which aspects of their behaviour are appropriate. Just praising children can make them believe that good behaviour is about pleasing adults. A proactive approach is therefore to give children plenty of feedback about what they are doing and why it is important. For example, 'You waited for Harry to finish his turn on the slide. That was good because he could get up safely.'

Supervision and attention

Another proactive approach may be to change the way in which staff are deployed in a setting. Time spent reacting to an unwanted behaviour is better spent preventing the unwanted behaviour from occurring in the first place. It is not unknown in settings for staff to be on the look-out and 'waiting' for the first incident to occur, when this time would be better used by engaging the child directly.

What this means in practice

Consider monitoring the time that is being spent reacting to behaviours and consider instead providing the child with the same amount of adult time but in a positive context.

- What level of support does the child need and is this being received?
- Does the child need an adult to help him or her play alongside or with other children?
- What situations are likely to cause the child to show unwanted behaviour and are staff actively looking to guide the child?
- Are staff reacting to incidents rather than looking for ways of distracting the child or diffusing a situation before it can build up?
- How are children gaining adult attention and time?

Change the elements of a situation

Taking a proactive approach can change patterns of behaviour. Being proactive means changing elements of a situation so that the child cannot use his or her normal responses. For example, a child in a nursery always tries to climb on to the table at lunchtime. Usually the staff react to this by taking the child off the table and telling her not to do this again. A proactive approach would be to set out a picnic rug outdoors. The child no longer has a table on which to climb and staff can give the child a plate of food to carry outside.

Modelling

Children learn a lot by about how to show appropriate and positive behaviours by watching others. This process is known as modelling. Children are particularly influenced by adults, especially those who are close to them. There is a huge onus on all adults working with children to be good role models as children will be constantly learning about appropriate behaviour from them. This means reflecting on how you act and the messages that the child is learning; for example, if you wish a child to learn to ask permission before touching someone else's toys, it is important for you to remember to do the same when you join in children's play. Children will also need to see consistent modelling from all the adults in the setting, especially if a child has seen unwanted types of behaviour being modelled, e.g. swearing or aggression.

What it means in practice

You might like to think about which aspects of wanted behaviour children need to have reinforced and also to ensure that, if you are working as a team, you have a consistent approach with children.

▶ Recognising difficulties in changing children's behaviours

It is important to understand the reasons why children's behaviour may take a while to change. This is because there is a significant link between the way a child thinks about him or herself and his or her behaviour. If children come to believe that they are 'naughty', they will show inappropriate behaviour. This becomes an ever-spiralling problem, as when the inappropriate behaviour is challenged, children's thoughts or schemas about themselves are confirmed. It is useful to understand how children develop such schemas about themselves.

Children are not born knowing about themselves. They learn about themselves primarily through the reactions of others. This is sometimes called the 'looking-glass effect'. Children who regularly receive negative messages will begin to believe that they are incapable of gaining adult approval or behaving appropriately.

What this means in practice

Challenging inappropriate behaviour must be done in ways that are positive and the child must understand what they need to do in order to behave appropriately. It is also important that adults think about the number of times that children may be hearing 'don't' or 'no' and check that this is counterbalanced by positive messages.

▶ Self-schemas are slow to change

Once children have developed schemas whereby they see themselves as being 'naughty' or 'difficult', it can be hard for them to see themselves in any other way. They can get used to behaving in certain ways and become comfortable with the results.

What this means in practice

In older children, self-schemas can be slow to change. It is therefore important to be patient and persistent. A child's behaviour may improve but then after a few days appear to get worse. This may be the child finding it hard to believe and accept the new 'them'. By reverting back to challenging behaviour, the child can test out his or her new schema to see how strong it really is. The danger for adults is that children can feel that the new strategy is not working and they lose their enthusiasm!

▶ Suggested activities

Activity 1 Help teddy play safely

Puppets and stooges such as a teddy can serve as non-confrontational ways of reminding children about the boundaries in the setting.

Aim

To help children remember boundaries and the reasons for them.

Resource

Teddy, puppet or other stooge.

Activity

Tell the children that teddy loves to come to the setting because he loves watching them play. He wants to learn how to play safely, but we will need to tell him how. Can the children remember anything that they should or should not do when playing in the sand? Encourage the children to tell teddy the reasons behind what they are saying.

Possible adaptations

Encourage children to take teddy to play with them so that they can show teddy how to play safely. Use teddy as the stooge to help children talk about playing safely in a variety of contexts.

Activity 2 Find your family

This type of traditional party activity can help children to get to know each other and can create a feeling of belonging.

Aim

To help children socialise with each other in a fun way.

Resources

Cards with pictures of animals, e.g. four dogs, four cats, four ducks.

Activity

Give each child a card with an animal on. Remind the children of the animals and the sounds that they can make. Tell the children to walk around the room and see if they can find their family. It is important that this is not a competitive game; competition can create barriers as some children quickly focus on 'winning' rather than on playing and enjoying.

Possible adaptations

- Put children into larger or smaller groups. Play the game so that 'pairs' of animals hunt for the rest of their family; this can allow an adult to join up with a child and thus discreetly help him or her.
- Use sound cues such as film canisters filled with rice.
- Play a game where children have to whisper their partner's name to find them.

Activity 3 Den making

Den or tent making can encourage children to come together because they have the same focus.

Aim

To help children co-operate and feel part of a group.

Resources

Sheets, boxes and anything else that will lend itself to being used to make a den.

Activity

Show small groups or pairs of children the materials and ask them if they would like to make their own den, play area or 'home'. Lend adult support when required but avoid taking over.

Possible adaptations

- Adults can play alongside children.
- Dens can be made indoors and also for certain purposes, e.g. a mark-making den where children can write and make marks.

Activity 4 Bounce the ball

Parachute games can help children feel part of a group as a collective effort is required to make the games work.

Aim

To encourage children to be part of a collective game.

Resources

Small parachute or large circular tablecloth, small football.

Activity

With a group of around six children, take out the parachute or tablecloth. Encourage children to raise and lower it. Give children time to enjoy feeling the breeze on their faces; try lifting and lowering the parachute quickly as well as slowly so that children gain some control. Introduce a ball on to the parachute and encourage the children to send the ball up into the air.

Possible adaptations

When children are able to gain control of the ball, they can see how long they can keep the ball bouncing without it falling off. There are plenty of other parachute games, for example children can take turns to run in and out from under the parachute.

Activity 5 Teddy needs some friends

Teddy or puppets can help children to think about how to join in play with others. This activity can be done with groups of children to help them learn the slogan, 'We all play, we don't turn away'.

Aim

To help children learn how to join in a game.

Resources

Teddy, other cuddly toys.

Activity

Tell the children that teddy is not feeling very special today. He wants to join in with his friends. Tell the children that you are going to talk to his friends to find out what is going on. Take out one of teddy's friends. Tell the children that teddy often tries to take over the game and if he doesn't get his own way, will spoil the game by pushing someone over. Ask the child to show teddy how to join in a game. At this point you may give suggestions to help the child. Ask the child to talk to teddy's friends to explain to them why it is important to let other children join in.

Possible adaptations

- Encourage the child to use small world people to model how to join in play.
- Consider using stickers in the setting to remind children of the importance of 'We all play, we don't turn away'.

Activity 6 Pick the sequins out of the rice

This type of non-competitive activity can encourage children to play alongside each other and help children to get to know each other.

Aim

To help children socialise in a non-competitive way.

Resources

Rice, green food colouring, tray, sequins, plastic bag.

Activity

Colour the rice by putting it into a plastic bag, adding some drops of green food colouring and shaking the bag. Spread the rice on to a deep tray and allow it to dry for a few minutes. Once the rice is dry, sprinkle a few sequins into it. Ask the children if they can spot the sequins and take them out. Model this process and see if children are interested in helping you. Leave the tray out so that children can go over at any time and do this. This will encourage children to drop in and out of the activity. The repetitive nature of the activity allows the children to talk easily to each other.

Possible adaptations

- Encourage two children to help you prepare the rice.
- Put out tweezers to create a physical challenge.
- Put other items instead of sequins in the rice, e.g. dried chick peas, ribbons or coins.

Chapter 12

Supporting children's sensory and physical development

▶ Introduction

Children's sensory and physical development is an important area, although it is easy to take it for granted. Children who have a sensory impairment or whose physical development is atypical will need extra support in order to enjoy experiences and to benefit from the learning environment. Increasingly, research is showing that children's sensory and physical development is linked to their cognition and ability to process information. This chapter looks at ways of supporting children who have a sensory need and then goes on to look at ways of promoting aspects of children's physical development.

▶ Understanding why sensory development is important

Our brain relies on our senses to bring in information. Children learn about themselves and their world from the sensory information that they receive. Children who have sensory needs or impairments affecting one or more of their senses will therefore not be receiving a range of information. This can affect the way they think, learn and remember and therefore has an impact on their cognitive development.

As well as sensory information being important to cognition, it is also linked to children's physical development. The feedback and information gained from our senses informs the movements and responses that we make. To lift a cup, for example, requires that we are able to adjust our hand movements according to the visual and tactile information that is sent to the brain. This can mean that a child who has a sensory impairment may also show atypical physical development and will need additional support.

A good starting point is to understand that sensory information sent to the brain helps children to remain alert. This is essential in order for children to concentrate. Children who have difficulty concentrating often have difficulties either in receiving sensory information or in processing it. In terms of supporting children, this means that activities that are multi-sensory are usually more effective in helping children to remain alert and concentrate.

❱ Touch

Most people take their sense of touch for granted, yet some children's sense of touch may be over- or underdeveloped. As touch provides the brain with a rich source of sensory information that helps the brain to remain alert, this can mean that children may appear to be easily distracted or find it hard to settle.

Not all children will enjoy sensory materials

Children who are over-sensitive to touch (tactile defensive)

Some children's tactile receptors can be over-sensitive. This means that increases in the arousal levels can reach a point which becomes uncomfortable for them. Touching paint or sand or other sensory activities may therefore distress them. These children may refuse to take part in 'messy' activities or wear particular clothes. This is known as tactile defensiveness. Understanding why some children react in this way is important as it is otherwise too easy to dismiss their fears. It would appear that the brains of children who are tactile defensive are instinctively adopting a protective approach, sometimes dubbed the 'fight or flight' response. This is a primitive reaction designed to keep us safe, for example we automatically remove our hands from flames or something that we are unsure of. While we all retain the protective instinct, most of us have also gained the ability to override this instinct in order to use our sense of touch to explore objects in our world and to discriminate between things. Given the choice of two peaches to eat, for example, we may touch them both and then choose the softest.

Children who cannot use their sense of touch effectively are therefore missing out because they are not learning about the properties of materials or gaining the ability to discriminate and notice similarities and differences.

What this means in practice

To help children who are tactile defensive we need to look for ways of helping the body suppress its instinctive desire to withdraw the hand. Firm touches and pressure are usually more successful in doing this. A child may become very distressed if asked to gently touch sand, but may respond if asked to clutch and grasp wet sand firmly. Confidence and support are also an important part of working with children. Adults must understand their fears and build their confidence gradually. The following ideas are suggestions only and if you are working with a child who is tactile defensive, you may also wish to seek further ideas from your local SEN advisory team.

- Do not dismiss children's fears.
- Do not force children's hands into things; this can make them feel panicky.
- Avoid making an 'issue' out of their reluctance to handle things; some children can then learn to use this as an attention-seeking device.
- Ask parents about materials that the child enjoys at home.
- Choose activities and games that encourage children to touch large-scale things with pressure, e.g. bouncing on a trampoline, trampling on wet sand, wearing wellington boots, wringing water out of fabric.
- Look for materials that are firm for children to explore, e.g. dried beans, marbles.
- Encourage firm movements using tools, e.g. cutting dough with knives, printing into wet sand with forks, drawing with sticks.
- Consider putting paint, sand or dough into zipper plastic bags so children can play with it through the plastic.
- Introduce more tactile materials such as cornflour and water only as children become more confident.
- Model language so that children can learn to express what they are feeling.
- Look for ways of helping children to remain in control, e.g. they can wipe their hands on a towel any time when playing in sand. The knowledge that they can do this can help children to gain confidence.

Children who under-react to touch

Some children find it hard to remain alert and are easily distracted because they are not reacting sufficiently to the sensory information provided by their tactile receptors. They may constantly fiddle with, touch and feel objects around them and may find it hard to keep their hands to themselves. Some children may also put things into their mouths beyond the age that this might be expected. At around two years, most children increasingly use their hands rather than their mouths to explore objects. It is thought that children who continue to use their mouths beyond this age are under-reacting to touch and they are effectively 'boosting' the amount of sensory information by constantly touching and using their mouths.

What this means in practice

There is a real danger of children who under-react to touch being labelled as 'naughty' or 'difficult'. Understanding that they find it hard not to boost their sensory input is therefore very important for everyone working with children. It means that you will need to increase the sensory level in activities and look for ways of helping them to gain the stimulation that they seek in more appropriate ways. You should also think about the safety implications if children are still putting objects into their mouths or fiddling with things.

- Provide daily sensory activities with sufficient materials to be satisfying for a child, e.g. large pieces of dough, large pieces of paper to paint on.
- Build upon children's interests and deliver the curriculum in ways that appeal to them, e.g. if a child plays well in the water tray, you may play a roll-the-dice game where a child fills up a bucket of water by putting in the number of scoops shown on the dice.
- Engage individual children by talking to them, showing them things and giving them things to hold. Left to their own devices, these children will find it hard not to touch other objects around them. They may also put objects into their mouths.
- During quiet times, such as story time, give the child something to hold and explore, e.g. a piece of dough, a shell or a ribbon. This means they can 'legitimately' fiddle.
- Do not take fiddling as a sign they are not listening; many adults doodle whon on the telephone.

We had one child in our setting who would be constantly 'butterflying' from one activity to another. She would also go to the drawers of toys and just tip them out. We eventually realised she needed much higher levels of stimulation in order to concentrate, so we planned more sensory activities and collected more natural toys and resources.

Gail, room leader, daycare centre

Tactile activities

- **Gloop:** Mix cornflour with water to form a sticky paste that can flow.
- **Sand:** Wet or dry sand can be used with children. Put sand into small trays so that children can play with it by themselves.
- **Water:** Use warm water as well as cold water. Add in food colouring, glitter or ice cubes for a change.
- **Cold cooked spaghetti:** Cooked pasta such as spaghetti can help children to explore. Consider colouring the spaghetti. (This is not suitable for children with coeliac disease, see page 217.)
- **Dry coloured rice:** Add a few drops of food colouring to dry rice and use this to help children make marks and scoop.
- **Brushes:** A selection of brushes, e.g. paint brushes and make-up brushes, can be left out for children to explore. Children can stroke their hands with them or use them to brush other materials such as sand, water or rice.

▶ Vision

Vision is an important source of information for the brain and there are many reasons why children may not be fully seeing. It is important that practitioners understand and look for children who are not fully seeing, as this can affect their hand–eye co-ordination and, later in their school years, their ability to learn to read and write. Early identification that children are not fully seeing can make a significant difference to children's learning and socialisation.

Lights and sounds can stimulate children's senses

What this means in practice

It is a good idea to watch children carefully and consider whether they are fully seeing. Here are some indicators that might indicate that a child needs a referral:

- Reluctant to look at objects or shows no interest in things that other children are doing.
- Frowns in order to focus.
- Moves whole head to look at objects.
- Complains of headaches.
- Draws and paints very close to the paper.
- Shows little interest in television or using computers apart from handheld items.
- Rubs eyes or has eyes that are often red.
- Has frequent accidents caused by bumping into others or falling over objects.
- Has poor spatial awareness.
- Avoids tasks or becomes frustrated with tasks requiring hand–eye co-ordination.
- Is slower to react and notice what others are doing.
- Is easily distracted and becomes tired and loses concentration more quickly than other children.

Visual discrimination

Being able to notice similarities and to pick out differences is an important skill. The brain must use the visual information being given. Visual discrimination is part of the process of learning to read. While some children readily look at objects and inspect them closely, other children need to gain the skills of doing so. Activities to help children's visual discrimination also build up their hand–eye co-ordination. Children will benefit more fully if adults also model language so that children can connect what they are seeing with words.

What this means in practice

Look out for activities that will help children to look at things carefully and also to pick out differences. You can do this in everyday ways such as buying different types and sizes of apples to see if children can spot the difference. Look out also for simple games such as 'What's missing', where children look at two images which are the same apart from three or four things that are missing. Other ideas include:

- Put out buttons for children to sort. Which one is their favourite?
- Use magnifying glasses and digital microscopes to allow children to inspect objects in more detail, e.g. shells.
- Mix up objects and see if children can separate them, e.g. oranges and satsumas.
- Encourage children to sort out clothing, e.g. pairs of socks, pairs of shoes.

◗ Supporting children's physical development

There are many reasons why a child's physical development may be atypical and we have already seen that there is a significant link between children's sensory skills and their movements. While it is not possible or desirable to 'fast track' children's development, we may be able to help children by building on their existing skills and stimulating them to make particular movements. Building children's confidence, in particular, is essential as many children quickly lose interest in activities that they do not enjoy or find frustrating. There are many components in physical development including balance, gross motor skills and fine motor skills. Co-ordinated movements require sensory and physical integration.

Before looking at some of the component parts of physical development, it is worth noting that children whose physical development is atypical may be unwittingly discriminated against. Other children may not wait for them to 'catch up' when playing games, or adults may repeatedly reward children who are first to fasten up their coats or move to the next activity. As many games and activities require increasing levels of physical skill, this means that children can quickly lose confidence and also lose out on friendships. They may decide to wait for help rather than try to be independent.

What this means in practice

Think about how you help children to develop self-care and independence skills in ways that are not competitive. Encourage children to take the time that they need and if children are struggling, think about how you might support them further, e.g. they could start to put their coats on before some of the other children so that they are not always last, or a ribbon could be threaded through the zipper to make it easier for the child to pull up.

◗ Balance and spatial awareness

Children's sense of balance is determined by movement receptors in the inner ear and in their muscles, and works in combination with their vision. Children also need to have adequate muscle tone, as to remain balanced requires tiny shifts in weight-bearing positions. Spatial awareness is about understanding where you are in relation to your environment. Good spatial awareness prevents you bumping into other objects. The combination of information from movement receptors and vision is used by the brain to develop a feeling of where you are. The more experiences children have of moving, the more easily the brain learns to process the information and make necessary adjustments.

Children who require mobility aids need to experience the world from different heights and angles as otherwise they will find it hard to develop the same level of spatial awareness as others. If you look at most children during the day, they may spend time in a variety of positions. It might be worth talking to a physiotherapist or occupational therapist about changing the levels for children with mobility needs, e.g. lying on the floor or raising a work area so they can look downwards for some of the time.

What this means in practice

The starting point if you have concerns over a child's balance or spatial awareness is to talk to the parents. It may be that the child has a visual impairment or that there is an underlying medical condition. Help might also be sought from a physiotherapist if concerns remain. Children who have experience of falling over quickly lose confidence and so the starting point for any activity is enjoyment. Begin by checking that an activity is achievable for a child and then gradually make it more challenging.

Make a list of the equipment and materials that you have available in your setting that would help children to develop a sense of balance and spatial awareness. This could include things that help children to experience rocking as well as stilts, trampolines and swings. These activities help children to develop balance and spatial awareness:

- Pushing a pram or shopping trolley on a pathway. Can the child stay on the path? Make the path gradually more challenging, e.g. narrower, and introduce bends and curves.
- Obstacle courses – these can involve the child in picking up items as they move across them. Try looking out for different textures for children to walk or crawl across, such as matting.
- Stop-and-go type games, e.g. when you hear a clap you must stop. These games are also good for children's listening and attention skills.

▶ Gross motor movements

Gross motor movements refer to whole limb movements such as throwing or kicking a ball. These movements are linked to children's balance and spatial awareness.

Climbing and crawling

Climbing and crawling require balance as well as sequencing and gross motor skills. The sequencing, in particular, is thought to help children's later acquisition of reading. Climbing and crawling also support children's spatial awareness.

What this means in practice

Look out for children who have passed directly from sitting to walking or who have 'bottom shuffled' or 'rolled'. These children may benefit from climbing and crawling activities. Here are some ways to create climbing and crawling opportunities:

- Play tunnels and tents for children to crawl through.
- Pretend games where children crawl as animals.
- Climbing and crawling over cushions and large foam blocks indoors.
- Crawling through and into large cardboard boxes that children can make into dens.
- Wooden tree trunks or crates that children can climb on and off.

Jumping

Jumping movements strengthen the legs and help children to gain spatial awareness. Children who find it hard to keep still often benefit from jumping movements before being expected to stay still. Note that some children appear to be fearless and will jump from heights that are unsafe. It is thought that some of these children are not gaining enough sensory information about where they are in relation to the ground. Increasing the amount of movements these children make is therefore useful, but close supervision will be essential.

What this means in practice

Learning to jump safely requires practice and children will go through stages as they learn to do this. At first children are likely to lead using one foot, and practising from a low step can work well for this. Other ways of supporting children include:

- Trampolining – children who are unsure can sit down on the trampoline while you gently bounce it to experience the sensation. They can then move to a crawling position before eventually standing and holding on to a bar.
- Hopscotch.
- Stepping from hoop to hoop.
- Jumping on large cushions.
- Jumping on giant bubble wrap.

Throwing and catching

Throwing and catching skills can help gross motor development and also teach children other skills such as judging speed, time and distance. Throwing is easier than catching, as catching requires the child to judge the speed of the oncoming object and continue to track it while also preparing and moving the hands. There is huge variation in when children can learn to catch and it is partly linked to opportunities and practice.

What this means in practice

The key to throwing and catching is to go at the child's pace and to build on his or her confidence. Vary the items that children throw and catch. Balloons, bean bags and knotted scarves are often easier for young children to manage. Look too at the size of the object that children are using; large, soft items can be easier to catch than smaller items. Here are some examples of throwing and catching activities that might be helpful:

- Roll the ball: sitting down, children roll a ball to you and then stop it when it comes back to them.
- Balloons in bags: put balloons in bags; this gives them a little more weight and makes them easier to aim and catch.
- Paper balls: encourage the child to scrunch up paper into a ball and throw it.
- Bubbles: blow bubbles into the air; can the children squash them?
- Passing games: pass the ball and gradually increase the distances.

▶ Fine motor movements

Hand movements are referred to as fine manipulative or motor skills. The development of fine manipulative skills is important as babies and children use their hands to explore their world and grasp things within their reach. Gaining control of their hands is also important for children, as many everyday tasks that make children independent of adults require the use of hands, for example dressing, toileting, pouring drinks, etc. As children get older, their fine manipulative skills become increasingly important as they are needed in order to write and manipulate tools such as scissors. Children who have poor fine manipulative control may avoid tasks where control is needed, and this can affect their learning and development.

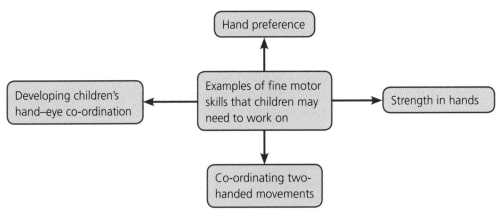

⌐Examples of fine motor skills that children may need to work on

Hand preference

Hand preference is biologically determined and by three years most children have a clear preference for using one hand for skilled movements. Older children who have not developed a hand preference are more likely to have difficulties with their fine motor movements and also in learning to read and write.

What this means in practice

While it is important to seek advice from educational psychologists and physiotherapists, the following suggestions might be helpful. Encourage plenty of two-handed activities where one hand is holding an object and the other carries out more skilled movements, e.g. holding a cup in one hand and putting beads into it with the other. Repeat the activities but vary the materials so that some pattern is established. In addition, here are some other suggestions that you might like to consider:

- Provide plenty of activities where children have to reach diagonally across, e.g. put a glue pot slightly off centre so that children have to reach to dip the spatula in.
- Observe carefully the way in which children use their hands. Do they consistently use the same hand for the same purposes? For example, sometimes a child may cut with the right hand but choose to draw with the left. In such cases, it is best not to interfere unless the child would be more accurate with the other hand.
- Consider pairing a child who shows slight left-hand preference with an adult who is left-handed. Sometimes children will awkwardly use their right hand because they are copying a right-handed adult.

Building strength in the hands

Children need to develop strength in their hands so that they can control them more easily. Many everyday tasks require a certain amount of strength, for example pulling on socks, opening screw-top lids or holding on to a rung of a climbing frame. The reasons why some children may not have sufficient strength in their hands can vary, and can include a child's previous reluctance to touch things.

This is a good example of an activity that can strengthen hand preference

What this means in practice

Building strength in children's hands must be done through play activities that children enjoy. This will help them to concentrate for longer periods and will also give them confidence. The key to successful activities is to gradually change one feature to make them slightly more challenging. Look out for activities that will encourage children to repeat movements, as the muscles in the hand are strengthened in the repetition. Here are some examples of activities that might increase hand strength.

- Put out a range of plastic bottles or containers with screw lids that have something inside that a child might want, e.g. a message or a small toy. Gradually tighten the lids so that more strength is required to open them.
- Look also for activities that encourage children to push or pull, e.g. pushing a wheelbarrow, pulling a wooden cart with bricks.
- You can also adapt sensory activities to support hand strength. A good example of this is to put a sponge and a measuring jug in the water tray. How much water can the child squeeze out of the sponge into the jug?

Co-ordinating two-handed movements

There are many activities that require children to use two hands at the same time, for example holding a toothbrush while putting toothpaste on to it or washing a plate with a sponge. Some of these activities can also support the strengthening of hand preference.

What this means in practice

Look for activities that are fun and that at first do not require a large degree of accuracy. Consider also the size of items, for example it is harder to glue a sequin on to a piece of paper than to glue a large bead. Here are some examples of movements that require both hands to work together:

- Dressing a large teddy or doll.
- Holding a mixing bowl and stirring the mixture.
- Making a sandcastle.
- Folding paper.
- Using a hole punch to make holes in paper.
- Using a stapler.
- Winding up a clockwork toy.
- Hanging up clothes using dolly pegs or a coat hanger.

Developing children's hand–eye co-ordination

Using the information from your eyes to inform hand movements is the basis of hand–eye co-ordination. There are a variety of reasons why children may have some delay in this skill, for example children who have a visual impairment that was previously undetected may have some delay in this area. Children will need some simple activities that encourage them to use their hands and eyes together.

What this means in practice

Begin with large objects and scale down as children become more skilled. As with other activities, children must feel that they are being successful and must enjoy what they are doing. Here are some activities that require hand–eye co-ordination:

- Threading beads, buttons or pasta tubes.
- Picking out seeds from a tray of rice.
- Catching bubbles.
- Jigsaw puzzles.
- Pouring drinks from a jug.

Helping children to use scissors

Learning to use scissors is a process. Children need to begin by having enough strength in their hands to manipulate the scissors and then need to be able to open and close them. The first movement that most children make is snipping. To help children gain satisfaction by being able to snip easily, it is worth beginning by putting out thin strips of dough or paper. Once the child is able to snip across, you can increase the width of the strips. It is important to remember that children need to be given paper that is slightly stiff, as thin paper is harder to cut. Most children will need plenty of practice before they are able to cut along lines or cut out circles. Begin by drawing lines on to patties of dough. Children can then cut across the dough. They can also make their own lines to follow. Introduce wavy lines and once children become more accurate, you can introduce circles. It is essential that children enjoy using the scissors, as the more they use them, the more skilled they will become. This means looking for materials that children will enjoy cutting and focusing on the feeling of cutting rather than the end product. Alternatives to putting out dough include using spaghetti or jelly.

Helping children's pencil grip

Children who are not holding their pencils in a 'lateral pencil grasp' are showing that their hands are not yet developed sufficiently. Many children who are trying to write will actually tense their bodies and their hands in order to gain control; this is reflected in their pencil grasps and their writing position. Instead of tracing and formal writing, they should be offered a range of activities that will strengthen their hands and help them to be more co-ordinated. A classic mistake, therefore, is to continue to make children practise handwriting when, in reality, children will benefit far more from going back a few steps and practising larger movements with their hands.

Early grasps usually seen at three years

Variety of pencil grasps

Grasps usually seen at around four and a half years

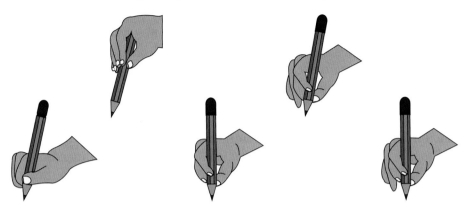

Mature grasps usually seen at six years

Variety of pencil grasps

What this means in practice

Children will need to master several skills before they are likely to attain a pencil grasp. In particular, their pincer grasp will need to be strengthened. This is the movement of the thumb and first finger. Activities that support pincer grasp include:

- Picking out sequins from a bowl of rice.
- Using tweezers to pick up dried chick peas and transfer them to another pot.
- Playing in water with pipettes.
- Picking up small pompoms and dropping them into a container.

They will also need to have plenty of opportunities to make marks using their hands and with a range of tools and implements. Activities that work for this include:

- Making patterns and shapes in wet sand.
- Painting and chalking on a large scale.
- Drawing shapes and patterns in gloop.
- Writing on a large whiteboard with a marker.
- Finger painting.
- Making marks and movements with fingers in shaving foam.

▶ Suggested activities

Activity 1 Obstacle course

Obstacle courses help children to plan their movements, as well as providing them with particular movements. Obstacle courses can be adapted in terms of complexity and so are very versatile.

Aim

To develop children's balance, perceptual skills and 'stomping' movements.

Resources

Plastic hoops, chalk.

Activity

This obstacle course can be done outdoors. Being outdoors can help children feel a sense of freedom.

Draw parallel lines with chalk on to the ground. These act as pathways for children to walk or run along. Lines can be made wide or narrow, depending on the level of skill of the children. The pathways are broken from time to time with hoops that the children have to 'stride into'.

Begin by showing children the obstacle course; you might consider doing it yourself with a teddy bear to show children what to do. Encourage children to go round the obstacle course.

Allow children to repeat the course as each practice will develop the fluency of their movements. Adjust the course if necessary to change the level of skill required.

Possible adaptations

- Make obstacle courses indoors and play music with a strong beat to encourage strong movements.
- Change the difficulty of the obstacle course by making the pathways more curved.
- Add in equipment that will encourage children to climb, such as cushions or beams.

Activity 2 Painting wall

Creating a painting wall can help in developing children's writing skills.

Aims

To develop children's grasp and arm movements using a sensory medium. To support children's two-handed movements. This activity will also help children to see a range of colours while helping with early letter formation.

Resources

Plastic sheeting, lining paper, masking tape, small tray, large paintbrushes, rollers, red, blue, yellow and white ready-mixed paint.

Activity

Begin by taping the sheets of plastic to a wall either outdoors or indoors. Tape a long strip of lining paper to the plastic. Put a squirt of each of the paint colours on to a small tray and provide large paintbrushes. Ask the children to take a brush, dip it into some paint and make circles. As children keep dipping into other colour paints, they will mix colours.

Possible adaptations

- Encourage children to make other marks, such as wavy lines, vertical strokes from top to bottom.
- Repeat the activity using crayons, markers and felt tips.
- Encourage children to produce large paintings.
- Use rollers instead of paint brushes.

Activity 3 Cutting dough with scissors

This sensory activity can be helpful for children who are tactile defensive as the cutting action is a 'firm' movement. This activity is especially useful for developing scissor skills and building the muscles in the hand. It works well because it does not focus children on an 'end product' and so children who normally avoid using scissors are more likely to spend time enjoying the feeling of cutting.

Aim

To develop children's grasp and arm movements using a sensory medium.

Resources

Left- and right-handed safety scissors, dough (a stretchy dough can be made by adding coloured water to self-raising flour and leaving it for a few hours).

Activity

Put out the dough and scissors on the table. Roll the dough into sausage shapes and begin to cut the dough. Most children will model the dough in the same way that they see adults do. Use this opportunity to talk and listen to the children. What are they pretending that they are cutting?

Possible adaptations

- Use different types of dough and adjust the stiffness of the dough. Provide plasticine for a more rigid feel.
- Provide cold cooked spaghetti for children to cut. Make dough patties and draw a line on them – can children cut along the line?

Activity 4 Squeeze and wash away the lines

This activity helps strengthen children's hands and also encourages them to make marks. It is a fun outdoor activity that does not have an end product.

Aims

To develop children's grasp and hand–eye co-ordination, and also to give them opportunities to make large marks.

Resources

Washing-up liquid bottle or container with a spray nozzle filled with water, jumbo chalks.

Activity

With the jumbo chalk, encourage a child to draw a line on to a wall. Show the children how they can squeeze water out of the bottle and aim it at the chalk line. Encourage children to make their own marks with the chalk and then erase them with water.

Possible adaptations

Use paintbrushes so that children paint with water to erase the line.

Activity 5 Thread and catch the keys

This activity helps children to track objects and also helps their hand–eye co-ordination. This activity can be played with more than one child.

Aims

To develop children's hand–eye co-ordination and also help them to track objects as they move.

Resources

A bunch of keys or other item that can be threaded and then moved along a long piece of string or cord, length of string or cord approximately 1–2 metres.

Activity

One end of the string or cord needs to be tied to a pole or attached to a wall at about 30 cm from the floor. Outdoors the string could be attached to a chain-link fence. The other end of the string is given to the child. Can he or she thread the bunch of keys on to it and then watch it as it travels along the string? As the child lowers or raises the string, the keys will move backwards or forwards.

Possible adaptions

- Look for other objects that can be threaded on to the cord or string.
- Play a game where one child threads the object and the other child has to try and catch it before it reaches the end of the string.

Activity 6 Flying birds

This activity helps children to track objects and also helps their hand–eye co-ordination. It encourages spatial awareness and gross motor movements.

Aims

To develop children's hand–eye co-ordination and also help them to track objects as they move. This activity also develops children's whole arm movements and spatial awareness.

Resources

Music for children to move to, a selection of square scarves.

Activity

Play the music and show children how to make their square scarf gently rise and fall. They might be able to do this in time with the music. Play a game with the children where they imagine that the scarf is a bird. Can they make their 'bird' fly up high, but also swoop down and around?

Possible adaptations

Play a game where one child tries to catch another child's bird. Encourage children to throw the scarves. Play games where you wear a tail (the scarf) and children have to run behind you and take the tail from you. Encourage children to make anti-clockwise and vertical downward movements with scarves. This will help them to get a feeling for letter shapes.

PART 3

Supporting children with specific needs

Part 3 is designed to give you some background information about the type of specific needs that some children may have. It has been written in response to requests from many practitioners for information about how to meet the needs of children with particular needs, disabilities or medical conditions. It has not been written as a tool for diagnosis. Concerns about children's development must be raised with parents so that a referral to a professional can be sought.

There is, of course, a danger in writing about specific needs, particularly medical conditions and disabilities, as the information given is generalised. As every child is unique, two children with the same 'diagnosis' are likely to have different responses, likes and dislikes. The aim here is to flag up some of the questions and issues that you may need to focus on in the setting to meet a child's needs. This part is also designed to help you consider further information that you may need from parents and the professionals who are supporting the child.

Part 3 is designed as a reference tool. It is arranged alphabetically and the information is presented using the following sections:

- Name of the specific need, disability or medical condition: an outline of the nature of the need, disability or medical condition.
- Incidence and diagnosis: a backdrop to the condition or impairment
- Health and development: a summary of the effects on children. Note that this is a generalised summary. You will need to talk further with parents and other professionals involved with the child.
- Information that we may need from parents and other professionals: questions to help you to find out more about how best to meet the child's needs.
- Key questions: use these to help you think about how your setting will adapt its practice to meet the child's needs.
- Some day-to-day questions: use these questions as a regular checklist and add to this list to help you remember the everyday needs of the child.
- Contact: the name, address and website of one or more leading support groups. Also ask parents and other professionals if they have additional information or contacts to help you better understand the child's needs.

Asthma

Asthma is a condition that affects breathing. During an asthma attack, the airways in the lungs tighten and become inflamed, making it difficult for air to pass through. Sometimes during an attack, excess mucus is produced by the body which again has the effect of narrowing the airways. While most asthma attacks leave a child struggling for breath and frightened, this medical condition can be life-threatening and so has to be taken seriously. Children with asthma are given medication in the form of inhalers.

▶ Incidence and diagnosis

According to the charity Asthma UK, 1 in 11 children in the UK is diagnosed with asthma. It is the most common long-term medical condition. It is usually diagnosed when a child shows some of the symptoms of asthma, which include wheezing, shortness of breath and coughing at night or after exercise.

▶ Health and development

Asthma does not cause any learning difficulties. It may impact on a child's physical development if it is not well managed or if a child loses confidence following an attack.

▶ Information that we may need from parents

- Does your child have an asthma action plan?
- What type of medication does your child have?
- How and when is the medication given?
- What are the known triggers?
- How do you manage the child's asthma at home?

▶ Getting it right for children

Medication for children with asthma is normally given using inhalers. There are two types of medication and they work in very different ways. It is important to understand the difference between them.

- **Relievers:** These are the 'emergency' medication and contain fast-acting drugs that can open the airways. They are normally in blue containers. Relievers should be used promptly when children first show signs of having an asthma attack or if they complain that is hard to breathe. Relievers can be life-saving and so should be accessible at all times. All adults in the setting (and preferably the child) should know where they are at all times.

- **Preventers:** These inhalers contain drugs that help the airways to become less sensitive to potential triggers and are usually taken daily. Children who need preventers usually take these at home. Children with mild asthma may not be prescribed a preventer.

Additional equipment used in the treatment of asthma

Many young children find it hard to use their inhalers properly and so inhalers are often attached to a gadget known as a spacer or volumatic. These are tube-like gadgets which allow children to breathe in the medication in more easily. They come with either a mouthpiece or a mask.

Children with asthma will need access to their 'reliever' inhalers

❱ Managing an asthma attack

At the first signs that a child is becoming breathless (look out for wheeziness and coughing), action needs to be taken to prevent a serious attack.

- Remain calm and reassuring, but react quickly.
- Encourage the child to find a comfortable position, sitting or standing but not lying down.
- Give the child their reliever and spacer, and if needed provide assistance to use it.
- One puff every 30–60 seconds (maximum of 10) until the symptoms improve.
- Talk to the child while monitoring the effect of the inhaler. If the child is getting worse or the inhaler is having little effect, call 999/112.
- Once the attack has finished, the child may still be slightly breathless and tired. They may also be frightened and shaken. It is important to reassure the child and acknowledge his or her feelings. Remember to record the attack and pass this information on to the parents at the end of the session.

▶ Removing triggers in the environment

To avoid children having asthma attacks, it is important to remove or limit as many triggers in the environment as possible.

Common asthma triggers

Trigger	Preventative action
Dust mite – thrives in dusty environments	Remove cushions with feathers in them. Put soft toys in the freezer for six hours before washing at 60°C. Wash all bedding at 60°C. Make sure that the setting is regularly damp dusted.
Air fresheners, scented products, aerosol/spray cleaners	Air fresheners and scented products such as pot pourri are known triggers and should not be used in settings. Aerosol and spray cleaners should not be used when children are around.
Fur	Find out if a child is allergic to cats, dogs or animal fur before exposing a child to them, e.g. visits to a petting zoo.
Straw and hay	Find out from parents whether these materials are triggers.
Mould	Have any damp walls or areas within the setting treated or sealed. Keep the setting ventilated to avoid mould caused by condensation.
Viral infections	Keep rooms well ventilated. Reinforce good personal hygiene.
Emotion	Maintain a calm, reassuring atmosphere. Recognise when a child is becoming upset and provide reassurance.
Physical activity	Plan physical activity so that children can rest or take it more slowly. Some children may need to take their time to adjust when going outdoors into cold air.

▶ Key questions

- Have parents brought in a reliever and spacer that is named?
- Have parents brought in an asthma action plan?
- Do all adults understand that the child has asthma?
- Does everyone know how the child may show signs of needing their reliever?
- Are there any triggers such as cuddly toys, feathers or chemicals in the environment?

❱ Some day-to-day questions

- How well is the child today?
- Is the child's inhaler accessible?
- What is the expiry date of the inhaler?
- Are activities planned to allow the child to pace him or herself?
- Is there good ventilation in the setting?
- Are the child's records accessible and emergency contact details up to date?

❱ Contact

Asthma UK

www.asthma.org.uk

Case study

Ashleigh came to us when he was two years old. He had just been diagnosed with asthma and his parents were understandably anxious. We asked if he had an asthma plan and also whether we could talk to the asthma nurse based at his GP's surgery. I think that being proactive in this way helped his parents to feel confident that we would be able to meet his needs. We also found it helpful as although we had had older children with asthma, talking to a specialist nurse gave us a better understanding of asthma and in particular the range of ways in which children might have an asthma attack. We also reviewed our environment and resources. This resulted in buying a better vacuum cleaner, reducing the number of cuddly toys and washing soft furnishings more often and at a higher temperature.

Ashleigh has two key persons as we operate a shift system. Both of them have up-to-date paediatric first-aid training. They also have learnt to read the signs that Ashleigh is becoming breathless and encourage him to use his blue reliever promptly. This means that so far, he has only had one asthma attack and that was quickly brought under control. It is great to see the way that Ashleigh comes into the nursery with a big smile on his face and also to hear from his parents that they no longer worry about him when they drop him off.

Attention deficit hyperactivity disorder

Attention deficit hyperactivity disorder (ADHD) was first recognised 100 years ago, but has only recently been more widely accepted by the medical community. Unfortunately, there are some professionals and members of the public who do not 'believe' that it is a condition, but it is a recognised condition. Children with this disorder find it difficult to sustain attention on any given activity, including play. They are easily distracted and fidgety. Children with ADHD have unusually high levels of impulsivity and activity. The exact cause of ADHD is not known but some researchers believe that it is linked to a difficulty in processing sensory information.

▶ Incidence and diagnosis

According to the Royal College of Psychiatry, it is thought to affect 3–5% of school-aged children, although accurate figures are hard to gauge. It appears to be more common in boys than girls and is also more common where a member of the child's family has similar traits. There is also a higher incidence in children who were premature, had a low birth weight or where there was smoking, alcohol or drug abuse during pregnancy.

Diagnosis in young children is not easy as impulsive behaviours are already common in young children, particularly between the ages of 2 and 3 years. In addition, children who are not sleeping sufficiently will also exhibit traits of hyperactivity. This means that few consultants will diagnose a child under five years with this condition, although on referral programmes to help parents manage behaviours will be offered. One of the striking features of children with ADHD is their persistent and sustained levels of activity and impulsivity. A child who is perfectly fine in one setting but not in another is likely to have emotional difficulties rather than ADHD

Treatment, once a diagnosis is made by a paediatrician, specialist psychiatrist or psychologist, follows the current guidelines as given by NICE (the National Institute for Health and Care Excellence). While drugs are sometimes prescribed for older children, they are not recommended for pre-school children. The first line of treatment is usually a parent training/education programme, as changing the environment or approach of the adult can moderate some of the behaviours shown by the child. In addition, some parents may also look for links between a child's diet and behaviours and they may be encouraged to keep a food diary to see if there is a link.

Health and development

ADHD is associated with difficulties in learning for a range of reasons.

Concentration

Children appear to lack concentration and may run around. As they find it hard to settle to an activity for any length of time, this makes it harder for them to acquire the skills and concepts that other children might acquire.

Social development

The difficulty in concentrating means that children may not stay in one place long enough to join and play a game. Other children can also be fearful of children who show apparently 'disruptive' behaviour. If the child is often being 'reprimanded', other children may decide to tell tales and scapegoat the child.

Emotional development

There is a danger that children with ADHD can become depressed and have low self-esteem. They may feel different from other children. They may see that their parents and other adults become frustrated with their behaviour and they may confuse this with not being liked or loved.

Information that we may need from parents

Many parents can feel worn out by their children and frustrated by professionals who often imply that this disorder has its roots in the parenting of the child. In young children, it is unlikely that a firm diagnosis has been made and so parents are likely to be working hard to get some support for their child. This means that working with parents and building a good relationship with them is very important. Parents need to feel that we are taking their needs and those of their child seriously. Positive parenting and consistency between home and setting will not eliminate ADHD, but it may help significantly. This is because realistic expectations and consistency seem to help young children. If parents have attended an education programme, it will also be important to find out what tips have worked and to try and replicate these in the setting.

Getting it right for the child

There is no single approach or way of helping children with ADHD, although it is essential that all adults remain positive and look for ways of acknowledging a child's efforts to show wanted behaviour. One of the key ways in which children can be helped is by maintaining a consistently calm environment. Many practitioners find that multi-sensory activities can help young children and that observing the child carefully can provide clues as to activities that might interest and 'hold' him or her. As children's concentration spans are limited, it is also important to consider this when planning an activity. Keep instructions short and have everything ready.

The following tips have found to be useful, although it is important to understand that strategies that are effective for one child might not work as well for another. Other professionals who work in your local area such as the educational psychologist may also provide you with other strategies.

- Create a calm atmosphere and react calmly to the child.
- Look for positive moments with the child and make sure that these are shared with the parents.
- Keep to strong routines and structures within the setting.
- Avoid situations where the child is kept waiting or hanging around – being still will be extremely difficult for them.
- Be flexible, e.g. can the child stand rather than sit?
- Make sure that activities are open ended and that a child can 'leave' them if his or her concentration wanes.
- Avoid confrontations and look for ways of making tasks, such as tidying, into games.
- Avoid long explanations; get your message across simply.
- Use visual cues and props rather than always relying on the spoken word.
- Provide frequent feedback as to how well the child is doing.
- Consider the use of stickers and other ways of visually giving children positive feedback, e.g. using a thumbs up sign.
- Consider looking at changing the layout to provide areas where the chid is less likely to be distracted.

▶ Key questions

- Who will be the child's key person?
- Does this adult have experience or training in working with ADHD?
- How will behaviour be managed to avoid stigmatising the child?
- How will positive aspects of the child's behaviour be identified and celebrated?
- How can the routine of the setting be adapted to ensure that the child is supervised and is engaged?

▶ Some day-to-day questions

- How well is the child today?
- How well did the child sleep?
- What sensory activities have been planned for the child?
- Are there any changes to the routine today? How will these be managed?
- What has the child achieved today that can be celebrated with the parent?

▶ Contact

There are several different organisations from which advice and information can be sought:

Royal College of Psychiatrists

www.rcpsych.ac.uk

Useful for fact sheets about ADHD.

ADDISS – the National Attention Deficit Disorder Information and Support Service

www.addiss.co.uk

ADHD Foundation

www.adhdfoundation.org.uk

HACSG – The Hyperactive Children's Support Group

www.hacsg.org.uk

This organisation focuses on dietary causes of ADHD, although these are not accepted universally by other experts and organisations.

Autism spectrum condition (autism and Asperger syndrome)

Autism spectrum condition or disorder is a life-long disability that affects children's ability to form relationships and communicate effectively with those around them. The condition also affects how children make sense of the world around them. Children may be over- or under-sensitive to sound, touch and taste. The term 'spectrum disorder' is used to reflect the many ways in and degrees to which the condition can affect children.

▶ Incidence and diagnosis

The exact incidence of autism among children is not at present known, but current estimates put it at around 1 in 100. The cause of autism is not completely known, but there appears to be some genetic disposition, with more boys being affected than girls. Diagnosis does not currently take place until a child is at least two years old and often much later, especially if the signs are subtle, as there are many reasons why social and communication development may be delayed in children. Increased awareness of Asperger syndrome has in some cases led to adults realising that they have this condition.

▶ Health and development

The extent to which children are affected by autism varies enormously. This means that you will need to get to know the child and seek information from parents and other professionals about how best to support the child's needs. There are three main areas that children with autism, including Asperger syndrome, find difficult. These are sometimes known as the 'triad of impairments':

- social interaction
- social communication
- social imagination.

Social interaction

Most children, once they have reached the age of three years, are able to play alongside and with other children. They notice the reaction on others' faces and use this information to adjust their behaviour accordingly. It is thought that children with autism spectrum conditions have difficulty in recognising and interpreting others' reactions and faces. This means that social interaction is difficult for children with autism. In cases where a child is severely affected, he or she may not be interested in playing with other children at all; children with Asperger syndrome may wish to join in but do not always show appropriate behaviour, for example they may hug another child, but not for any particular reason.

Social communication

Language is used for a variety of purposes, but it is also an important tool to communicate with others. Children with autism may find it hard to use language to socialise and are limited in their interpretation and use of non-verbal cues such as facial expression and gestures. The amount of language and communication used by children with autism spectrum conditions varies, with some children finding it difficult to communicate at all, while others may have a good vocabulary but talk inappropriately and find it hard to listen to and think about what others are saying. Children may also repeat phrases that they have heard over and over again, although they are not being used meaningfully. This is known as echolalia and while this is a part of normal language development in children up until two and a half years, it is sometimes a clue that a child may have difficulties. Many children also have difficulty in expressing their feelings and getting their needs met.

Social imagination

Being able to imagine what someone else is thinking and to understand why someone has decided to do something is very significant. It allows us to make sense of what others do and what other people might be thinking. Without this ability, the world and other people can seem a frightening place. Children with autism have varying levels of difficulty with this skill. Limitations of imagination can mean that children who have some language will also take things literally and so phrases such as 'it's raining cats and dogs' will be taken to mean that there really are cats and dogs falling out of the sky. Imagination is also important in play and the usual pattern of development means that most children from three years start to use pretend play. This type of play can be enriching and a way for children to make sense of the world, but this is difficult for children with autism as pretending requires imagination. Changes in routine are also difficult for children with autism as they find it hard to understand and predict what is going to happen next.

▶ Sensitivity

The way that children respond to sensory information can vary. Some children are hypersensitive and will react badly to noise, light and tactile experiences. Something such as playing in sand can cause great distress and so it is important to find out from parents whether a child is hypersensitive. On the other hand, other children can be under-sensitive and so it is important not to make assumptions before getting to know a child. Some children with autism also continue to put objects in their mouths beyond the typical age (usually 18 months). It is important to know if this is the case as it may affect what can be safely put out for the child.

▶ Information that we may need from parents

- How do you communicate with your child?
- What strategies do you find helpful to manage your child's condition and meet your child's needs?
- Is your child hypersensitive and what experiences do they find difficult?
- Does your child mouth objects?
- What situations does the child find particularly difficult?
- What play does the child enjoy?
- Is the child receiving support from the speech and language team?
- Are there any other professionals involved in meeting the child's needs?

▶ Getting it right for the child

No two children who have been diagnosed with autism will have the same needs. This means that your first step is to get to know the child and their strengths as well as their areas of need. Parents should be helpful in this respect as they will usually have found out using a trial-and-error approach what works best for their child. Some parents may also be trying out one of the many programmes designed to help children with autism and so you may need to follow the programme in the setting.

A key person who is sensitive to the needs of the child is essential and in a group care setting, where there may be a need for co-key workers, it will be important for a routine to be established. As well as meeting the child's needs for security and understanding, the key person will also need to play a role in keeping the child safe. Children with autism do not always understand possible dangers, even if they have been warned. They may also try physically escaping if they are unsettled or distressed. The key person will be needed to help structure situations so that the child with autism can play with or alongside other children. The key person should also work with the parents and other professionals to look at strategies to support social communication. This might mean using Makaton or an augmentative communication system such as the picture exchange communication system (PECS).

For many children settling in to a setting will be difficult. Adults will need to be sensitive to this and to work carefully with parents to find ways to help children make the adjustment (see page 104).

Communication strategies to help children with autism

The following strategies are often used to aid communication, although how well they will work will depend on the individual child.

- Use the child's name at the start of the sentence so that the child knows that you are addressing them.
- Use simple language, short sentences and keep words to a minimum, e.g. 'Harry, coat on.'
- Do not use idiomatic expressions or jokes, e.g. 'laughing his head off' or 'things are up and down at the moment'.
- Use objects, pictures or symbols to help children understand instructions.
- Consider using visual timetables so that children know what is going to happen next.

Choosing toys and play activities

Children with autism may find it hard to choose what to play with and may not play in ways that are typical. Repetitive play actions are typical and children may become upset if another child interferes with their play cycle, e.g. lining up several cars or bouncing ten times on a trampoline. It will be important to talk to parents about their child's interests and what they enjoy using. It will also be helpful if, over time, the range of toys and resources that a child can use is expanded in order that more skills and concepts can be learnt. Children may also need to be shown what to do and how to use a toy or resource. Examples of resources that are often popular include:

- construction toys, including Lego
- jigsaws
- bubbles
- jack-in-the-box or other pop-up types of toys
- books that have flaps or touch buttons
- physical activities that allow for repetition, e.g. bouncing on a trampoline, rocking horse.

As children with autistic spectrum conditions find it hard to play with other children, it can be helpful to look for group activities that can form part of a routine, e.g. a song that is sung at the start of the session or rhyme time. Music sessions can work well, but may be distressing for children who are hypersensitive as other children may make loud and sudden noises.

▶ Key questions

- Who will act as the child's key person?
- Do all the adults recognise the needs of a child with autism?
- How will the safety of the child be supported?
- What does the child enjoy doing and how will this be built on?
- Is there a communication and language programme that can be followed?

▶ Some day-to-day questions

- Are there any changes to routines or staffing that may create difficulties for the child?
- Are resources and toys suitable and safe for the child?
- Are activities structured to allow the child to interact with other children with supervision?

▶ Contact

The National Autistic Society

www.nas.org.uk

A good source of information, resources and training.

Cerebral palsy

Children with cerebral palsy have difficulties controlling their movements and muscles as a result of an injury to the brain before, during or after birth. There are several reasons why the brain may be injured, including lack of oxygen during the birthing process, maternal infection in the first weeks of a pregnancy and atypical brain development. There are three main types of cerebral palsy, with some children having a combination of two or more.

- **Spastic cerebral palsy**: This form of cerebral palsy creates stiffness in the muscles which in turn decreases the amount of movement that is available. The tightness of the muscles means that it can be a painful condition with muscles going into spasm. This is the most common form of cerebral palsy and can affect different areas of the body.
- **Dyskinetic cerebral palsy**: This form of cerebral palsy is also referred to as dystonic, athetoid or choreoathetoid cerebral palsy. This form creates jerky, irregular movements because muscles rapidly contract and relax, going from tense to floppy. Children may be unable to control their movements and may find it difficult to maintain an upright position. Speech can also be affected because of the difficulty in controlling tongue and breathing movements.
- **Ataxic cerebral palsy**: This form of cerebral palsy causes difficulty in maintaining, balancing and judging spatial awareness. Hand movements and speech can also be affected, although most children with just this form of cerebral palsy are likely to be mobile.

Note: The term 'spastic' is no longer used to describe individuals with cerebral palsy and is considered to be deeply offensive.

▶ Incidence and diagnosis

It is thought that 1 in 400 children will have some form of cerebral palsy. Some children will be diagnosed at birth, while others will be diagnosed during their first year as their motor development will not be progressing at a typical rate.

▶ Health and development

The extent to which a child may be affected by cerebral palsy can vary enormously, with some children having only slight indications of cerebral palsy. While children with cerebral palsy may have difficulties with motor co-ordination and speech, it is important not to assume that they will have learning difficulties. The huge variance between children means that it is essential to gain information about the child from the parents and other professionals involved with the family.

Children's physical development will be affected, with many children requiring mobility aids such as standing frames, walking aids and wheelchairs. Gross and fine motor control are affected to varying degrees.

Spatial awareness

Some children will struggle with spatial awareness. This can be very frustrating for them as they may be able to reach out to grasp a cup, but miss it slightly and knock it over.

Touch

Some children's sense of touch will be affected. This means that some sensations can be unpleasant or distressing. Close observations of a child's reaction when introducing sensory play materials such as sand will be essential.

Communication

Some children's speech and language will be affected and they will usually be supported by speech and language therapists. You will need to find out how to support this work. It is common for augmentative methods of communication to be used (see page 131).

Toilet training

This can be difficult for many children with cerebral palsy because of the difficulty in controlling the relevant muscles and so it may be delayed or difficult to achieve. Constipation can also be a problem and so monitoring and sharing information about bowel movements with parents will be important.

Feeding

Some children can have difficulty in feeding as the muscles in the throat and mouth can be affected. Advice as to how to help with feeding should be sought from parents and also other professionals working with the child. Children are usually supported by speech and language therapists, occupational therapists and physiotherapists, as feeding is a complex process involving swallowing as well as movement. It is likely that many children will need additional time and support in order to feed and they may be messy. It is important though that children are given as many opportunities as possible to be independent.

Other needs

Some children with cerebral palsy may also have other needs that must also be taken into consideration when supporting them. These may include:

- epilepsy (see page 248)
- hearing impairment (see page 239)
- visual impairment (see page 268).

▶ Information that we may need from parents

As no two children will have the same needs, it is essential to gain as much information as possible from parents. Be ready also to ask parents to demonstrate how they manage the care needs of their child.

- What does your child enjoy doing at home?
- Is there anything that makes your child frustrated?
- What mobility needs does your child have?
- What care needs does your child have, e.g. toileting, feeding?
- How do you manage these needs at home and what equipment do you find helpful?
- Is the child receiving any physiotherapy and is there a programme that should be followed?
- Is the child receiving any speech and language support, and if so how can this be supported in the setting?
- Does your child have a hearing or visual impairment?
- Does your child take any medication that needs administering in the setting?
- Are there any professionals who work with your child whom we should be in contact with?

▶ Getting it right for the child

Cerebral palsy affects children in so many different ways that it is essential to learn as much as possible about the individual child. This information should come from parents and also from other professionals who support the child and their family.

Once information is available, it is essential for everyone to consider how to include the child in the day-to-day activities of the setting. A good deal of flexibility and creativity are often needed and this may include the use of technology.

Empowering the child by encouraging him or her to make choices and to be independent is essential as it is not uncommon for adults to 'take over' and 'baby' a child.

▶ Key questions

- Who will liaise directly with the parents and other professionals?
- Who will act as the child's key person?
- What resources and equipment do parents and occupational therapists recommend?
- Do members of staff need lifting and handling training?
- Do members of staff need to learn how to support the child at mealtimes?
- Do staff know how to keep the child physically comfortable?
- Does the environment need to be altered to allow access?

▶ Some day-to-day questions

- How well has the child slept?
- Are the necessary resources and equipment available?
- How is the environment organised to allow access?
- Is information being shared with parents at the end of the session about the child's involvement in the session and how their care needs have been met?

▶ Contact

Scope

www.scope.org.uk

Coeliac disease

Coeliac disease is an auto-immune condition. When a substance called gluten is taken into the body, it triggers the immune system into attacking healthy tissue in the lining of the intestine. This results in the body not being able to absorb the nutrients in the food such as vitamins, iron and calcium. This can leave children malnourished and lacking in energy.

Gluten is found in three cereals that are often used in making food: wheat, rye and barley. This means that common foods such as bread, cakes and pasta cannot be eaten unless they are made with gluten-free flour.

▶ Incidence and diagnosis

Coeliac disease was once thought to be rare, but now it has been realised that it is more common than previously thought. It is now thought to affect 1 in 100 people, with many adults now being diagnosed with the condition. Symptoms in childhood include failure to thrive, weight loss, frequent episodes of diarrhoea, vomiting and tiredness. The tiredness is normally a result of anaemia (lack of iron). A blood test is normally carried out followed by a biopsy to confirm the diagnosis. Once a child has been diagnosed, a gluten-free diet must be followed.

▶ Health and development

Once a child is diagnosed and is on a gluten-free diet, there should be no effects on the child's health and development. It is important that steps are taken to make sure they do not feel isolated or different because of this condition.

▶ Information that we may need from parents

- Do you have recipes, products or a diet sheet that we could use?
- Would you prefer to bring in food for your child?
- Are there immediate signs that your child has inadvertently ingested gluten?

▶ Getting it right for the child

Children must be given food that is gluten-free. It is important that all adults in the setting understand the severity of this condition. It is not an allergy, an intolerance or a food fad! It is important therefore to put into place careful steps to prevent the child coming into contact with gluten. This means good supervision at meal and snack times and also recognising that play dough made with ordinary wheat flour will not be suitable. A recipe for gluten-free play dough is given here.

Gluten-free play dough

- 230g (8oz) of rice flour
- 230g (8oz) corn flour
- 230g (8oz) salt
- 4 teaspoons cream of tartar
- 2 cups (500 ml) water
- 2 tablespoons vegetable oil
- Food colouring

Method

1 Place all ingredients in a saucepan.
2 Cook over a low heat for about five minutes, stirring all the time. The mixture is very runny to start with but will gradually thicken.
3 Remove from the heat and knead on a hard surface to remove any lumps.
4 Roll into a large ball and store in an airtight tub. It keeps for several months.
Reproduced with kind permission of Coeliac UK.

Wall charts help keep everyone aware of dietary needs

As well as ensuring that the child avoids gluten, it is also important that children are not made to feel different. This may mean altering foods that are served at snack time so that the child does not have to eat different snacks all the time, e.g. rice cakes rather than crackers. It will also be important in day care where a cook is employed that they have had sufficient nutritional training to make sure that the child has a balanced diet.

❱ Key questions

- Is everyone in the setting aware that this child has coeliac disease?
- What steps are taken in the kitchen to prevent contamination when foods with gluten are being prepared, e.g. separate boards, containers?
- What strategies will be used to prevent the child being given food containing gluten, e.g. coloured plate, photo in the kitchen?
- Who will act as the child's key person and liaise with parents regarding food and other requirements?
- How can the meals and snacks of the setting be altered so that the child's dietary needs can be integrated?

❱ Some day-to-day questions

- Has the child brought in their own food and snacks? If so, where are these going to be stored?
- Are planned cooking activities involving children gluten-free?
- Is the play dough gluten-free and so safe for the child to use?
- Are any other parents bringing in food today, e.g. birthday cakes?

❱ Contact

Coeliac UK

www.coeliac.org.uk

Cystic fibrosis

Cystic fibrosis is an inherited condition in which abnormally thick mucus is produced by the body. This creates difficulty with lung function and with digestion. Medical advances have significantly prolonged children's lives over the years, but they still need frequent medical treatment and daily physiotherapy.

▶ Incidence and diagnosis

Cystic fibrosis (CF) is a genetically inherited disease. Children will only have the condition if both of their parents are carriers of the gene. It is estimated that 1 in 25 adults will be carriers and that around 1 in 25,000 newborns will have the condition. Diagnosis can occur shortly after birth if the baby's pancreas has already been blocked by mucus, otherwise failure to put on weight and/or frequent bouts of coughing and vomiting may be noticed. Confirmation of the condition usually follows a 'sweat test' in which the amount of chloride in a baby's sweat is measured.

▶ Health and development

The condition does not affect children's capacity to learn, but repeated absences due to infections and the physical toll that this condition has on children can affect their opportunities to play and learn.

Lung infections

Children with CF are prone to repeated lung infections that can damage the lungs and create difficulties in breathing. Daily physiotherapy is used to help loosen the mucus in the lungs, which the child then coughs up. Young children are also taught to control their breathing to maximise their lung function. As well as regular physiotherapy, children take antibiotics to fight off infections.

Difficulties with digestion

The abnormally thick mucus that is produced as part of this condition prevents insulin produced by the pancreas from working effectively and the body lacks enzymes that are used to process and break down food. Replacement enzymes are therefore given to children before each meal.

Growth

Many children with CF are underweight and have delayed growth. This is caused by the body's difficulties in absorbing food properly, added to the strain of repeated infections.

▶ Information that we may need from parents

- What physiotherapy does your child require during the session?
- How would you like this to take place?
- What are the signs in your child that he or she may be unwell?
- What would you like us to do if we suspect that your child is poorly?
- What nutritional requirements does your child have?
- What types of food and snack does your child enjoy?
- What type of medication does your child need?
- How does your child feel about CF?
- What activities does your child enjoy?

▶ Getting it right for the child

It will be essential for staff to work closely with parents and also to listen to and observe the child. Children may not feeling like joining in some activities if they are feeling tired or may want to engage in play that is comforting and repetitive. Early signs that a child is poorly and is fighting infection must be taken seriously. It will also be important for parents to be aware of the amount of food that the child has had in the day.

Meal and snack times

Making sure that children gain sufficient nutrition is essential. All foods provided should be nutrient-rich and high in protein to make sure that the child will gain enough calories, vitamins and protein. It is also important for children to have regular snacks and drinks. As with other food-related or digestive conditions, it is important to avoid making the child feel different. Children will also need to have replacement enzymes to take before snack and meal times. It is essential that a member of staff takes on responsibility for this.

Preventing infections

It will be essential to have good hygiene routines in the setting to avoid cross-infection. Children will need to be reminded to wash their hands frequently and good ventilation will be important. Where another child is showing early signs of being poorly, it will be important for the child with CF to be kept away to reduce the risk of them picking up an infection. Measures such as those required for children with asthma (see page 200) should also be put in place. One way to cut the risk of infections, particularly airborne viruses, is for children to spend time outdoors.

Coughing

One effect of the constant mucus production is frequent coughing. Children are encouraged to spit out the mucus as soon as they are able rather than to swallow it. This means that a ready supply of tissues should be with the child and that adults in the setting should understand that coughing is part of the condition.

Physiotherapy

For children who spend long periods in the setting, physiotherapy may be required during the day. Parents and professionals should be able to show the techniques involved, which are carried out to loosen the mucus in the lung to allow the child to cough it up more easily.

Emotional needs

As well as getting the physical care needs right for the child, children will also need to be given emotional security and opportunities to play and develop. While this is potentially a life-threatening condition, children still need enough freedom and play in order to develop and fulfil their potential. This means encouraging children to enjoy being outside and joining in physical activities at their own pace. Repeated absences will mean that good settling in and the key person relationship are essential so that children can quickly pick up from where they left off. Role play can also help the child to express their feelings and so it may be helpful to create hospitals and homes in the role-play area.

Some children can also be aware that they are growing at a slower rate than their peers. This means that activities such as measuring each other's height may not be appropriate.

▶ Key questions

- Who will be the child's key person?
- Who will liaise with parents regarding physiotherapy, amounts of food that the child has eaten, etc.?
- Is everyone in the setting aware of the effects of this condition?
- Where will any medication be stored?
- Who will be responsible for giving the child their medication?
- Who will ensure that the child is eating snacks and meals?
- How will the risk of cross-infection be managed in the setting?
- Is there a quiet area where the child can nap or have physiotherapy if required?
- Are emergency contact details for the child easily accessible?

▶ Some day-to-day questions

- Has the child brought in his or her medication?
- How well does the child seem?
- Does the child need to rest more today?
- Has the child been eating well?

▶ Contact

Cystic Fibrosis Trust

www.cysticfibrosis.org.uk

Diabetes

Diabetes is a serious and potentially life-threatening condition in which the body is unable to regulate the amount of glucose in the bloodstream. Glucose from the food that we eat is vital as it powers the cells in our bodies. Glucose is helped to enter the bloodstream by a hormone called insulin, which is manufactured by the pancreas. Diabetes is caused when the pancreas produces either no insulin or insufficient quantities. Symptoms of diabetes include thirst, frequent urination, weight loss and extreme tiredness. There are two types of diabetes.

- **Type 1 insulin dependent diabetes** – this is the type of diabetes that young children are most likely to have. It is not linked to obesity or lifestyle and is thought most likely to be genetic in cause. This type of diabetes is controlled by regular insulin injections as well as through diet. The amount of insulin needed is determined by a blood test before each meal. As children get older they are encouraged to monitor their own blood and to self-inject. This helps them to take responsibility for managing their diabetes.
- **Type 2 non-insulin dependent diabetes** – this is the type of diabetes that used to be associated with older people, but is becoming more common among primary and secondary school-aged children. Unlike Type 1 diabetes, the pancreas is still producing insulin, but it may not be sufficient. This type of diabetes can usually be managed by diet alone.

The four Ts

Type 1 diabetes can develop very rapidly and so as well as supporting children who have the diagnosis, it is also important to look out for the signs of diabetes in other children. A campaign by Diabetes UK is helpful in looking out for the symptoms of possible diabetes. It is known as the 'four Ts':
- **Toilet:** Going to the toilet a lot, bed wetting by a previously dry child or heavier nappies in babies.
- **Thirsty:** Being really thirsty and not being able to quench the thirst.
- **Tired:** Feeling more tired than usual.
- **Thinner:** Losing weight or looking thinner than usual.

▶ Incidence and diagnosis

The UK has a high incidence of Type 1 diabetes, with Diabetes UK suggesting that 24.5 per 100,000 children aged 0–14 are diagnosed with it each year. Once a child is suspected of having diabetes, a simple urine or blood test will be carried out to diagnose its presence.

▶ Health and development

Diabetes should not in itself cause any learning difficulties although children may need emotional support. When diabetes is properly controlled, it should not cause any additional health problems for children, but at times it can be hard to control.

Meal and snack times

It is important that children with Type 1 diabetes eat regularly so that the body does not lack glucose. This means that children will usually need snacks and small meals. Diet is important for children with diabetes and it is important to follow the dietary guidelines that will have been given to the family. There are likely to be clear guidelines as to the amount of carbohydrate a child can have, including foods such as pasta and bread, as well as sugary foods.

Hypoglycaemia

Children with diabetes develop hypoglycaemia when the level of glucose in their blood is too low. It can cause unconsciousness if not acted upon. Hypoglycaemia can occur rapidly and can be frightening for the child and other children. There are many reasons why a child may have hypoglycaemia but common causes include:

- Lack of food – the child may not have eaten sufficiently or may be late having a meal.
- Insulin dosage – the dosage of insulin may not have been correct.
- Additional demands on the body – vigorous exercise such as swimming or running may cause the body to metabolise glucose more quickly, thus creating a shortfall.

Signs that a child has hypoglycaemia include the following:

- sudden or gradual lack of colour
- irritability, anxiety or confusion
- tiredness and lethargy
- hunger
- shakiness
- sweating
- unconsciousness.

Treatment is simple as the child needs to take in fast-acting carbohydrate, such as a sugary drink, sweets or glucose tablets. If the child has become unconscious, an ambulance needs to be called as intravenous glucose may be required. Once the child is feeling better, he or she will need to eat some slower-acting carbohydrates such as a banana, sandwich or pasta. Parents must be informed that a child has been hypoglycaemic, even if it has been detected quickly, so that they can monitor the insulin levels more closely or if necessary seek professional help.

Hyperglycaemia

This sounds similar to hypoglycaemia, but is the direct opposite. Hyperglycaemia occurs when children's glucose levels are too high. While the condition should not be left untreated for long periods, its short-term effects are less severe than when there is insufficient glucose. Hyperglycaemia often occurs when children have colds, flu or are feeling unwell. The body's metabolism changes in these situations and this means that the usual dose of insulin needs to be changed. Some of the symptoms, such as tiredness or irritability, are the same as for hypoglycaemia but the key difference tends to be the slower onset, although this may not be sufficient a sign for you to detect the difference. As the signs are similar but the consequences of hypoglycaemia can be more dangerous, it is thought best to err on the side of caution and take steps as if the child has hypoglycaemia.

▶ Information that we may need from parents

- What type of diabetes does your child have?
- How is the diabetes managed?
- How does your child cope at home with diabetes?
- What are the signs that your child is hypoglycaemic? (This is very important to ask as signs can vary from child to child.)
- What are the dietary needs of your child, e.g. snack times, frequency and timing of snacks?
- Do you wish to bring in your own food/snacks for your child?
- What type of food should we keep in stock in case your child needs a snack or meal?
- Are there any foods that should be given to your child and what should be avoided?
- What would you like us to do if your child refuses food or snacks?
- What type of information about your child's food and drink intake would you like us to record?
- Will your child need his or her glucose level monitoring during the session?
- Will your child need an insulin injection while he or she is with us?

Most children's insulin levels are monitored and controlled by parents at home. However, if there is a need for children to have an insulin injection while in the setting or to have their glucose level checked, it will be essential for parents or other professionals to train staff. If children are to eat food and snacks provided by the setting, it is also essential that parents advise the setting as to the quantity as well as the type of foods that are suitable.

◗ Getting it right for the child

It is essential that everyone working with a young child who has diabetes be observant and listen to the child. They must understand what they should do if the child is becoming hypoglycaemic. Avoiding hypoglycaemia is essential as not only is this frightening for the child and their parents, it may also have longer term effects on the child's health.

For children with Type 1 diabetes, the dosage of insulin in relation to food often depends on the type of activity that a child has done and will be doing. To help parents adjust dosages, it is important to let them know what the child has been doing, as well as any vigorous physical activities that might be planned, such as swimming, outings or long walks. Parents will also need to know if the child has eaten less than usual as this will affect the amount of insulin that is required later in the day.

As well as making sure that the child's physical needs are met, it is also important that children feel good about themselves. Children with diabetes can feel very 'different' and so in group care settings, it is a good idea to think about using a rolling snack method so that children can serve themselves when needed, or having several snack and meal sittings.

Finally, it is also important that staff think about cooking activities and any parties that involve food as children with diabetes may be unwittingly excluded. Plan cooking activities and parties in a way that will allow the child to make or eat the foods that he or she needs.

◗ Key questions

- Is everyone in the setting aware that this child has diabetes? (A photo of the child with a note in the kitchen to remind staff that a child has diabetes can be a useful strategy and is often reassuring for parents.)
- Does everyone understand the dietary needs of the child?
- Are staff aware of the importance of regular food and snacks for this child?
- How will food and drink intake be monitored and recorded?
- Does everyone know the signs for this child that he or she is becoming hypoglycaemic?
- Who will act as the child's key person and will liaise with parents regarding food and other requirements?
- Are emergency contact details easily accessible?
- What system will be in place to alert parents to changes in the normal routine or activity level which might affect the child's energy requirements?

▶ Some day-to-day questions

- How well is the child looking?
- Will the child be engaging in any vigorous physical activity that requires extra energy?
- Has the child brought in food or snacks?
- Does everyone know what time the child needs snacks, drinks and food?
- Who will be letting parents know about the child's food and drink intake over the day?

▶ Contact

Diabetes UK

www.diabetes.org.uk

Down's syndrome

Down's syndrome is a genetic condition caused by the presence of extra genetic material. There are three types of Down's syndrome, although by far the commonest type is Standard Trisomy 21 in which a child has an extra copy of chromosome 21. The extra genetic material causes a range of characteristics that were first documented in 1866, although not linked to DNA until 1956. These include specific physical characteristics as well as learning difficulties and some medical conditions. While children may share some of the characteristics associated with Down's syndrome, it is important to stress the wide variance between children and so getting to know individual children and their strengths and weaknesses is essential.

▶ Incidence and diagnosis

Down's syndrome affects about 1 in 1,000 children. It is not yet understood why an extra copy of chromosome 21 sometimes occurs. The condition is either diagnosed at birth by the presence of several physical characteristics, including facial shape and poor muscle tone, or prenatally as there is now a widespread screening programme.

▶ Development and health

All children with Down's syndrome will have some form of learning difficulty, although the extent will vary enormously. Many children will find the processing of information difficult and may also find concentrating on tasks hard. Communication and language are often delayed and some children may need to use Makaton or a picture exchange system to help them to communicate. Progress is made at the child's own pace although stimulation and a supportive environment are essential.

Fine and gross motor development

Many children with Down's syndrome will be slower to gain physical skills than their peers. They are likely to have poor muscle tone and this is likely to mean that they are slower to become mobile and develop the same level of strength as other children of their age. It will be important to bear this in mind when providing activities and resources, e.g. toys that can be handled more easily.

Hearing loss

Many children with Down's syndrome will have some form of hearing loss. Around 20 per cent will have permanent loss known as sensorineural hearing loss. A higher number of children are prone to temporary conductive hearing loss as a result of physical differences to the inner ear that are exacerbated by colds, infections and a higher than average production of ear wax. This means that children may not always be able to fully hear, which in turn affects their language development. The type of hearing loss can fluctuate and so children on some days may have better hearing than on others. This means that adults need to be aware of whether or not a child is hearing properly and if necessary to adapt the activity accordingly. It is also important that ear infections are detected as early as possible and so signs that a child is in pain or is rubbing his or her ears need to be taken seriously. (For strategies to help children with hearing impairment, see page 239.)

Vision impairment

Many children with Down's syndrome may have some form of vision impairment, including squints, long- and short-sightedness. These are usually corrected by the wearing of glasses and so checking that a child has his or her glasses is important. As learning by watching is a key strategy by which we can help children to learn, it is particularly important to monitor how well children are seeing. This is especially the case for those children who have not been prescribed glasses and whose vision may change. (For strategies to help children with vision impairment, see page 268.)

Heart problems

A third of children with Down's syndrome have some form of heart condition, although the severity ranges enormously, with some babies requiring surgery early on in their lives. It is a good idea to work with parents in order to modify activities to make them appropriate for children who are affected by heart problems.

Respiratory and other infections

Many children with Down's syndrome are prone to chest and other infections. These are usually treated with antibiotics but may result in the child being frequently absent. Good hygiene routines in the setting are very important so as to avoid unnecessary cross-infections. It is also important for staff to look out for signs that a child is unwell and then to contact the parents.

▶ Information that we may need from parents

- What type of activities does the child enjoy at home?
- What situations are difficult for your child?
- What communication methods do you use with your child?
- How well can the child adapt to changes in routine?

- Does the child wear glasses or have any visual impairment?
- Does the child have a hearing impairment or are they prone to temporary hearing loss because of ear infections and/or glue ear?
- Does the child have any medication that should be given or held by staff?
- In cases where the child has a heart condition, are there any activities that should be avoided or adapted?
- Are there any particular signs that we should be aware of that may indicate that the child is unwell?
- What stage of toileting has your child reached?

Getting it right for the child

Remember that children with Down's syndrome develop and learn in much the same way as other children, although their progress is likely to be slower. Walking, toileting and talking will often be later than for most other children. No two children with this syndrome will share exactly the same characteristics, of course, or have the same personality! This means that it will be important to assess each child's stage of development when providing activities and resources, rather than to consider the child's chronological age. A good example of this is concentration levels. Many children will find it hard to concentrate and may become easily distracted. They may also find it hard to process information. This means that it will also be important to repeat activities where a child has enjoyed them as reinforcement and practice will be a key way in which concepts and other skills will be learnt by the child.

Many children with Down's syndrome are likely to have language needs and it will be important to find out how to support their communication and language from parents and also from the speech and language therapist who may be supporting the child.

In terms of children's emotional development, it is important to consider how the setting will help the child if he or she has frequent absences due to illnesses. Such absences can lead to the child showing separation anxiety when he or she returns, unless the child has a strong attachment to their key person and during the absence has been able to stay in contact in some way. This can mean the key person sending the child a postcard or an email with a photograph so that the child can maintain the relationship. It may also mean that the child will benefit from flexible arrangements such as returning at first for only half of a session.

Key questions

- Who will act as the child's key person?
- How will we help this child to settle in?

- Who will be responsible for any medication and where will this be kept?
- What communication needs does this child have?
- Do we have toys and resources that are appropriate for this child's level of motor and cognitive development?
- Are we planning activities to suit this child's stage of development?
- How can we encourage this child to develop self-help skills?
- Are the hygiene measures taken in the setting sufficient to eliminate the risk of unnecessary infections?

▶ Some day-to-day questions

- Is the child looking well today?
- Does the child need any medication?
- How well is the child hearing today?
- If needed, has the child brought his or her glasses into the setting?
- Are the other children 'mothering' this child and preventing him or her from becoming self-sufficient and developing self-help skills?
- Are there stimulating play activities and experiences that are right for this child?
- Are we remembering this child's stage of development when dealing with any unwanted behaviour?
- Are we using a visual timetable to help the child understand what will be happening today?

▶ Contact

Down's Syndrome Association

www.downs-syndrome.org.uk

Duchenne muscular dystrophy

There are 20 known types of muscular dystrophy, with Duchenne being the most common in children. Muscular dystrophies are genetic conditions that cause cells in the muscles to break down and gradually be lost. This causes increasing loss of movement and can eventually reduce life expectancy.

▶ Incidence and diagnosis

Duchenne muscular dystrophy usually affects boys and is quite rare, with around 100 boys a year being born with the condition. Failure to meet the expected milestones of walking is often the first indication that a boy has the condition, unless the condition is already known in the family. A blood test is then carried out to confirm the condition.

▶ Health and development

Although the condition mainly affects a boy's health, some boys do have slight difficulties with speech and language, although these are not usually severe.

Mobility

The gradual loss of mobility is one of the main features of this condition; young children are still likely to be mobile, but may need assistance or extra time in order to move. Children may be able to climb stairs on all fours or using the banisters. The weakness in the muscles also means that children may fall down or need to sit down. To counteract the deterioration in muscle strength, most children will have a programme of physiotherapy and be encouraged to remain physically active.

Nutrition

It is important that children with muscular dystrophy do not become overweight as this makes it harder for the body to move. This means that you should check with parents if the child has particular nutritional needs.

▶ Information that we may need from parents

- What does your child enjoy doing?
- What does your child find difficult?
- What mobility needs does your child have?
- Are there any adaptations or equipment that would be useful for your child?

- Are there any activities we will need to adapt to help your child participate?
- Does your child have a physiotherapy programme that we should adopt?
- Does your child become frustrated, and if so, how do you help him or her?

▶ Getting it right for your child

This can be a distressing condition for parents and carers, as little by little they see the strength in their child ebb away. Giving children a good quality of life is therefore essential and the focus of work should be to look for ways of helping the child to join everyday activities alongside other children. This may mean changing the layout of equipment to allow the child to move to it more easily.

While play and physical activity remain important for children with this condition, it will be important to be flexible and let children rest or go at their own pace.

The way that the condition progresses also means thinking about what the child's future needs might be and how best to meet these. Ramps may need to be installed or activities moved to a different place to allow for access. Thinking ahead and following the advice of an occupational therapist and other professionals involved with the child is therefore important.

▶ Key questions

- Who will be the child's key person?
- Do they understand the effects of the condition on the child?
- What activities does the child enjoy?
- How can we plan activities that will take into account the child's physical needs?
- What adaptations to the setting are required?
- Are emergency contact details for the child easily accessible?

▶ Some day-to-day questions

- How well is the child?
- Are activities planned that will allow the child to participate?
- Will the pace of the day allow the child to rest?

▶ Contact

Muscular Dystrophy UK

www.musculardystrophyuk.org

Development co-ordination disorder (dyspraxia)

Over the past few years, there has been a change to the terms used to describe what was previously known as dyspraxia. The term 'development co-ordination disorder' is now used by some professionals in preference to the term 'dyspraxia'. Development co-ordination disorder (DCD) causes children to have difficulties with their physical co-ordination. Some children also have organisational and planning difficulties.

▶ Verbal dyspraxia

Where children have difficulty with their speech, this is known as verbal dyspraxia. Signs include inconsistency in making sounds and forming words and difficulty in sequencing words. While some children with dyspraxia may show signs of verbal dyspraxia, many children will not. Equally, some children diagnosed with verbal dyspraxia will not show any difficulty with motor communication. Verbal dyspraxia is seen as a speech and language difficulty and where this is diagnosed, children will be supported by a speech and language therapist.

▶ Incidence and diagnosis

The incidence of DCD is hard to calculate because children can be affected so mildly that it may not be picked up. Having said this, the NHS estimates that around 1 in 20 children aged seven to eight years may have it to some extent. The cause of DCD is not known, but it is thought to link to the brain's ability to process and co-ordinate information. Diagnosis is often made by one or more of the following professionals: paediatrician, paediatric physiotherapist or educational psychologist. Parents or professionals will often suspect a problem because of delayed motor skills and poor co-ordination. Some children may show that they have DCD because of difficulty in speech. In addition to DCD, some children may also have related conditions including autism spectrum condition, dyslexia and attention deficit hyperactivity disorder (ADHD).

▶ Health and development

The extent and way in which DCD affects children can vary enormously and some of the signs of DCD are the same as those for other disorders, such as Fragile X (see page 254). It is important to remember, while children may have difficulties with their movements, organisation or speech, their overall intelligence is usually average or above average.

Gross motor and locomotive skills

Children are often slower to reach the developmental milestones and may not follow the expected sequence of development. It is not uncommon to find that a child has not crawled as a baby but has bottom-shuffled or gone straight to walking. Young children may find it hard to throw or kick a ball as this requires a complex sequence of movement. Their running and movements may look jerky and they may often trip over or bump into others. Children with DCD may find it hard to sit still as sitting requires co-ordination and muscle control.

Fine motor skills

Some children with DCD may have difficulties in making movements that require co-ordination, such as threading beads and cutting food, and may actively avoid activities that require a high level of manual dexterity. Older children may have difficulties producing legible handwriting or drawing.

Concentration, language and thought

Some children with DCD are very sensitive to touch. This is called tactile defensiveness (see page 181). They may not enjoy playing with sensory materials such as sand or may object to having their hair combed or teeth brushed.

Behaviour

Children may show inappropriate behaviour. This can be a result of frustration or as a way of avoiding situations where they think that they may fail. A child, for example, may run around the setting rather than pick up the toy bricks as the child knows that he or she will be slower than other children. It is also worth remembering that children may find it hard to sit still as this requires a good level of co-ordination. Looking for ways of shortening the time that children have to sit still, such as at meal times and group times, is therefore important.

▶ Information that we may need from parents

- What activities does your child enjoy at home?
- What does your child have difficulty with?
- How do you support your child at home?
- Does your child receive any support from other professionals, e.g. speech and language, physiotherapy?

▶ Getting it right for the child

It is often parents who first notice that their child's physical development is atypical and so listening to parents and supporting them is an important part of getting it right for the child. If you are working with a baby or toddler, you should also be observant and thoughtful as to whether or not a child might be showing signs of DCD.

For the child, it is important that we look for ways of breaking down movements or tasks into smaller steps so that they can be achievable. We may also need to look for ways to help children practise fine and gross motor tasks so that they can gain some level of fluency in their movements. This means carefully considering the physical stage of development of the child when planning activities so that they do not become frustrated.

As writing can be difficult for children, it is important not to fast-track writing skills, but instead to focus on the larger movements first such as making shapes using a paintbrush and water rather than using a pencil.

For some children, we may need to focus on organisation and sequencing skills. Visual timetables showing each step of what to do can help some children, e.g. a step-by-step visual aid that shows children how to dress or get their things to go outdoors.

Helping children to concentrate

Some children with dyspraxia find it hard to concentrate and are easily distracted. Breaking down tasks into smaller components can therefore be helpful. Consider ways of minimising distractions for the child, e.g. carry out activities in areas where other children are not walking by. Also ensure that activities are interesting and relevant for the child. It will also be important to remember that sitting still may be difficult for many children. Think carefully through the routines of your setting and think about how you can keep these moments to a minimum for the child.

Emotional needs

Children with DCD can develop low self-esteem. They know what they want to achieve but find it hard and frustrating to make their bodies work for them. Children who have started the primary phase of their education may begin to notice that their handwriting, painting or ability to dress is not the same as other children. This can lead to frustration and feelings of inadequacy. Some children also begin to believe that they cannot learn and are 'stupid'. This in turn can lead to children showing task avoidance or disruptive behaviours.

There is also a danger that some children can become over-reliant on adult support as adults can unwittingly take over activities such as self-care tasks to speed the child along. This stops children from using and developing everyday skills and thus independence. To help children build a positive view of themselves, it is therefore important for adults to allow children enough time to complete tasks and also to adapt activities to ensure that children are working at their developmental level.

▎ Key questions

- Who will be the child's key person?
- Is everyone in the setting aware of the difficulties that the child has?
- How will the planning of activities and routines take into consideration the child's needs?
- How will the child be encouraged to take part in activities that require fine motor skills?
- Do we need to liaise with other professionals, e.g. occupational therapists, physiotherapists and the speech and language service?
- How will we support the development of a positive self-esteem?

▎ Some day-to-day questions

- What activities have been planned to promote this child's motor skills?
- Do activities take into consideration the child's interests?
- Are activities broken down into smaller steps to make them achievable?
- Is an adult available to offer support and encouragement?
- Are there any specific activities planned that will support any ongoing physiotherapy and/or speech and language programme?

▎ Contact

Dyspraxia Foundation

www.dyspraxiafoundation.org.uk

Deafness/hearing loss

While some websites, medical journals and textbooks use the term 'hearing impairment' as an umbrella term to describe any amount of hearing loss, it is not a term favoured by organisations that work with children and their families, who tend to prefer the terms 'deafness' or 'hearing loss'. A starting point when working with children is to be sensitive and use the term that is preferred by individual parents.

There are two types of hearing loss, sensorineural and conductive, which we will look at separately to start with although it is important to recognise that some children may have both types of hearing loss.

▶ Sensorineural

Sensorineural hearing loss occurs in the inner ear or beyond. It prevents sounds from being processed. This type of hearing loss tends to be permanent and occurs for a variety of reasons including premature birth, genetic factors and diseases such as meningitis and mumps. The extent to which a sensorineural hearing loss can impact on a child's hearing can vary.

▶ Incidence and diagnosis

According to the National Deaf Children's Society, 840 babies a year are born with permanent deafness caused by sensorineural hearing loss. Other children develop deafness during childhood as a result of infections such as meningitis or injury to the head. Most children who are born deaf are diagnosed fairly quickly during routine screening or as a result of parents noticing that their child is not responsive to sounds. Once a child is diagnosed, tests are carried out to determine the extent of the child's deafness. Children with mild and moderate deafness are likely to be offered hearing aids. Hearing aids do not cure the deafness but instead amplify sound. Children with profound or severe deafness may be offered a cochlear implant. Cochlear implants work by converting sounds into electrical signals that stimulate the auditory nerve. Cochlear implants require a surgical procedure.

▶ Conductive hearing loss

Conductive hearing loss is common among children and results in varying degrees of reduced hearing. Blockages such as ear wax or fluid build-up in the Eustachian tube prevent sound from reaching the inner ear.

▶ Incidence and diagnosis

The commonest type of conductive hearing loss is known as 'glue ear'. It is thought that 80% of children under eight years will at some time be affected by 'glue ear'. Glue ear is caused by a fluid build-up in the Eustachian tube.

Glue ear diagnosis is usually made following parents' or carers' observations that a child is not responding to speech and/or is not developing as expected. It is not always easy to spot as the level of children's hearing can fluctuate and children's level of responsiveness can change. Parents may report that their child only hears when they want to or that they are often in their 'own world'. Once it is recognised that a child is not fully hearing, a hearing test carried out by an audiologist will confirm the child's level of hearing. In the case of glue ear, sometimes the child may need repeated tests as the first test may be carried out when the child is having a 'good' week and so may prove inconclusive.

While some children can be offered hearing aids for conductive hearing loss, children whose deafness is caused by glue ear and whose hearing is significantly affected will be offered an operation whereby a drain known as a grommet is inserted into the ear.

▶ Health and development

Deafness and hearing loss do not affect children's level of intelligence, but may create a significant barrier to learning if steps are not taken to help the child access information.

Speech, language and communication

One of the effects of even slightly reduced hearing is that it makes communication more difficult. The way in which children's speech, language and communication are affected depends on many factors, including when deafness was acquired, how quickly it was recognised and the steps taken to support the child. Children who have become deaf, for example as a result of meningitis, may have already acquired a good level of speech and language, while some children who are deaf from birth may need significant support to help them to acquire language. The decision as to the best strategy to help the child to communicate is usually taken by speech and language therapists in conjunction with parents. There are several options and which option is considered will depend on the needs of the child. Options for children include learning to sign, lip reading, using the spoken word, or a combination of techniques.

Learning

Any level of hearing loss can impact on children's learning if support and modifications to the environment are not made. Children, even with a mild conductive hearing loss, may not learn to read as they may not be able to hear the sounds and therefore connect them to letter shapes. Children may also miss out on hearing instructions, comments or questions from other children and so may not learn from these.

Behaviour

Some children may show inappropriate behaviour at times. This is usually due to frustration caused by being unable to communicate their needs or being unable to understand what is happening. Reduced hearing or deafness can be very isolating for children. It is important for adults to deal with the cause of the child's frustrations as a starting point.

Social and emotional development

Some children whose hearing loss is not diagnosed quickly may miss out on opportunities to socialise with other children. This can mean that they may need to be shown how to interact with others, as some children will have adapted to playing alone and creating their own world.

▶ Information that we may need from parents

- What type of hearing loss does your child have?
- How does your child's level of hearing/deafness affect his or her daily life?
- Does your child receive any speech and language support?
- Would you be happy if we contacted this service to gain further advice?
- What strategies do you use to communicate with your child?
- Does your child use a hearing aid or have a cochlear implant?
- What advice have you been given about how best to use the hearing aid/ cochlear implant?
- What type of activities does your child enjoy doing?
- Are there any activities that can cause your child to become frustrated?

▶ Getting it right for the child

Your starting point should be to talk to the parents. They will be able to advise you as to the communication strategy that they are using with the child. They will also be able to tell you what type of hearing aid/cochlear implant, if any, their child uses and how it is used with their child. While many children will be using the spoken word as their main communication method, some children may be learning British Sign Language if they have a severe hearing impairment. If this is the case, at least one member of staff in the setting will need to spend time learning this language. Just knowing a few signs will not suffice! Note that British Sign Language is not the same as Makaton. Makaton is a visual signing system and not a language. It is used alongside the spoken word to make it easier for children to understand what is being said. It might be used for some children with mild hearing loss.

The key to helping all children is to consider the way in which we are communicating with them.

Remember to:

- Check that you have the child's attention before talking.
- Maintain good eye contact with the child.
- Identify the topic of the conversation early on.
- Use a normal pace of speech, but make sure that you speak clearly.
- Be expressive and use good intonation in your speech.
- Make sure that the lighting in the setting is sufficient so that children who are lip reading or relying on facial cues can see you.
- Use props and visual aids to reinforce your communication with children, e.g. show the child an apron rather than talking about one.
- Use props to support story time and make sure that the child can see the pictures.
- Emphasise key words in your speech.
- Use meaningful facial expressions and gestures to support verbal messages.

Do not:

- Obstruct your face, e.g. put your hand over your mouth.
- Look away from the child while you are speaking.
- Exaggerate your facial movements or speech.
- Shout or speak in a loud voice as this distorts sounds.

As well as being able to communicate effectively with the child, it is also important that you are able to listen carefully to the child. Many children may have speech patterns that are atypical or may not speak as clearly as other children of their age. Children who are not feeling listened to will quickly become frustrated and may withdraw. Show the child by nodding, paraphrasing and smiling that you understand what is being said. Allow children plenty of time and avoid competitive situations where children shout out. Make sure that children have some time working with an adult by themselves or in small groups.

Supporting children who wear hearing aids

Hearing aids amplify sounds. Advice about supporting children who wear hearing aids should be gained from parents and the audiologist who supports the child. The following general pieces of advice may be helpful:

- Always make sure that the hearing aid is in the correct ear. Children who have a hearing loss in each ear may have two hearing aids; they must be put in the correct ear.
- Handle hearing aids gently; they are sophisticated pieces of equipment.
- Check that the battery is not flat; try to have spare batteries in the setting.
- Check that the earpiece is not covered in earwax – this is normally removed by washing the ear mould with warm soapy water.

▶ Key questions

- Who will be the child's key person?
- Do they need deaf awareness training?
- Is staff training required to learn how best to support communication with the child?
- How will everyone who works with this child become aware of their communication needs?
- Is the lighting sufficient in the setting?
- Who will take responsibility for implementing any speech and language programme for the child?
- How will quiet areas be created within the setting?

▶ Some day-to-day questions

- How well is the child hearing today?
- How will we ensure that background noise is kept to a minimum?
- Is the child wearing their hearing aid, if needed?
- Is the device in the correct ear?
- Is the child's hearing aid functioning properly?
- Are spare batteries available?

▶ Contact

The National Deaf Children's Society

www.ndcs.org.uk

Dyslexia

Dyslexia is a specific learning disorder causing persistent difficulties in processing information, which results in children's reading, writing and spelling being affected. While it is not fully understood, it would appear that the brain finds it hard to process certain types of information. This means that an older child or adult with dyslexia may have excellent language, knowledge and creative skills but find it hard to process symbolic information. Dyslexia and development co-ordination disorder (dyspraxia) are often linked disorders, although some children with dyslexia may not have any apparent difficulties in controlling their movements.

It is unlikely that children will be diagnosed with dyslexia in their early years as the formal teaching of reading, writing and spelling is not suitable for children under six years old. However, it is possible to notice some of tendencies such as a child not hearing rhymes in words, not being able to follow a rhythm or mixing up sounds in words. Some children will have also have problems with tasks involving sequencing, such as getting dressed or following two or more instructions at the same time, e.g. 'Find your coat and take it back to the hall.' A few children may also find it difficult to acquire hand preference, which is typically in place at two and half years old.

Children with suspected dyslexia will be diagnosed by an educational psychologist. While there are no 'cures' for dyslexia, children may be taught using special programmes. Assistive technology such as voice-activated writing software is increasingly being used to support children with dyslexia to fulfil their potential.

▶ Contact

British Dyslexia Association

www.bdadyslexia.org.uk

Eczema

Eczema, also known as dermatitis, is part of a group of skin conditions. Skin becomes dry and itchy, and when a child has severe eczema the skin may become raw, cracked and bleeding. There are many different forms of eczema:

- **Atopic eczema** – this is the commonest type of eczema. It is thought to be inherited and is triggered by allergens in the child's environment which cause the body's immune system to over-react.
- **Allergic contact dermatitis** – this type of eczema occurs when the body's immune system reacts to a minute amount of a chemical over a period of time.
- **Irritant contact dermatitis** – this type of eczema occurs when the body comes into contact with chemicals, e.g. in detergent.

▶ Incidence and diagnosis

Eczema is a very common condition. It is thought that up to 1 in 5 children may have some type of eczema, although the severity can vary enormously. Symptoms include soreness, dryness of skin and itchiness. While there is no cure, the majority of children will be free of symptoms by their mid-teens. Where children have severe eczema, paediatricians are likely to refer them to see a specialist dermatologist. Most children's eczema is treated by using emollient creams that help to prevent the skin from becoming dry and itchy. Children may also be prescribed a cream that contains a topical corticosteroid that reduces the inflammation.

▶ Health and development

Eczema does not cause any learning difficulties but some children can find it hard to concentrate properly as they can be distracted by the itchiness or through tiredness.

Tiredness

Eczema can interrupt sleep as the itchiness can keep the child awake. This may mean that the child will feel tired and this may be reflected in his or her behaviour. Children may be irritable or find it hard to concentrate. Some children may also be prescribed antihistamine tablets which can cause drowsiness.

Social and emotional development

Some children may not feel good about the way that they look and this can prevent them from socialising. It is important therefore to look for ways of boosting children's self-image.

▶ Information that we may need from parents

- How is the child's eczema being managed?
- Are there any creams or medications that the child needs in the setting? If so, when should these be used?
- Are there any known triggers?
- Are there any materials in the setting, such as sand or dough, that might further irritate or dry out the skin?
- Does the child have any dietary requirements?
- What would you like the setting to do if the child begins to scratch uncontrollably?

▶ Getting it right for the child

Eczema can be extremely distressing for children. The itchiness can become unbearable and so it is unfair to tell children not to scratch. Working with parents to find ways of helping the child is therefore important.

Emollients

These are creams that help to moisturise the skin. They can also help with the itchiness. As with any form of treatment, it is essential to find out from parents how and when the cream can be applied. Make sure that the child's skin and your hands are clean. Bacteria are easily introduced into the inflamed part of the child's skin. Avoid any cross-infection by making sure that each child with eczema has his or her own labelled cream. Apply or help the child to apply the cream very gently. Rubbing can irritate the skin and cause further itching.

Topical steroids

These creams contain steroid drugs that are used when children have flare-ups. They are very effective. These creams are likely to be applied at home, but where a child spends time in full day care, you may be asked to apply them.

- Only use topical steroids when asked to by parents.
- Check that the cream is in date.
- Read any instructions on the tube carefully, as well as the prescribed dosage.
- Wash your hands thoroughly before and after applying the cream.
- Apply the cream sparingly and only to the area of skin affected.
- Make sure that steroid creams are labelled with the child's name.
- Do not use the steroid cream on any other child.

Antihistamines

These drugs are given to reduce the itchiness and help children sleep. They are usually given at home. Some antihistamine formulas can make children drowsy.

Antibiotics

Some children may have an antibiotic cream or medicine to take if they have an infected area of skin.

Bandages

Children may wear bandages that contain emollient, sometimes known as wet wraps. Bandages help by soothing the skin while also moisturising it. They help to prevent children from scratching the affected area. Parents will usually apply bandages at home. It is important that wet wraps are not used on infected skin.

Removing triggers in the environment

Eczema triggers are similar to those for asthma. In addition, stress can play a huge part for many children. This means you must provide a calm and relaxed environment and observe children closely for the first signs of distress.

Emotional development

Thought has to be given as to how to support children's self-image. Sometimes other children may be reluctant to touch or play with a child with eczema. It is important to look out for this and, if appropriate, to talk this through with the children. It is also important to make the child with eczema feel good about themselves and the way that they look.

▌ Key questions

- Who will be responsible for liaising with parents on a day-to-day basis?
- Are staff aware of the symptoms and effects of eczema?
- Who will be responsible for administering any medication or treatment?
- How will the child's dietary needs be met?

▌ Some day-to-day questions

- How well is the child today?
- Which, if any, areas of the skin are affected?
- How well has the child slept?
- Are activities suitable for the child?

▌ Contact

National Eczema Society

www.eczema.org

Epilepsy

Epilepsy is a neurological condition that results in a person having seizures. The seizures are caused when the brain's normal pattern of electrical activity is temporarily disturbed. Epilepsy is a complex condition as there appear to be several types. There are also over 40 types of seizures. Seizures can, however, be grouped into two broader categories: generalised or partial. In the past, the terms 'grand mal' or 'petit mal' were used to describe seizures. These terms are now no longer used as they do not convey the wide range of different seizures.

Note: The term 'fit' used to be used to describe a seizure. It is no longer used to describe seizures and should therefore be avoided.

▶ Incidence and diagnosis

Epilepsy is thought to affect around 1 in every 240 children under 16 years old and so is relatively common. The majority of people with epilepsy have their first seizure before the age of 20. There are several reasons why a child may develop epilepsy, including brain damage sustained during birth or as a result of an injury to the head. Some children may also develop epilepsy as a result of having an infection such as meningitis or as part of a chromosomal disorder. However, in many cases the exact cause is unknown. Diagnosis is not always easy and information needs to be gathered about what happened during a seizure. When epilepsy is suspected, referrals are usually made to a neurologist. A range of tests may then be performed including an EEG, which measures brain activity, and an MRI or CT scan, which usually provides pictures of the brain. Once diagnosed, anti-epileptic drugs are usually prescribed. These are usually efficient but can cause side-effects.

▶ Health and development

Epilepsy alone will not necessarily cause any learning or health difficulties, although sometimes the drugs that a child is taking may have some side-effects. It is therefore important not to underestimate a child's potential.

Seizures

While seizures can be grouped into two broad categories, there are many different types of seizures. You should talk to parents about the form in which their child is likely to have any seizure. The form a seizure takes depends on the part of the brain that is being affected. Some children can have more than one type of seizure.

Partialised seizures (local focal)

In partialised seizures, the brain activity begins or is involved in one area of the brain. The child's experience of the seizure will therefore be determined by the area of the brain that is being affected. Some seizures begin as partial seizures and then spread to other areas of the brain, causing a secondary generalised seizure.

Simple partial seizures

In simple partial seizures, the child remains, or is at first, conscious. There may be motor activity such as twitching or unusual sensations in the limbs, depending on the area of the brain that is being affected.

Complex partial seizures

Children having a complex seizure may appear to be dazed or show repetitive automatic movements such as fumbling with clothes, mumbling or chewing. They may be able to respond or reply, but afterwards will have little memory of the seizure.

Generalised seizures

Children having generalised seizures will lose consciousness as wide areas of the brain are being affected. Some of these types of seizures can be dramatic, with the child falling to the ground such as in tonic/clonic seizures, although with some children generalised seizures can take the form of absences (see below).

Tonic/clonic

This type of seizure is the most common. In the first part of the seizure (tonic), the child becomes stiff and falls to the ground. The seizure continues but changes (clonic), with the child's muscles relaxing and then tightening rhythmically. This causes convulsing movements. Once the seizure is over, the child will need to rest. They may be drowsy and have a headache.

Tonic

This is a dramatic and frightening seizure to watch. The child's muscles stiffen and the child loses consciousness. The child's eyes are likely to roll back and because of the contraction of the muscles in the chest, the child may have difficulty breathing. This in turn can result in their lips and face turning blue. Tonic seizures are short and usually last less than a minute.

Atonic

These types of seizures are also known as 'drop attacks'. The child loses all muscle tone, causing them to drop to the floor suddenly. The seizure is very brief and usually the child can get back up again.

Myoclonic

This type of seizure results in a brief episode of twitching, which often takes place in the arms but sometimes a child's head or body may jerk.

Absences

Absences are common in young children. The child loses consciousness for a few seconds. They may appear to be staring aimlessly or look blank. These types of seizures often go unnoticed, but the child may have missed out on what has been said or has happened in this time. This can result in children looking puzzled and disorientated.

▶ Possible side-effects of drugs

Finding the right dosage and drug for children can be difficult in the early days. It is important to recognise the side-effects that some drugs can cause and to report these to parents.

Drowsiness

Some medication causes children to become drowsy. If this is the case, allow children to rest and sleep as their body dictates. Overtiredness can trigger seizures in some children.

Memory and concentration

Sometimes medication can affect a child's ability to concentrate as brain activity is being slowed down. It is important to notice changes in the level of attention and concentration that a child shows as this can indicate some changes in the brain's activities.

Over-activity

Some children are affected by the medication by becoming more active and restless. This again should be noted and talked through with parents.

▶ Information that we may need from parents

- Is your child's epilepsy fully or partially controlled by medication?
- When do they take their medication?

- Are there any side-effects of this medication on your child?
- Are there any triggers that may cause a seizure?
- What type of seizures does your child have?
- How long do they normally last and what form do they take?
- How much rest does your child usually need afterwards?
- Does your child have emergency medication to take?
- Would you like to be contacted immediately if your child has a seizure?
- Are there any activities that should be limited or modified?
- How does your child feel or what does he or she understand about having epilepsy?
- Does your child have any other medical condition?

❱ Getting it right for the child

Firstly, it is useful to understand that there is still widespread ignorance about epilepsy. This dates back hundreds of years to when people with epilepsy were thought of as being in some way possessed by the devil or as having mental illness. In reality, most children with epilepsy will lead straightforward, normal and active lives, as having epilepsy in itself does not create any further health or learning difficulties.

To get it right for the child, it is important to gain information from the parents about the frequency of any seizures and any effects of medication. It is also important for all staff to provide a supporting, calm, reassuring atmosphere so that if a seizure occurs, the child does not feel stigmatised. It is also known that stressful situations can, for some children, trigger seizures.

Where children have repeated seizures, it is also important for staff to be able to correctly describe the type of seizures and what happened. This is particularly important if a child is in the process of being diagnosed.

❱ Managing risks

It is essential that children are not cocooned and that while some precautions may need to be taken, children are not prevented from taking part in activities such as swimming, climbing and using wheeled equipment such as scooters or tricycles. Simply supervising most children closely yet unobtrusively will be sufficient. For children with high levels of unexpected seizures, you should take advice from parents. In some cases, protective headgear can be worn so that children can still take part in activities.

What to do if a child has a seizure

Many practitioners are concerned that they will not know what to do if a child has a seizure, although in reality little if any first aid is required. A few children with epilepsy may have emergency medication to take if the seizure is prolonged. If this is needed it should be administered by a trained member of staff. It is, however, useful if all adults working with the child know how to place the child in the recovery position after a seizure is over.

Remember to:

- Remain calm and stay with the child.
- Guide the child away from any danger.
- Cushion the head if the child is falling.
- Time the seizure and note what is happening to the child's body so that you can report accurately back to the parents afterwards.
- Place the child in the recovery position when the seizure has finished.
- Stay with the child until they have regained consciousness.
- Be aware that the child may have lost bladder or bowel control in some instances and respond sensitively.

Do not:

- Move the child unless they are in danger.
- Attempt to restrain or hold the child.
- Give the child any drink until they are fully conscious.

When to seek emergency help

You should phone for an ambulance if:

- It is the child's first seizure.
- The seizure is generalised and continues for longer than five minutes or if the seizure is longer than the usual for the child.
- Another seizure occurs when the child has not yet gained consciousness.
- The child has been injured as a result of the seizure.

▶ Key questions

- Who will be responsible for administering emergency medicine if needed?
- Does everyone in the setting who works with the child know that the child has epilepsy?
- Does everyone know what to do if a seizure occurs?
- Is everyone aware of any side-effects of the medication?

- Does everyone understand that epilepsy should not be seen as a barrier to many everyday activities?
- How will risks be managed to allow the child to take part in all activities?
- What strategies will be used to help other children understand what is happening if the child has a seizure (particularly tonic/clonic)?

▶ Some day-to-day questions

- How well is the child?
- Are there any changes to the child's level of concentration, memory or signs that they are drowsy?
- Does the child need extra supervision or protection in order to engage in any physical activities?
- Are emergency contact details available?

▶ Contact

Epilepsy Action

www.epilepsy.org.uk

Look out for the free online courses on this website.

Fragile X

This is an inherited genetic condition, which is called 'fragile X' because the X chromosome is slightly damaged. It results in most of the affected children having some form of learning disability. Boys are more seriously affected than girls as girls usually have another X chromosome that is undamaged which appears to mitigate the effects of the damaged chromosome. Fragile X is the most common form of inherited learning disability, although it was not recognised until the late 1970s.

▶ Incidence and diagnosis

Fragile X affects about 1 in 4,000 boys and 1 in 6,000 girls. Diagnosis can be difficult unless one of the child's parents already knows that his or her family is affected. Some of the characteristics of fragile X are similar to those of autism spectrum condition, including hand flapping, difficulty in social situations and resistance to changes in routines, but it is a separate condition. Once suspected, however, diagnosis can be made from chromosomal testing.

▶ Health and development

There are marked differences between girls and boys with fragile X syndrome. Generally boys are affected more severely and show more challenging behaviour as a result.

Behaviour

Boys particularly show unwanted and challenging behaviour as they can be impulsive, overactive and irritable. They can also have aggressive outbursts. This behaviour needs to be seen in the context of children having difficulty in processing information, which causes them to be easily overwhelmed and stressed. Sitting still is hard for most children and again this can be interpreted incorrectly as poor behaviour when in reality it is linked to the difficulty in processing information.

Physical development

Children can have difficulties with their hand–eye co-ordination and may at times appear to be 'clumsy'. Children with fragile X syndrome may also have poor spatial awareness.

Cognitive development

Boys and girls can find it difficult to concentrate, but boys will have particular difficulties. Their attention span can be limited, according to the type of activity presented. There can also be difficulties in understanding and remembering new information. Many children find it particularly hard to deal with tasks that require sequencing, e.g. sounding out a word when learning to read, with other children seeming to have difficulties in situations where there is too much going on, i.e. over-stimulation.

Communication

Children's language is often delayed. Speech can be disorganised and fast. It is common for children to repeat themselves and also to echo back what has been said to them. This is thought to help them process information more easily. Children may often jump from topic to topic. Children are likely to have difficulty in following instructions, particularly if the instructions require motor movement.

Emotional and social development

Many children find social situations difficult and find eye contact hard, particularly with people they do not know or in stressful situations. Children also find it hard to cope with changes in situations because of their difficulty in sensory processing. Most children are, however, affectionate and interested in social interactions, although sometimes shyness and inappropriate social responses such as hand flapping create barriers for them. Between 10 and 30 per cent of people with fragile X syndrome can develop epilepsy.

Ear infections

Children with fragile X are prone to ear infections and glue ear, which causes a fluctuating hearing loss. It will be important to look out for signs of ear infections and report any symptoms to parents. It will also be important to look out for signs of glue ear (see page 240) and if a child is not fully hearing, to take steps to support them (see page 241).

▶ Information that we may need from parents

- What does the child enjoy doing at home?
- What type of strategies do you use to manage the effects of fragile X?
- What situations does your child find difficult?
- Does your child have epilepsy and if so does he or she need medication?
- Does your child take any medication to help with any over-activeness?
- Does the child have particular ways of communicating that we should be aware of?

▶ Getting it right for the child

It is very important to provide close supervision and to be very patient with children, especially boys, who have fragile X syndrome. It is important to remember that they are not being deliberately difficult. Staff will need to make sure that they focus on the child rather than on the behaviour. They will also need to understand that expecting eye contact from the child in conversations will not be appropriate.

Activities will need to be carefully planned so that children can leave them easily if their concentration wanes, for example a shorter game or a shorter story. New activities or 'exciting' events such as trips out or parties may provide too much stimulation for the child and so good preparation will be required to help the child adjust.

▶ Key questions

- Who will act as the child's key person?
- How will the child be supported during the session while remaining independent?
- Are there any areas where close supervision will be essential to avoid accidents?
- Who will be responsible for any medication and where will this be kept?
- What strategies will be used to develop the child's communication and language skills?
- How will we avoid situations where the child may be over-stimulated?
- How will we help the child in new social situations?
- How will we break down concepts and learning into smaller steps to allow the child to process information more easily?

▶ Some day-to-day questions

- Have we planned activities and this session remembering that this child may find it hard to concentrate?
- Do we need to prepare the child for any changes or events that may cause him or her to become over-stimulated?
- Are activities planned that will help the child to process information at their own pace?
- Have we prepared visual timetables to help the child cope with changes?

▶ Contact

Fragile X society

www.fragilex.org.uk

Hydrocephalus

Hydrocephalus occurs when the fluid in the brain is unable to flow freely away. This causes a build-up of fluid and thus pressure in the brain. This in turn can cause permanent brain damage, although the extent is variable. There are several causes of hydrocephalus, including spina bifida, meningitis and brain haemorrhage. Hydrocephalus is treated by inserting a drain known as a shunt into the brain which allows the fluid to be released. The shunt is usually permanent. Signs that the shunt is not working include headaches, vomiting, dizziness, visual disturbances and drowsiness. If any of these signs is apparent, the parents should be contacted immediately and emergency medical attention sought.

▶ Incidence and diagnosis

Around 1 in 1,000 babies is born with hydrocephalus and it is usually diagnosed at or shortly after birth. Other children develop hydrocephalus as a result of conditions such as brain tumours or infections of the brain. Premature babies and babies with spina bifida will be closely monitored as these are two common causes of hydrocephalus. Head circumference measurements may indicate a large head-to-body ratio and the fontanel may show signs of swelling. Once diagnosed, a shunt is immediately inserted as otherwise the condition can be fatal.

▶ Health and development

The extent to which children are affected by hydrocephalus varies enormously and depends on the amount of damage to the brain.

Blockage of the shunt

The shunt is invisible as it is completely inserted into the child's head. It can, however, become blocked and this can be potentially life-threatening. This is why noticing the signs of a blockage is important.

Physical development

Children may have difficulties with hand–eye co-ordination and gross motor skills.

Learning difficulties

While many children with hydrocephalus will have learning difficulties, this is not the case with all children. It is therefore important not to make assumptions and instead to talk to the parents. Some children may have difficulties in reasoning and may need plenty of reinforcement activities with the focus on providing visual information. Children may also need tasks to be broken down into smaller steps.

Memory and concentration

Some children may have difficulties with short-term memory and concentration. Frequent reminders may be required and instructions are best given one at a time. Poor short-term memory can also affect children's behaviour as they may not remember what they should be doing or even that they have been told to stop certain behaviours.

Social and emotional development

Many children dislike any change in routine and find change hard to cope with. As short-term memory can be affected, children may not remember why changes are happening. This can make children very anxious and upset. They may also have seemingly irrational fears and dislikes.

Noise sensitivity

Some children are very sensitive to everyday noises such as vacuum cleaners and washing machines. They may become very distressed, although the reason why this should happen is not known.

▶ Information that we may need from parents

- What does your child enjoy doing?
- Does your child have any fears or strong dislikes?
- What situations does your child find difficult?
- Have you noticed any difficulties with your child's memory?
- What type of strategies do you use at home to overcome short-term memory difficulties?
- Does your child find it hard to cope with changes in routines?
- Who should we contact if we suspect that the shunt is not working properly?
- Are there any activities that your child should not take part in? In addition to activities, are there any specific movements that your child should not do, e.g. bending forward?

▶ Getting it right for the child

As many children have difficulties with their short-term memory, it is essential that all staff understand the implications of this. It can mean that a child will quickly forget any instructions and will need to be reminded several times. Visual cues can be very helpful in this respect. Strong routines are also suggested as this can make children feel more secure. In terms of children's learning, it is important to use sensory and visual activities as these may help children to process and retain information more easily. As some children have short-term memory difficulties, it is important to provide close supervision to avoid accidents, as children may not remember warnings about risks or dangers.

Finally, it is important that everyone in the setting is familiar with the signs that the child's shunt is not functioning and knows that they should act promptly.

▶ Key questions

- Who will act as the child's key person?
- Does everyone in the setting know the signs that the shunt is not working properly?
- How will activities be presented to ensure that the child can concentrate and process information at their level?

▶ Some day-to-day questions

- Are there any signs that the shunt is not working effectively?
- Are there any vigorous physical activities planned that the child should not engage in?
- Is the routine likely to be disrupted and how will the child be helped to deal with this?
- Are there sufficient activities planned that are sensory and visual?
- Are staff and helpers aware that the child may have difficulties in remembering information?
- Is there adequate supervision to prevent incidents or accidents?

▶ Contact

Shine

www.shinecharity.org.uk

This organisation also provides information about spina bifida (see page 264).

Sickle cell anaemia

Sickle cell anaemia is a genetically inherited blood condition that affects the red blood cells in the body. The haemoglobin in the red blood cells is abnormal and there are changes to the shape of the red blood cells. Haemoglobin is important because it carries oxygen around the body. Children with sickle cell conditions are likely to have bouts of severe pain caused by the abnormally shaped blood cells becoming blocked in the small blood vessels. They are also likely to be anaemic because the red blood cells that are affected by the condition are unable to survive as long as normal red blood cells. This results in lower levels of haemoglobin.

▶ Incidence and diagnosis

Sickle cell anaemia is inherited as it is a genetic condition. It affects around 1 in 2,000 children in England. For a child to be affected by the condition, both parents must carry the faulty gene. The term 'sickle cell trait' is used where only one parent has the gene. In this case, the child will not be affected by the condition but will carry the gene. In the UK, sickle cell condition primarily affects children and adults whose families once originated in the Caribbean and Africa.

▶ Health and development

Anaemia

Children with sickle cell conditions are often anaemic. This results in lethargy and extreme tiredness. Children may need to rest frequently and may have difficulty concentrating. A diet high in folic acid is often recommended as a supplement for those with anaemia.

Pain and 'crises'

Sickle cell conditions create pain as the abnormal blood cells become blocked or trapped in small blood vessels. These blockages cause pain in the arms, legs, back and stomach. Severe episodes of pain are known as 'crises'. Sickle pain can happen anywhere and at any time, although there are some triggers such as the child fighting an infection, becoming dehydrated or cold. The onset of a crisis is usually gradual but can result in a child needing to be hospitalised. It is therefore important to contact parents when a child reports being in pain.

Splenic sequestration crisis

In young children, there is a danger that a crisis can affect the spleen. This can be life-threatening and so you should always act on any of these signs: paleness, weakness and pain in the abdomen, especially in the spleen area (underneath the left breast).

Stroke

For children with sickle cell conditions, 10% will have a stroke by the time they are 20 years old. A stroke is caused when the blood supply in the brain is cut off. It is important to quickly recognise the signs of a stroke and to get emergency help. The slogan 'FAST' is used to help people remember the signs of a stroke:

F – Facial weakness – can the child smile? Has their mouth or eye dropped?
A – Arm weakness – can the child raise both arms?
S – Speech problems – can the child speak as clearly as usual and understand you?
T – Time to call 999.

Infections

Children with sickle cell anaemia are at increased risk of bacterial infections. It is important to take steps to avoid cross-infection within the setting. It is also important to contact parents quickly if a child develops a temperature, as medical attention is likely to be needed. As a result of susceptibility to infections, children may also be on courses of antibiotics.

Priapism

Priapism occurs in boys during a crisis. The penis becomes stiff because the red cells become blocked. It is rare in boys under six or seven years old. It is painful yet some boys may not mention the pain because they are embarrassed. It is important, however, that medical attention is sought after two hours because it can later lead to impotence.

Learning

Sickle cell conditions do not affect children's ability to learn although frequent absences due to crises or to attend medical appointments may mean that children can miss out on learning activities.

Social and emotional development

As with other conditions, children can feel isolated and 'different' because of their medical condition. Other children may, for example, ask why they are not playing outdoors in cold weather. It is important therefore to help children develop a strong self-esteem.

❱ Information that we may need from parents

- How do you manage this condition at home?
- What are the signs that your child is at the start of a crisis?
- Are there any triggers that may cause a crisis?
- How much fluid should your child be given and what should we do if your child is not drinking much?
- Is there any medication that your child needs to take?
- Is your child able to communicate how they are feeling?

❱ Getting it right for the child

It is essential for everyone to understand that this condition may affect the child's level of activity and so taking our cue from the child is important, especially if the child asks to nap or opt out of a physical activity. A child who complains of pain must be listened to as this might be the onset of a crisis.

Keeping children warm and dry

The condition becomes worse when children are cold and when the weather is damp. Sudden drops in the child's temperature can trigger a crisis. It will be important therefore to make sure that your setting is adequately heated and also to encourage the child to stay indoors when it is particularly cold and damp. Swimming is not advised unless the water is very warm and the changing rooms are heated. Some children can also be sensitive to cold drinks and food and so this may need to be discussed with parents.

Avoiding dehydration

Children with sickle cell conditions need to maintain their fluid levels. It is important that they do not dehydrate. This means that they should be encouraged to take frequent drinks and that drinks should always be on stand-by for the child. The risk of dehydration increases in the summer and during physical activity. Particular attention should be paid to checking that children at these times are drinking sufficiently. As a consequence of increased fluid, children will need more trips to the toilet, or in the case of babies their nappies to be changed more often.

Emotional support

As well as managing the physical needs of the child, it is also important that the child feels emotionally secure. A young child will benefit from a strong relationship with a key person who will be able to recognise the child's feelings and also frustrations. The key person will also be important in noticing early signs of the onset of a crisis.

▶ Key questions

- Who will be the child's key person?
- Who will ensure that the child is regularly offered drinks and monitor their fluid intake?
- Is everyone in the setting aware of the effects of this condition?
- Where will any medication be stored?
- Who will be responsible for giving the child any medication?
- Does the planning for the child include periods of rest as well as activity?
- What will be on offer for the child if other children go outside when it is cold or damp?
- Is there an area where the child can nap or lie down if required?
- Are parents' emergency contact details accessible?

▶ Some day-to-day questions

- What is the weather forecast?
- What activities are planned for the day?
- How is the child feeling?

▶ Contact

Sickle Cell Society

http://sicklecellsociety.org

Spina bifida

Spina bifida is a condition that occurs early in pregnancy. The vertebrae in the spine do not fuse properly, leaving part of the spinal cord exposed. As the spinal cord serves as the pathway for messages to be passed to and from the brain from the limbs, any blockages can result in loss of sensation and loss of the use of limbs. Hydrocephalus often accompanies spina bifida at birth (see also Hydrocephalus, page 257).

There are different forms of spina bifida:

- **Spina bifida occulta**: This type of spina bifida is the commonest and the mildest form of spina bifida. It rarely causes any disability and many people will not even know that they have it. It is not usually detected until a person needs an x-ray of their back. While this type of spina bifida does not normally result in any consequences, it can sometimes be more significant. While rare, a few children with spina bifida occulta may have difficulties in controlling their bladder and bowel and this usually reveals itself during toilet training. Parents are usually advised to seek medical help if, after the age of three years, a child is not making any progress.
- **Spina bifida cystica**: This is so named because a cyst or blister is formed on the spine. There are two forms of spina bifida cystica:
  - **Meningocele** – the nerves are not usually badly damaged and are able to function, therefore there is often little disability present. This is the least common form.
  - **Myelomeningocele** – this is the most serious and more common form of cystic spina bifida. The spinal cord is damaged or not properly developed. As a result, there is some paralysis and loss of sensation below the damaged region. The amount of disability depends very much on where the spina bifida is and the amount of nerve damage involved. A significant proportion of children with this type of spina bifida will also have hydrocephalus.

▶ Incidence and diagnosis

The number of people with spina bifida varies regionally, although the mildest form of spina bifida occulta is thought be present in 5–10% of the population, many of whom will not have any symptoms. The cause of spina bifida is still being researched although a mix of genetic and environmental factors appears to be at work. An increased intake of folic acid before conception and during the first 12 weeks of pregnancy is currently recommended as a preventative measure. Diagnosis of spina bifida is often made during routine ultrasound examinations and at also at birth.

▶ Health and development

It is important to understand that spina bifida does not cause learning difficulties for children and there is no reason why children with this condition cannot achieve academically.

Hydrocephalus

Many children with myelomeningocele spina bifida will have hydrocephalus. As we saw on page 257, it will be important to watch out for signs that the shunt is not working.

Mobility

Some children with myelomeningocele spina bifida are likely to need aids so that they can stand or be mobile. Occupational therapists working with the family are likely to provide advice and equipment where it is needed.

Toilet training

For some children toilet training will take a while, but for others with myelomeningocele spina bifida it may not be possible to achieve full bladder and bowel control.

Emotional and social development

As with other conditions, children as they become self-aware may experience low self-esteem unless they are supported. Some children with significant mobility difficulties may also at times become frustrated.

▶ Information that we may need from parents

- What does your child enjoy doing?
- Are there any activities that your child finds difficult?
- How does spina bifida affect your child, e.g. hydrocephalus, mobility difficulties?
- Does your child need any equipment to help with mobility or standing?
- Does your child have a physiotherapy programme in place and would you like us to incorporate it into the session?
- Does your child have any toileting needs?
- Does your child have any dietary requirements?

◗ Getting it right for the child

Children with spina bifida myelomeningocele are likely to need equipment or support to be mobile. This does not necessarily mean a wheelchair, as many younger children can get around by using a standing frame or even by crawling. It will be important to talk to the parents about their child's mobility needs and also to create an environment that allows the child to have maximum movement and access to activities. This might mean adjusting where toys and resources are put and in some cases adjusting table heights. Advice from occupational therapists can be useful in this respect.

Lack of mobility can sometimes cause pressure sores and advice might need to be sought from parents or other professionals about how to prevent these.

Where children's mobility is constrained, it will also be important to find ways to empower children as it can be easy for adults and other children to overcompensate and 'help' a child. This prevents children from developing a sense that they are capable and so impacts on their confidence.

As we have seen, bowel and bladder control can be tricky or not possible. It will be important to work with parents when children are being toilet trained. As there are likely to be more accidents with this group of children, adults will need to be sensitive and supportive.

For children where toilet training is not appropriate, thought will need to be given as to where to change a child and also whether any aids or adaptations such as hoists will be needed. To preserve the child's dignity, it will be important that the child is changed only by familiar adults who they like and trust.

◗ Key questions

- What are the mobility needs of the child?
- Are any adaptations required in the setting?
- Who will be responsible for ensuring that the personal hygiene needs of the child are met?
- Where will the changing of nappies/pads take place and will this meet the child's need for privacy?
- Who will be responsible for ensuring that any physiotherapy or movements are carried out?
- Who will be responsible for ensuring that the child's dietary requirements are met?

▶ Some day-to-day questions

- Are the activities accessible for the child?
- Are there sufficient supplies of nappies/pads to change the child?
- Are there any signs that pressure sores are starting to develop?
- How are the emotional needs of the child being met?

▶ Contact

Shine

www.shinecharity.org.uk

Vision impairment/sight loss

Vision impairment is one of the terms used when a child has sight loss that cannot be fully corrected with glasses. There are many degrees of sight loss. Contrary to popular belief, blindness as characterised by a total lack of light is very rare. In fact, the contrary is often true and many children with eye conditions will find bright glaring light a problem and so may wear shaded eyewear.

There are many causes of sight loss including genetic factors, diseases and damage to the eye or optic nerve. In some cases, the eye and optic nerve are healthy, but eye movement is irregular, while for some children the shape of the cornea causes refractive errors such as long- or short-sightedness.

▶ Incidence and diagnosis

It is hard to calculate the number of children with vision impairment, but it is thought to be around 25,000. The speed of diagnosis depends on many factors including the level of sight. Routine health checks often detect that a child is not fully seeing and children are then referred to a specialist.

▶ Health and development

Vision impairments do not cause learning difficulties in children, but can act as a barrier to learning if children are not supported.

Gross and locomotive skills

Children with vision impairments may not have gained confidence in their movements. Vision is used to support spatial awareness and young children tend to move in order to explore the world that they see. Sighted babies will try to reach out for objects that are within their grasp or take their first steps when attempting to reach something out of range.

Children with vision impairments may be reluctant to run or move quickly. They may bump into objects, find it hard to negotiate stairs and find it hard to make co-ordinated movements such as kicking a ball.

Fine motor skills

Many fine motor movements involve the use of hand–eye co-ordination. If unsupported, children may not gain some skills and concepts as a result of not being able to access toys and resources such as jigsaws, construction play or role play. Children may also miss out on opportunities to learn independence skills such as dressing and pouring drinks unless they are supported.

Behaviour

Many children will have moments of frustration caused by being unable to make movements that require hand–eye or foot–eye co-ordination. There are many ways in which frustration may manifest itself, including a reluctance to engage with an activity or by contrast an outburst of anger.

Social development

Some young children may find it hard to engage with other young children as many aspects of communication are linked to being able to see others' body language and reactions, e.g. a toddler may imitate another toddler's gestures.

Communication and language

The motivation to talk is often triggered by the need to engage with others. Children who cannot see others' responses may be slower to talk or not show the same range of non-verbal responses. This is because babies often learn gestures and body language through a process known as mirroring. It is very important for adults to provide plenty of language and description that is linked to what children can touch, feel and perceive.

▶ Information that we may need from parents

- What does your child enjoy doing?
- What activities does your child find difficult?
- Does your child need glasses? If so, when does he or she need them?
- Is your child happy to wear glasses or does he or she need encouragement?
- How do you usually encourage your child to wear glasses?
- What light levels does your child need? What lighting should be avoided?
- Does your child have sunglasses for outdoor use?
- How have you adapted your home to suit your child's needs?
- Are there any pieces of equipment or adaptations that we should provide?
- Do you get support from a qualified teacher of the visually impaired (QTVI)?

▶ Getting it right for the child

It is important first of all to find out about the extent of the child's sight loss from the parents and if necessary from other professionals. You should also find out about situations which seem to affect the level of vision, as children's vision may not be constant during the day or from day to day. If a child has a high degree of sight loss, a qualified teacher of vision impaired children (QTVI) may be supporting the child and their family. A QTVI will be able to offer advice about how to adapt the environment and routine of your setting, as well as practical strategies for how best to work with the child.

Settling in will also need to be given some thought. Going to an unfamiliar place and being looked after by unfamiliar people is daunting, but doing so with low vision is likely to result in increased anxiety. Together with parents, we can reduce children's anxiety and gradually help them to explore the setting. It can be worth starting off in a small, quiet area that the child learns to explore and become comfortable with. Items in this space will need to be named so that the child has a way of referencing what each item is. Other children can be introduced into this space one by one or in pairs so that the child is not overwhelmed. Gradually, as the child becomes more confident, they can explore other areas. Clear routes need to be created so that the child can operate independently within the setting and know how to move safely from one area to another.

One of the effects of sight loss is that opportunities to learn by watching others are reduced. This means that skills that other children may pick up 'naturally' will need to be specifically introduced or taught to a child. Children will also need to be introduced to toys and resources as, unlike other children, they may not be able to see what is available in the environment. Again, it will be important to accurately name and describe objects so that children have a way of referencing them and also asking for them again.

Children may also need longer and repeated opportunities to explore concepts or skills because it may be harder for them to process and retain information as the brain usually relies on sight to help it.

It is also important to remember that completing a range of activities, including dressing or playing with a jigsaw, will require the child to put in more effort and time. This can mean that children can become tired from the additional concentration or become frustrated. It will be important to factor this in when planning activities for children and also when supporting them.

The toys and resources we choose for children can make a difference. It is thought that objects and toys that have clear contrasts between colours or features will be easier for children to manage. Materials that have good sensory feedback, such as sand and water, can also be helpful as these are stimulating. It will be important also to look for ways of using technology. Voice-activated resources can be used, as well as books and toys that make sounds as they are touched.

It will be important to encourage some children to wear their glasses and so finding books and other positive images showing children who wear glasses might be helpful. We may also need to look at ways of supporting other areas of development, such as language and movement, that have been affected as an indirect consequence of the vision impairment. It is important that children are encouraged to become self-reliant and to learn as many everyday skills as possible. This will help their self-esteem. Advice as to how best to help children will come from parents, other professionals and also support organisations such as RNIB. You may find the following guidelines helpful:

- Take advice as to how to illuminate the setting to avoid glare and shadows.
- Make sure that steps, ramps and other changes to the floor levels are clearly marked, e.g. with fluorescent strips or textured flooring.
- Teach other children to pick up any objects that fall on to these strips and walkways.
- Keep the floor areas around the child free of obstacles.
- Make sufficient sound or call out the child's name when approaching the child to avoid him or her being startled.
- Keep closely to routines so that the child can understand what is happening around him or her.
- Seat children close to adults during activities where visual images are being used, e.g. sharing a story.
- Look for ways of adapting activities to encourage children to participate, e.g. trays so that objects do not fall off tables and out of sight, balls that have bells in them, velcro on dressing-up toys.
- Look out for non-slip surfaces on tables.
- Keep up to date with assistive technology, e.g. magic pens that 'read' a story.

▌ Key questions

- Who will act as the child's key person?
- What support and adaptations does the child need?
- Is everyone in the setting aware of the child's needs?
- How will the child be encouraged to develop physical skills?
- How will the resources and activities encourage independence?

▌ Some day-to-day questions

- Has the child brought his or her glasses into the setting?
- Is the lighting sufficient in the setting?
- Are staff aware of the child's needs in relation to sight?
- Are other children 'mothering' the child?
- Is the setting tidy and clear of obstacles?
- Are there any changes to the layout of the setting?

▌ Contact

Royal National Institute of Blind People

www.rnib.org.uk

Index